Practical Psychology for Forensic Investigations and Prosecutions

Wiley Series in

The Psychology of Crime, Policing and Law

Series Editors

Graham Davies and **Ray Bull**

University of Leicester, UK

The Wiley Series in the Psychology of Crime, Policing and Law publishes concise and integrative reviews on important emerging areas of contemporary research. The purpose of the series is not merely to present research findings in a clear and readable form, but also to bring out their implications for both practice and policy. In this way, it is hoped the series will not only be useful to psychologists but also to all those concerned with crime detection and prevention, policing, and the judicial process.

For other titles in this series please see www.wiley.com/go/pcpl

Practical Psychology for Forensic Investigations and Prosecutions

Edited by

Mark R. Kebbell
Griffith University, Australia

and

Graham M. Davies
University of Leicester, UK

WILEY

Copyright © 2006   John Wiley & Sons Ltd, The Atrium, Southern Gate, Chichester,
West Sussex PO19 8SQ, England
Telephone (+44) 1243 779777

Email (for orders and customer service enquiries): cs-books@wiley.co.uk
Visit our Home Page on www.wiley.com

Designations used by companies to distinguish their products are often claimed as
trademarks. All brand names and product names used in this book are trade names,
service marks, trademarks or registered trademarks of their respective owners. The
Publisher is not associated with any product or vendor mentioned in this book.

This publication is designed to provide accurate and authoritative information in
regard to the subject matter covered. It is sold on the understanding that the Publisher
is not engaged in rendering professional services. If professional advice or other expert
assistance is required, the services of a competent professional should be sought.

Other Wiley Editorial Offices

John Wiley & Sons Inc., 111 River Street, Hoboken, NJ 07030, USA

Jossey-Bass, 989 Market Street, San Francisco, CA 94103-1741, USA

Wiley-VCH Verlag GmbH, Boschstr. 12, D-69469 Weinheim, Germany

John Wiley & Sons Australia Ltd, 42 McDougall Street, Milton, Queensland 4064,
Australia

John Wiley & Sons (Asia) Pte Ltd, 2 Clementi Loop #02-01, Jin Xing Distripark,
Singapore 129809

John Wiley & Sons Canada Ltd, 6045 Freemont Blvd, Mississauga, ONT, L5R 4J3

Wiley also publishes its books in a variety of electronic formats. Some content that
appears in print may not be available is electronic books.

Library of Congress Cataloging-in-Publication Data

Practical psychology for forensic investigations and prosecutions /
edited by Mark R. Kebbell and Graham M. Davies.
    p. ; cm. – (Wiley series in the psychology of crime, policing and law)
  Includes bibliographical references and index.
  ISBN-13: 978-0-470-09213-2 (cloth : alk. paper)
  ISBN-10: 0-470-09213-0 (cloth : alk. paper)
  ISBN-13: 978-0-470-09214-9 (pbk. : alk. paper)
  ISBN-10: 0-470-09214-9 (pbk. : alk. paper)
  1. Forensic psychology. I. Kebbell, Mark R. II. Davies, Graham,
1943- . III. Series.
  [DNLM: 1. Criminal Psychology–methods. 2. Forensic Sciences.
W 740 P8947 2006]
RA1148.P73 2006
614'.15–dc22   2006014663

British Library Cataloguing in Publication Data

A catalogue record for this book is available from the British Library

ISBN-13   978-0-470-09213-2 (hbk)   978-0-470-09214-9 (pbk)
ISBN-10   0-470-09213-0 (hbk)   0-470-09214-9 (pbk)

Typeset in 10/12pt Century Schoolbook by TechBooks Electronic Services, New Delhi,
India
Printed and bound in Great Britain by TJ International, Padstow, Cornwall
This book is printed on acid-free paper responsibly manufactured from sustainable
forestry in which at least two trees are planted for each one used for paper production.

The Editors would like to dedicate
this book to their families.

Contents

About the Editors

Mark Kebbell is Associate Professor of Forensic Psychology and the Director of the Forensic Psychology Programme at Griffith University. His expertise and research is in the area of interviewing particularly with regards suspects and vulnerable witnesses. He wrote the guidelines for police officers in England and Wales (with Wagstaff) for the assessment of eyewitness evidence. He has worked on more than 70 criminal cases, principally involving murder or serious sexual assault, and has given expert evidence on numerous occasions including uncontested psychological evidence in an Old Bailey appeal case. Academically, he publishes in international journals and has been awarded a British Academy Postdoctoral Fellowship for Outstanding Younger Scholars.

Graham Davies is Professor of Psychology at the University of Leicester. His main research interests lie in the area of eyewitness testimony in children and adults on which he has co-authored over 100 papers in scientific and professional journals and 6 books. He evaluated the live link and videotaped interview innovations for child witnesses for the Home Office and edited the current official guidance on interviewing: *Achieving Best Evidence*. He acts as an expert witness in cases involving children's evidence and is a serving magistrate. He is a past Chair of the Society for Applied Research in Memory and Cognition and the current President of the European Association of Law and Psychology.

About the Contributors

Laurence Alison is Professor of Forensic Psychology and Director of the Centre for Critical Incident Research at the University of Liverpool. His research interests include investigative decision making, police leadership and law enforcement personnel's use of expert advice. He has published widely on these topics at an international level in a variety of academic and practitioner outlets. He has contributed advice to several major cases in the last 10 years, including rapes, murders, armed robberies and terrorist attacks. He has produced several books on profiling and investigation, most recently as editor of *The Forensic Psychologist's Casebook: Psychological Profiling and Criminal Investigation*.

Jennifer Beaudry is a doctoral candidate at the Department of Psychology, Queen's University under the supervision of Rod Lindsay. Before pursuing graduate studies at Queen's University she worked as an emergency services child protection worker for the Sudbury Children's Aid Society. Her main research interests are eyewitness identification evidence, radical lineup procedures and juror decision making. She has co-authored a chapter, entitled "Belief of Eyewitness Identification Evidence", for the *Handbook of Eyewitness Psychology: Memory for People*. Her research has been presented at several international conferences, including the American Psychology-Law Society and the Society for Applied Research in Memory and Cognition. She currently holds a Canadian Graduate Scholarship from the Social Sciences and Humanities Research Council.

Ray Bull is Professor of Forensic Psychology and Director of Forensic Psychology at the University of Leicester. His main interests focus on investigative interviewing (e.g. of suspects and witnesses) and witness testimony (e.g. of children and voice identification). His major books include *Investigative Interviewing: Psychology and Practice* (with Milne), *Handbook of Psychology in Legal Contexts* (with Carson), *Psychology and Law: Truthfulness, Accuracy and Credibility* (with Memon and Vrij). He has co-authored numerous articles in research journals. He has been commissioned by government to co-author guidance documents on good practice in interviewing child witnesses, achieving best evidence from vulnerable witnesses and the taking of evidence on commission. He has written expert reports for many dozens of court cases (including Courts of Appeal) and has testified in criminal trials and civil hearings in a number of countries. He recently received the rare honour (for a "civilian") of a Commendation from the London Metropolitan Police Service for his work on a particular case.

Deborah Davis is an Associate Professor in the Psychology Department of the University of Nevada-Reno. With regards to forensic psychology, her areas of expertise are witness memory, false confessions, issues of sexual consent, rules of evidence and jury research. She has also conducted a variety of research in the areas of social psychology of ageing, and attachment and relationship behaviors, and has written papers concerning research ethics. She was the editor of *From the Mind's Eye*, a newsletter designed to report social science research on law and courtroom psychology. She has also been a member of the editorial boards for *Representative Research in Social Psychology*, the *Journal of Experimental Social Psychology*, and the *Journal of Personality and Social Psychology*.

Paul Dupuis is a Psychology Instructor at Red Deer College in Alberta, Canada. He obtained his PhD from Queen's University. His research interests are in social psychology and eyewitness testimony. He has a particular interest in identification evidence and how lineups are constructed. He has published in this area including a study testing the influence of simultaneous face, body and sequential voice lineups (with Pryke, Lindsay and Dysart) and has demonstrated that multiple identifications (by the same witness) from independent lineups of different features are highly diagnostic of suspect guilt.

Elizabeth Gilchrist is Reader in Forensic Psychology and Director of Forensic Psychology at the University of Kent. Her research interests are in the area of domestic violence and the needs of vulnerable victims, and in criminal justice processes, particularly decision making and in the effectiveness of interventions in the domestic violence arena. Her recent work has included work with women and children who have experienced domestic violence, and a large national study on perpetrators and victim/survivors of domestic violence, which was funded by the Home Office. She is also working on an evaluation of a community-based intervention for domestic violence, funded by the local probation area, and an evaluation of support for victims of sexual offences, funded by the Home Office. She is currently involved in establishing research priorities for the parole board and is developing further work in the area of domestic violence and underlying neural mechanisms, exploring decision making within the parole board and the implications of intimate offending for future risk.

Don Grubin is Professor of Forensic Psychiatry at the University of Newcastle and Honoury Consultant Forensic Psychiatrist at 3 NNNs Trust, St Nicholas Hospital. His research interests are risk assessment and treatment of sex offenders, prison health screening and fitness to plead. His current work focuses on the use of polygraphy in the treatment and supervision of sex offenders and in the treatment of personality disordered prisoners and patients. He is also carrying out a study into the use of SSRI medication in the treatment of sex offenders.

Kevin Howells is Professor of Forensic Clinical Psychology at the University of Nottingham, Head of the Peaks Academic and Research Unit in Nottinghamshire Healthcare Trust and also a member of the Centre for Applied Psychological Research at the University of South Australia. He has been involved in assessment, treatment and research work with offenders in both the United Kingdom and Australia.

Emily Hurren is a PhD candidate within the School of Psychology at Griffith University. Her research interests include child maltreatment, the links between child maltreatment and juvenile offending, sex offending and improving police interviewing of suspected offenders to increase rates of confession. Most recently she has interviewed approximately 60 convicted sex offenders concerning their perceptions of how they were interviewed by the police and how police interviewing of suspects can be improved.

Richard Leo is an Associate Professor of Criminology, Law and Society and an Associate Professor of Psychology and Social Behaviour at the University of California, Irvine. He is a leading international authority on police interrogation practices, *Miranda* requirements, coercive persuasion, false confessions and wrongful convictions. In the last decade, he has authored numerous publications on these subjects in a variety of leading social science journals and law reviews. He is also co-author (with Thomas) of *The Miranda Debate: Law, Justice, and Policing* and is the recipient of The Ruth Shonle Cavan Award from the American Society of Criminology, the Saleem Shah Career Achievement Award from the American Psychological Association and a Soros Senior Justice Fellowship from the Open Society Institute. He has lectured widely to police, judges, criminal defence attorneys, prosecutors and other professionals. He is currently completing a book on police interrogation and American justice for Harvard University Press.

Rod Lindsay is Professor of Psychology at Queen's University. His main interests focus on eyewitness identification techniques (lineups and showups) and the credibility of witness testimony (e.g. of children). He is a co-editor of the 2006 two-volume *Handbook of Eyewitness Psychology: Memory for Events* and *Handbook of Eyewitness Psychology: Memory for People* (both with Ross, Read and Toglia). He has co-authored over 80 articles and book chapters and over 100 conference presentations, mostly on topics related to eyewitnesses. His publications include several articles in law journals and he was recently awarded a career achievement award from the Canadian Psychological Association for his Distinguished Contribution to the Application of Psychology. He participated in the sessions leading to the National Institute of Justice (US) publication *Eyewitness Evidence: A Guide for Law Enforcement*. He has participated extensively in the training of Canadian judges, prosecutors and law enforcement officers regarding issues of eyewitness accuracy and police procedures for obtaining and evaluating eyewitness evidence, particularly identification evidence. He has written expert reports for many court cases and has testified in criminal trials and civil hearings in a number of countries including consultation with prosecutors in the Rwandan war crimes trials.

Becky Milne is Principal Lecturer in Forensic Psychology at the Institute of Criminal Justice Studies of the University of Portsmouth. Her main interests focus on the cognitive interview, investigative interviewing (e.g. of suspects and witnesses), the investigation process and miscarriages of justice and the interviewing of vulnerable groups. She has written *Investigative Interviewing: Psychology and Practice* (with Bull). She has co-authored numerous articles in research journals and has been commissioned by the UK government to co-author guidance documents on achieving best evidence from vulnerable witnesses and the taking of evidence on commission. She sits on the Association of Chief Police Officers Strategic Steering Committee for Investigative Interviewing as the academic lead and acts as an interview advisor on many cases concerning the best ways to interview witnesses and victims. In addition, she trains investigators from numerous organizations with regard to the enhanced cognitive interview.

Jacqueline Stacey works as a researcher in the Peaks Academic and Research Unit in Nottinghamshire Healthcare Trust and is doing a PhD on the role of forgiveness in forensic populations, based at the University of Nottingham.

Aldert Vrij is Professor of Applied Social Psychology at the University of Portsmouth. His main research interests lie in deception, and he examines nonverbal and verbal correlates of deception and people's ability to detect deceit. He has received grants from the Leverhulme Trust, ESRC, British Academy and the Nuffield Foundation to support this research. He has published almost 300 articles and six books on the above topics. His book *Detecting Lies and Deceit* provides a comprehensive overview of nonverbal, verbal and physiological correlates of deception. He presents seminars to professionals on a regular basis in Europe and other parts of the world. He also gives lie-detection training sessions to fellow academics. He acts as an expert witness on lie-detection issues in criminal cases in both his native country, the Netherlands, and in the United Kingdom. He is editor of *Legal and Criminological Psychology* and sits on the editorial boards of *Law and Human Behavior, Human Communication Research, Psychology, Crime, and Law* and *Journal of Nonverbal Behavior.*

Helen Westcott is Senior Lecturer in Psychology at The Open University. She is a member of the International Centre for Comparative Criminological Research (ICCCR) at The Open University, and has a longstanding interest in issues concerning child sexual abuse and interviewing children, along with cross-examination practice, and the abuse of children who are disabled. She publishes and presents widely on topics related to children's evidence, for example her book *Children's Testimony* published by Wiley in 2002, with Davies and Bull. She was a member of the writing team that produced the 2002 Home Office guidance, *Achieving Best Evidence in Criminal Proceedings*, and she works closely with practitioners and policy makers.

Series Preface

The Wiley Series on the Psychology of Crime, Policing and the Law publishes integrative reviews of important emerging areas of contemporary research. The purpose of the series is not merely to present research findings in a clear and readable form, but also to bring out their implications for both practice and policy. In this way, it is hoped that the series will not only be useful to psychologists, but also to all those concerned with crime detection and prevention, policing and the judicial process.

This is particularly the case for the current volume with its emphasis on practical psychology in investigations and prosecutions. As the editors point out, there have recently been made a number of technological advances that assist investigations and prosecutions but most still heavily rely on human abilities.

The chapters in this volume each cover one of the major aspects of investigations and prosecutions. Obtaining comprehensive and reliable information from witnesses has, until fairly recently, not really been a priority for police forces around the world. However, this is beginning to change, largely based on research, theory and input from psychologists. Similarly, the interviewing of suspects and the topic of false confessions is, at last, being influenced also by peer-reviewed, published research rather than solely by the views of experienced professionals. The topic of eyewitness identification has over recent decades been the focus of substantial research by psychologists, which has culminated in practical and useful recommendations for increasing their reliability.

Another very important topic that has received considerable attention from research psychologists is that of the detection of deception, particularly regarding the mistaken beliefs that many people have about reliable cues to deception. People also have mistaken beliefs about what offender profiling involves and how effective it has been.

Understanding the psychological characteristics of offenders can be useful to decision making both regarding investigations and prosecutions. Indeed, deciding to prosecute involves a range of psychological factors. One crucial factor here is the likely risk to society posed by the alleged wrong-doer.

An important issue that can influence decisions to prosecute and the effectiveness of prosecutions is investigators' and courts'/jurors' understanding of why many reports of sexual abuse are only made a long while after the alleged offences. Of similar importance is an understanding of why some (alleged) victims may subsequently try to withdraw their complaints.

This volume provides comprehensive chapters on each of the above topics. The editor and authors have succeeded in explaining psychological contributions in a clear way and of providing links across the chapters. I am confident that you will find this volume both very interesting and of immense practical use.

RAY BULL
University of Leicester

Preface

Crime is a blight on our societies. From Australia to the United States, Russia to South Africa, Iceland to Argentina, crime has a major impact on how people live their daily lives. Minor crimes such as vandalism and petty theft are a nuisance, and while they typically have comparably little economic impact, they create an environment of distrust and suspicion that can poison communities. More serious crimes such as assaults, kidnappings, rapes and murders have a more profound impact both on victims and their communities, leading to fear, hatred and isolation.

Technological advances, for example DNA testing and CCTV, have improved our methods of investigating and prosecuting crime, but despite these advances the majority of forensic investigations and prosecutions still rely on human factors. In this respect forensic investigations and prosecutions have changed little over the past couple of centuries. Investigators still rely on their own conceptualizations of who commits certain crimes to identify potential offenders, eyewitnesses are still integral to most investigations and prosecutions, and a suspect confessing still has a major impact on decisions to convict a suspect. It is in these human factors where psychology has its role. In this book, we outline current, cutting-edge research and its application to investigating and prosecuting offences.

Acknowledgements

We would like to acknowledge gratefully the contribution of Emily Hurren to the editing of this book.

Introduction

GRAHAM M. DAVIES AND MARK R. KEBBELL

Almost a century has passed since the publication of *On the Witness Stand* by Hugo Munsterberg (1908), one the first books to treat legal issues from a psychological standpoint. Munsterberg was an acknowledged pioneer of applied psychology, who moved from his native Germany to set up the first experimental psychology laboratory at Harvard at the invitation of William James (Hale, 1980; Moskowitz, 1977). Munsterberg's book, based on a series of successful magazine articles, aimed at promoting the role of psychology in the courts, the police and the prisons. Despite its somewhat bombastic tone, the book's central message, that the law and its agencies had ignored the importance and potential of psychology, shines through. Sadly, the research he was able to offer to support his claim was limited, took little account of the principles of jurisprudence or the realities of law enforcement and was leavened with trenchant criticism of lawyers (labelled as "obdurate") and other law-enforcement professionals. Not surprisingly, the book was a popular success, but did little in the short term to promote the union of psychology and law. Indeed, it drew from the distinguished American jurist John Henry Wigmore a satirical review (1909), which though savage in its treatment of Munsterberg's pretensions, did foresee a time when psychology might have something to offer the law.

We hope that on the evidence of the contributions to the current volume, Wigmore might well have concluded that psychology's time had come. The contributors illustrate the many practical applications of psychology to forensic problems and the manifest opportunities for mutual cooperation that currently exist. There are many topics included in

Practical Psychology for Forensic Investigations and Prosecutions.
Edited by Mark R. Kebbell and Graham M. Davies. © 2006 John Wiley & Sons, Ltd.

Munsterberg's classic that feature in this book. They include the accuracy of memory of witnesses, the detection of crime and deception, untrue confessions and the use of suggestive questioning in court. In addition, the current volume covers other topics that Munsterberg could only have dreamed of: offender profiling, risk assessment procedures, sexual violence and offender behaviour, to name but a few. As the contributors illustrate, all are issues on which psychologists are currently working fruitfully with their professional colleagues in the police, social services and the law.

We trust our readers will find the tone adopted by all our contributors is more measured and constructive than Munsterberg and takes proper cognisance of the differences in the ways that psychologists and lawyers think and reach decisions. It would be foolish to think that there is not some residual friction between the different professional groups involved in the legal arena, but it is fair to say that guarded respect and mutual understanding is increasingly the norm. This process has been accelerated by the many positive impacts of forensic psychology on legal processes described by the various distinguished contributors to this volume.

Together, the contributions provide an overview of appropriate psychological methods for investigating and prosecuting offences. Practical information is provided designed to maximize the possibility of guilty persons being convicted and those innocent of charges being exonerated. Importantly, the book illustrates ways of ensuring that victims and suspects, both innocent and guilty, are treated with respect and in a professional way. A theme running through many contributions is the need for a more holistic approach to criminal justice that links the different stages of the investigative and prosecution process together by maximizing reporting rates, thorough investigation, effective presentation of evidence in court and effective sentencing. Clearly, forensic psychologists cannot by themselves ensure that such joined-up thinking prevails, but they can make a contribution to this ideal by working with their professional colleagues in law and law enforcement.

AN OVERVIEW OF THE CONTRIBUTIONS

In the opening chapter, Becky Milne and Ray Bull discuss the interviewing of victims of crime, with a particular emphasis upon children and those with intellectual disabilities. They emphasize the role of the interviewer's expectations and agenda in shaping both the witness's responses and any subsequent written report. Given these influences, they argue for the value of full recordings of all witness interviews conducted by the police. Effective styles of interviewing are discussed with a particular emphasis upon the staged interview recommended in the Home Office guidance, *Achieving Best Evidence* (Home Office, 2002). The practical problems of interviewing vulnerable victims are explored and some solutions offered to common problems with such witnesses.

Jennifer Baudry, Rod Lindsey and Paul Dupuis present some practical guidance on the conduct of identification procedures for suspects by the police. The simplistic view that identification is a matter of common sense has long since been demolished due to serious miscarriages of justice caused by confident but wrong identifications by witnesses. The authors draw attention to the most recent list of convicted persons exonerated through new DNA evidence where a primary cause of error was mistaken identification (Innocence Project, 2005). The authors produce a series of evidence-based recommendations on procedures to be followed in conducting mugshot searches and the composition of line-ups and show-ups, designed to maximize the likelihood of an offender being identified, while minimizing the likelihood of an innocent suspect being selected.

Next, Laurence Alison and Mark Kebbell provide an evenhanded review of the research evidence for and against the authenticity of recovered memories. The issue of recovered memories – memories of traumatic events remembered after long intervals of apparent amnesia – initially polarized the psychological and psychiatric community between those who saw such 'memories' as invariably fabrications springing from suggestive therapeutic practices and those who believed they were the plausible consequences of global traumatic amnesia. Today, there are indications of a middle ground emerging in this debate (Davies & Dalgleish, 2001) and the current chapter is another constructive contribution. The authors also offer some cautionary words of advice for experts and investigators who may be drawn into cases involving the delayed reporting of sexual abuse.

Kevin Howells and Jacqueline Stacey examine the psychological characteristics of offenders: what makes a criminal. The authors stress that no one single factor characterizes all criminals and that some fashionable nostrums – such as "lack of self-esteem" – are not necessarily associated with criminality. The authors focus on serious offending, with an emphasis upon sexual and physical assaults, and draw on their experience of designing and running offender treatment programmes to argue that a range of factors, including impulsiveness, levels of anger and on occasion, cultural and political factors, need to be taken into account in reducing reoffending and countering crime in society.

Aldert Vrij's chapter on detecting deception via verbal and nonverbal cues would have made disappointing reading for Hugo Munsterberg, an early exponent of the use of the lie detector. Vrij's review of the research suggests that not only is the polygraph an unreliable instrument in the detection of deception, but also such contemporary successors as the voice-stress analyser and thermal imaging. He recommends more traditional solutions, such as getting suspects to elaborate on their alibis and withholding police evidence until after suspects have had the opportunity to give their version of events.

Mark Kebbell and Emily Hurren discuss techniques for interviewing suspects to obtain accurate information. They point out that a genuine confession from a guilty suspect has many advantages, not least the savings in time and cost and obviating the need of the victim to testify in court. They outline some of the psychological models that have been proposed to explain the process of confession and review ethical interview procedures that might encourage confession in guilty suspects: disclosing the mass of evidence against an accused is a far more effective and reliable method of securing a confession than the adoption of an aggressive and bullying posture.

The use of inappropriate interviewing techniques can lead to false confessions, another important source of miscarriages of justice according to DNA exoneration records. Deborah Davis and Richard Leo review the investigative techniques that are likely to lead to false confessions. These include prolonged interviewing and a certainty of guilt of the suspect that is not warranted by objective evidence. They emphasize the difficulties for both interrogators and the courts in readily distinguishing between true and false confessions and echo Milne and Bull in calling for all interviews to be videotaped. Once a confession is made, it is difficult for a suspect to re-establish their innocence, even when other evidence is inconsistent with the suspect's account.

Laurence Alison and Mark Kebbell explore the myths surrounding one of the most prominent activities undertaken by forensic psychologists: offender profiling. They argue against the predominant view among profilers and indeed, the police, that it is possible to confidently infer from a crime scene, the character and the background of the offender. They describe research that suggests that crime-scene characteristics may owe as much to the situational factors as to the nature of the offender. They are critical of many profiles, which they assert, contain many generalized statements and unverifiable assumptions and call for a more overtly evidence-based approach to profiling.

Elizabeth Gilchrist discusses the factors underlying the decision to prosecute in criminal cases. The research she reviews undermines the belief that decisions are made purely on the basis of a rigorous consideration of the evidence and the demands of the public interest.

She argues that any comprehensive model of legal decision making requires consideration of such factors as police practices on decision to charge, prosecutors' beliefs and stereotypes, class attitudes and political influences. She points to the procedures adopted in Tasmania that list factors that should *not* be taken into account as well as those that should, in reaching decisions to prosecute.

Graham Davies and Helen Westcott look at the problem of the premature withdrawal of complaints by victims of crime, which can leave an offender free to perpetrate the same or more serious offences against other persons. This problem is particularly acute among witness victims who are vulnerable by reason of age or mental disability. They examine what can be done to reduce overt intimidation of witnesses and to support complainants, both during the investigative phase and at trial. They argue that while much can and is being done for vulnerable witnesses through alterations in legal process and social support, the demands of cross-examination will continue to be a formidable obstacle to justice for many victims.

Don Grubin tackles the contentious topic of communicating risk to the court. Advising on the likelihood of an offender committing further serious offences is a high-profile task for a forensic psychologist or psychiatrist. Success goes unnoticed, but failure is public and likely to lead to denigration by the press for the professional involved. Grubin highlights common confusions, such as that between the likelihood of further offending and the consequences for the victim. He illustrates how actuarial approaches are rapidly overtaking clinical judgement as the most accurate and transparent method for assessing risk with violent and sexual offenders. He emphasizes that while the final decision lies with the courts, it is up to the assessor to communicate clearly the reasons for their assessments, both immediate and in the longer term.

In the concluding section, the editors note the roles that forensic psychologists are already taking in progressing the investigative, prosecution and trial process, as described by the contributors to the current volume. These contributions illustrate also the different methodological approaches that have been adopted, not merely quantitative but qualitative, not merely experimental, but also field and case-study approaches. Finally, they emphasize the crucial importance of communicating with the other players in the legal process: police officers, social workers, lawyers and judges. This communication process needs to be two-way: forensic psychologists passing on their own insights, but also learning more about important and unexplored issues, which can better shape their research to the practical realities of the police station and courtroom. Only then perhaps, can forensic psychology be said to have fully learned the lessons of Hugo Munsterberg and *On the Witness Stand*.

REFERENCES

Davies, G.M. & Dalgleish, T. (2001). *Recovered memories: Seeking the middle ground*. Chichester: John Wiley & Sons, Ltd.

Hale, M. (1980). *Human science and social order: Hugo Munsterberg and the origins of applied psychology*. Philadelphia: Temple University Press.

Home Office (2002). *Achieving best evidence in criminal proceedings: Guidance for vulnerable or intimidated witnesses, including children*. London: Home Office.

Innocence Project (2005). Accessed at http://www.innocenceproject.org.

Moskowitz, M.J. (1977). Hugo Munsterberg: A study in the history of applied psychology. *American Psychologist, 32*, 824–842.

Munsterberg, H. (1908). *On the witness stand: Essays on psychology and crime*. New York: McClure.

Wigmore, J.H. (1909). Professor Munsterberg and the psychology of testimony: Being a report of the case of Cokestone *v*. Muensterberg. *Illinois Law Review, 3*, 399–445.

CHAPTER 1

Interviewing Victims of Crime, Including Children and People with Intellectual Disabilities

BECKY MILNE AND RAY BULL

INTRODUCTION

This chapter examines the importance within investigations of victims of crime and witnesses to crime and will emphasize that assisting victims/witnesses to provide as full an account as possible of "what happened" is a complex process for which interviewers need to be properly trained. Psychology needs to rise to the challenge of (i) translating what is known from laboratory and field research into this applied arena and (ii) developing new theories and techniques to the extent that current laboratory research on memory and communication provides insufficient guidance.

This chapter will first of all examine the role of witnesses and victims within the investigation process and then it will discuss the importance of the appropriate interviewing of witnesses and victims within the criminal justice system. This will lead to a discussion of the necessity of the accurate recording of information gleaned from such interviewing and we will try to answer the question: "To video or not to video?". The chapter will then examine the interviewing of children and people with learning disabilities. The discussion will make recommendations for best practice.

Practical Psychology for Forensic Investigations and Prosecutions.
Edited by Mark R. Kebbell and Graham M. Davies. © 2006 John Wiley & Sons, Ltd.

INTERVIEWING VICTIMS OF CRIME

The main question that needs to be addressed is: "What is the main aim of an investigation?". The answer to this question is a simple one, and is one likely to be true for investigations conducted in all countries irrespective of legislative and criminal justice system differences. The answer applies to all types of investigations, within many organizations. The main aim of an investigation is to answer two primary questions: (i) "What happened?" (if anything did happen) and (ii) "Who did it?" (see also the chapter in this book by Beaudry, Lindsay & Dupuis concerning identification procedures for identifying "who did it?").

The next question that needs to be addressed is: "How do investigators seek to answer these two primary questions?". Investigators have noted that in order to seek answers to these core investigatory aims they invariably gather material/information from a number of sources (Kebbell & Milne, 1998) and usually these sources of information are people: witnesses, victims, suspects, complainants, emergency services, experts or colleagues (e.g. the first officer at the crime scene). Information is therefore the currency of the criminal justice system. In order to gather such valuable information from these sources investigators need to communicate, and any communication with a purpose, is an interview. The aim of such interviews is to obtain the best *quality* and *quantity* of information, which can in turn be used to find out what has happened, who committed the crime and to feed this into the investigative process. Commonsense tells us that the more information that is obtained, which is of good quality, the more likely a solution will be found.

Why are witnesses to crime and victims of crime so important? How do they help within the investigative process? In the USA, Sanders (1986) asked police officers; "What is the central and most important feature of criminal investigations?". The majority replied "witnesses". A similar view applies in the UK where Kebbell and Milne (1998) asked 159 police officers for their perceptions of the utility of witnesses within investigations. It was found that witnesses/victims were perceived usually to provide the central leads in criminal investigations. Furthermore, investigators frequently have little (or no) other forensically relevant information to guide an investigation. Therefore, the primary source of information and evidence for the investigator is usually witnesses/victims. As a result, information gained from the interviewing of witnesses/victims often forms the cornerstone of an investigation (Milne & Bull, 1999; Milne & Shaw, 1999). (See also the chapter by Kebbell and Hurren in this book who discuss the critical role of evidence in suspects' decisions to confess).

Information gleaned from witnesses/victims in the first instance governs the initial direction of the investigation, helping the investigators outline avenues of exploration and lines of enquiry to be pursued. As stated above, information obtained from witnesses/victims is pivotal in answering the two primary questions. First, "What happened?" (which in turn helps to outline the choice of offence to be charged and the points to prove the particular offence under investigation; in essence what crime is being investigated). Witness/victim information also helps answer the second question of "Who did it?" (if this question cannot be answered then there will not be a prosecution; witnesses/victims help in the selection of possible suspects). When a suspect is apprehended and charged with an offence, a good witness/victim interview can also be helpful in the planning and preparation stage that should take place prior to the interview of the suspect (Milne & Bull, 1999). In addition, a comprehensive account from a witness/victim, obtained in an appropriate manner, may help in the gaining of a confession from a suspect (Kebbell, Hurren & Mazarolle, 2005). This is because research has shown that strength of evidence is associated with suspects confessing within an interview (Gudjonsson, 2003).

However, obtaining the maximum quantity and quality of information from a witness is not an easy task. The information about the incident has to endure what we (Milne & Bull, 1999) have termed an obstacle course that involves imperfect eyewitness memory processes (Kebbell & Wagstaff, 1999), the difficulties associated with interviewing and the problems concerning the statement-taking process itself. Interviewers need to know about memory processes in order to be able to interview appropriately, as such knowledge will help interviewers to develop appropriate strategies to achieve maximum quantity of information from an interviewee without jeopardizing the quality of the information gained. This is because memory is fragile. It can easily be altered, changed and manipulated. It is, therefore, imperative for interviewers to learn how easily they can influence what interviewees tell them. The cognitive interview (and enhanced cognitive interview) was developed to do just this: help interviewees give a full and detailed account without decreasing the quality of the additional information obtained (see Fisher & Geiselman, 1992; Milne & Bull, 1999 for fuller accounts of the cognitive interview).

The initial interview and the accurate recording of that interview is crucial and can very often determine the success of the investigation. It would, therefore, be reasonable to assume that the interviewing of witnesses/victims and the resources needed to do this properly (e.g. time, money and facilities) would be a high priority. Unfortunately, research has shown that this is not usually the case and that the interviewing of witnesses/victims is often of a lower standard than the interviewing of suspects (Clarke & Milne, 2001; McLean, 1995). Indeed, police training courses around the globe tend to focus on the interviewing of suspects. Furthermore, in many countries interviews with witnesses/victims are still not tape/electronically recorded but merely written up as a statement.

There are three primary reasons why the electronic recording of interviews with witnesses/victims is important. The first concerns the investigative process itself. The best way to retain the information gained from witnesses to enable investigators to use this information to its full effect is to record it electronically. The second is from the witness/victim standpoint. The third concerns the presenting of the evidence within an ensuing court case, where the necessity of obtaining and maintaining an accurate record of the original account of an event from witnesses is crucial – "the bedrock of (the) adversarial process is the evidence of witnesses for the prosecution, not the confession of the accused" (Wolchover & Heaton-Armstrong, 1997a, p. 855). The decision of whether to electronically record interviews with witnesses/victims (or to merely take a written statement) is thus an extremely important decision.

We will examine the investigative reasons first. During an interview, what the interviewee communicates verbally and nonverbally has to be encoded by the interviewer. However, the many tasks required in a witness[1] interview put a lot of cognitive demands on the interviewer, especially so when there is no recording of the interview (e.g. the interviewer has to conduct an appropriate interview and also write down what the interviewee is saying). We all have only a limited amount of cognitive resources available at any one time (Navon & Gopher, 1979). As a result, the quality of the interview will suffer (Clarke & Milne, 2001) and there will be incomplete encoding of the available information (i.e. what the witness is reporting). In other words, not all the information mentioned by the interviewee will be encoded; some of it will never enter the interviewer's memory at all. The information that does enter the interviewer's memory has later to be recalled (for example, to produce a written statement or report). Thus, the information reported by the interviewee must travel through the memory processes of the interviewer. Research has found that even if a police report is written immediately after the interview, the report may contain only two-thirds of the relevant information reported by the interviewee (Koehnken, Thurer & Zoberbier, 1994). This would not be so bad if only irrelevant information is left out of the statement (presuming that the interviewer at that time in the investigation knows what information will be crucial to the case). Lamb, Orbach, Sternberg, Hershkowitz and Horowitz (2000) found that, even when investigators took notes within

---

[1] The use of 'witness' in this chapter also includes 'victims'.

an interview, 25% of the forensically relevant details provided by child interviewees were not included (many of these details were considered to be central to the investigation). Lamb et al. (2000) concluded "interviewers cannot be expected to provide complete accounts of their interviews without electronic assistance" (p. 705).

It has also been well documented that even before an interview begins interviewers form judgements about the event in question (Shepherd & Milne, 1999). For police investigators, these primarily arise from the crime category to which the alleged offence belongs and what typically occurs in such offences (i.e. offence knowledge) (Mortimer & Shepherd, 1999). Investigators will, wittingly or unwittingly, utilize this information to guide the direction of the case (Ask & Granhag, 2005). These judgements also guide their attention, comprehension and memory and in turn enable interviewers to make decisions pre-interview. If, however, interviewers are guided too much by their own views about the event, then relevant and vital information may (wittingly or unwittingly) be overlooked, screened out, ignored, forgotten, disposed of or deleted, even at this pre-interview stage. In the interview itself interviewers are also influenced by these pre-interview judgements. The interviewer may hold certain hypotheses about the event in question, and as a consequence, information which is consistent with the interviewer's pre-existing view will receive preferential treatment while inconsistent details may be distorted or even filtered out completely (Milne & Shaw, 1999; Mortimer, 1994a, 1994b). It is this which often compels interviewers merely to confirm what they already know or think they know (i.e. they enter the interview room with a confirmatory bias) and to close prematurely the interview (i.e. once they have attained the information that they sought, without exploring in the interview other possibilities). This may result in vital information never being sought and/or being lost. It is therefore imperative to electronically record interviews with witnesses, so that everything that is reported to the interviewer can be preserved.

Research has shown that the "standard interview" (i.e. how police typically interview) tends to involve poor questioning strategies that are not conducive to maximum retrieval (Clarke & Milne, 2001; Fisher, Geiselman & Raymond 1987; McLean, 1995). This is largely due to the fact that there usually exists minimal training for police officers with regard to witness/victim interviewing. Research examining police officers' abilities to interview witnesses has shown that this aspect of police work is usually poor (e.g. use of appropriate questions; Clifford & George, 1996; Fisher et al., 1987; McLean, 1995). For example, McLean (1995) concluded "the treatment of witnesses appears far worse (than that of suspects)" (p. 48). This is even more remarkable when one notes that this senior officer asked his team to record their witness interviews for this research and they therefore knew that their abilities would be assessed. Even more worryingly, the national research conducted by Clarke and Milne (2001) found that after investigative interview training (that did tend to focus on the interviewing of suspects) the interviews with witnesses and victims were rather poor. (The interviewers in this study also knew that their witness interviews would subsequently be assessed.)

Research has also shown that the information obtained from witnesses is often far from complete, especially when a standard interview is used (which tends to be characterized by a question–answer format). For example, compared to a standard interview, the cognitive interview elicits up to 40% more information (see Koehnken, Milne, Memon & Bull, 1999). In essence the typical witness statement only contains the "tip of the iceberg" of information available. Interestingly, the report by Macphearson, Cook, Sentamu and Stone (1999) that examined the critical failure points of the investigation into the murder in London of Stephen Lawrence (April, 1993) noted that interviewers may well have missed important facts that later turned out to be crucial.

Another investigative reason for electronically recording witness interviews concerns the use, value and reliability of the information obtained within the investigation. When a written statement has been obtained there is no record of the questions asked to elicit the information. Thus, the actual quality of the resulting information is unknown. When interviewing, interviewers should at the outset gain a free recall (free narrative or first account) from the witness. Research shows that information obtained from this stage in the interview is usually reliable and of good quality (e.g. Milne, Clare & Bull, 1999). However, as the interviewer probes using questions to elicit more detail, the quality of the information is jeopardized and typically becomes less reliable (Milne & Bull, 1999). Investigators should examine how the crime-relevant/important information from witnesses/victims was obtained. Unfortunately, at present, reliability judgements may be determined by "stereotypes" (e.g. good character, confident witness etc.), rather than by examination of the interviewing itself.

From the witnesses' perspective, there are also good reasons for the electronic recording of interviews. The interview itself tends to be shortened by the electronic recording of the interview as handwriting a statement draws out the length of the interview (while the interviewer is trying to write down what the interviewee is saying). The interviewer should be concentrating fully on helping the witness remember in detail, attending their needs, as opposed to trying to write down what they are saying.

With regard to statement taking, police interviewers also tend to rewrite what the witness actually reports, using more "standard" legal language, putting events in a chronological order, making sure the account contains no contradictory evidence or information the interviewer deems to be irrelevant, addresses specific points to prove the offence in question, including legal jargon, and is confirmatory (Ainsworth, 1995; Rock, 2001). Witnesses thus often sign a statement that is dissimilar to what they originally said (Ede & Shepherd, 1997; Milne & Bull, 1999). This is problematic as a statement, in addition to initiating an investigation, also initially provides an outline of the evidence and enables a case to be prosecuted and defended coherently (Heaton-Armstrong, 1995).

However, a written statement may not have a "refreshing" effect prior to giving testimony in court if it differs from what was originally said. Furthermore, a statement which is inconsistent with the witness's subsequent account of the event in court leaves it open to the lawyers to blame the witness for inconsistencies, and inconsistency is often seen as an indicator of unreliability, which may result in significant doubt being applied (by the court/jury). Rock (2001) noted that a statement is often used "as a weapon against a witness (p. 70)" in court. (See Milne & Shaw, 1999; Wolchover & Heaton-Armstrong, 1997a, 1997b for fuller accounts.)

In England and Wales recent legislation and national directives stipulate that interviews with adult witnesses (in addition to the more "traditional" vulnerable groups – see below) should be videorecorded. The *Youth Justice and Criminal Evidence Act, 1999* sought to improve access to justice for vulnerable people. Prior to this 1999 Act, only children, primarily in abuse cases, were allowed to use a prior recorded video interview as their evidence-in-chief in criminal trials. The definition of vulnerable is dealt with under Sections 16 and 17 of the Act.

Section 16 (which has now been enacted) specifies that vulnerable witnesses include:

(i) Children under 17 years of age at the time of the court hearing.
(ii) People whose quality of evidence is likely to be diminished because they have a mental disorder, or have a significant impairment of intelligence and social functioning, or have a physical disability or are suffering from a physical disorder.

Some examples of what constitutes such vulnerability are:

> people with a psychopathic or any other personality disorder, schizophrenia or any other mental disorder. In some circumstances, this might include a clinical diagnosis of depression; people with learning disabilities; people with Alzheimer's Disease or other forms of dementia; people suffering from impairments of hearing or speech.

Section 16 thus defines a person as vulnerable because of "who" they are; the vulnerability is associated with the person. (For more on interviewing such witnesses see below.)

In Section 17 (which has only yet been enacted in Northern Ireland and is planned to be enacted in England and Wales at the end of 2006/ 2007) vulnerability stems from the actual (alleged) crime or circumstances surrounding the nature of the (alleged) offence (i.e. the witness/victim is vulnerable through intimidation, fear, distress). Crime types that need to be thought about within this category include: serious sexual assault, racially motivated attacks, murder/manslaughter, elder abuse and domestic violence (to name a few). Witnesses to such crimes are termed "intimidated" witnesses.

In addition, numerous national guidance manuals for the police (e.g. the *Murder Investigation Manual*, *Domestic Violence Manual*, *Serious Sexual Offences Manual*) all suggest that such significant witnesses should be interviewed on video as part of the investigative process. Furthermore, the *Criminal Justice Act, 2003* (Section 137) allows that any interviewee, regardless of vulnerability, may be afforded a video interview as their evidence-in-chief in a court of law in indictable offences (to be enacted along with Section 17 of the *Youth Justice Criminal Evidence Act, 1999*). Thus the question in the UK soon will be "Why did you not video the interview?".

INTERVIEWING CHILDREN AND PEOPLE WITH INTELLECTUAL DISABILITIES

While everybody knows that children's brains are not as fully developed as those of adults, few people have indepth knowledge of how children's memories and communication skills differ from ordinary adults. Similarly, although everybody knows that some people have intellectual disabilities, few of us know much about how to assist such people to tell us what has happened to them.

It is a sad fact that some crime perpetrators specifically choose to prey on vulnerable victims such as children and people with intellectual disabilities, partly in the hope that such victims will not be able to provide comprehensive accounts of what has happened to them. Fortunately, several countries have recently introduced legislation and interviewing guidance designed to make it more likely that vulnerable victims will achieve the justice they deserve.

In Scotland, for example, the *Vulnerable Witnesses (Scotland) Act, 2004* specifies a number of procedures and 'special measures' that are now available. This recent legislation has many similarities with the *Youth Justice and Criminal Evidence Act, 1999* and the *Criminal*

Justice Act, 1991 both introduced in England and Wales for the same purpose as the Scottish legislation. All of this legislation has been accompanied by official government guidance documents for interviewers, this guidance being firmly based on psychological research.

For example, *Achieving Best Evidence In Criminal Proceedings: Guidance For Vulnerable Or Intimidated Witnesses, Including Children* (ABE) was introduced in England and Wales in 2002. Two of its major chapters focus on how best to interview witnesses who are (i) children or (ii) vulnerable adults. (The 2001 writing of ABE was coordinated and partly authored by psychologists from the University of Leicester.) While vulnerable adult witnesses are, of course, not children, effective interviewing of these two groups has many similarities.

One crucial aspect of skilled interviewing of such people is not to rush them. While time pressures can sometimes justify a quick interview with a vulnerable witness (e.g. a victim is assaulted in the street, the police arriving very soon after so that with a description from the victim they can immediately search the vicinity for the perpetrator), organizational pressures should not be used as an excuse for conducting rushed, hasty, ill-planned and ineffective interviews (Aarons & Powell, 2003).

Children and vulnerable adults do need more time (Milne & Bull, 1999)

- to understand the nature of the task;
- to comprehend the questions being put to them;
- to think about the questions;
- to try to retrieve from memory the relevant information;
- to put this information into words;
- to say these words (or communicate in a way that suits them if they cannot speak).

Investigative interviews with children and vulnerable adults will only be as good as the planning put into them beforehand. Such witnesses will usually have a poor understanding of how their own memory works and will have limited strategies for retrieving the relevant information that is in their memory. It is the responsibility of interviewers to realize this and to try to overcome these limitations. Furthermore, many such victims will not be able to concentrate for long periods and therefore interviewers need to take account of this.

The *Achieving Best Evidence* document (available at http:/www. cps.gov.uk/publications/prosecution/bestevidencevol1.html) provides comprehensive guidance concerning the determination of whether an adult witness/victim may have special vulnerabilities. Of course, vulnerable victims will possess some relevant skills. Indeed,

"... mildly mentally retarded persons... In their interactions with others... often have a hidden agenda... trying to protect their self-esteem by... disguising incompetence" (Kernan & Sabsay, 1997, p. 243) and "to avoid the embarrassment of having to admit that they have not understood something that has been said to them or that they have been asked to explain, an admission that might reveal them as incompetent, mildly retarded individuals will sometimes feign understanding" (p. 245). Thus, determining whether a victim is especially vulnerable is not always an easy task. Indeed, even regarding children, many professionals seem to falsely assume that those over 12 years of age do not have relevant comprehension problems (Crawford & Bull, 2005). Also, the cues people seem to use to determine if an adult has intellectual disability (e.g. by their speech – Kernan, Sabsay & Shinn, 1989) or may be suggestible (e.g. by their facial appearance – Nurmoja, 2005) do not seem to be that reliable.

Interviewer Behaviour

When it has been determined that a witness/victim is vulnerable (e.g. because of young age or/and intellectual disability) interviewers need to be aware that this may unduly affect their own behaviour, especially if they are not experienced at interacting with such people. ABE points out that "Research has made it clear that when people meet others with whom they are unfamiliar their own behaviour becomes abnormal" (p. 67). The interviewees will probably notice this and may view it as a sign of discomfort, unease and/or impatience. Interviewers should also be aware of the appropriate terminology for the various intellectual disabilities. While interviewers need to be fully aware of victims' vulnerabilities, they should not focus too much on these to the exclusion of building on the interviewees' relevant strengths.

A sizeable proportion of vulnerable victims will want to place themselves (e.g. be seated) closer or further away from the interviewer than will ordinary witnesses. Asking witnesses for advice on how best to communicate with them will assist with this and many other relevant issues, and will also empower witnesses which will have several benefits, including reducing compliance to questions. Establishing good rapport could also reduce compliance.

Rapport

In 1992 the *Memorandum Of Good Practice On Video Recorded Interviews With Child Witnesses For Criminal Proceedings* (MOGP) was published by the Home Office (the relevant government department).

(Its recommendations were incorporated into the 2002 *Achieving Best Evidence*.) This MOGP stated that "A rapport phase ... should not be omitted ... " (p. 16). This opening phase of the interview is especially important for children and people with intellectual disability. They, unlike the interviewers, will be unfamiliar with the purpose and format of investigative interviews. This unfamiliarity will add to the stress of (possibly) having been victimized to make it even more difficult for them to retrieve information from memory (Milne & Bull, 1999). They will need time to adjust to the setting and to the interviewer, and will need explanations of what is about to take place.

The rapport phase should also be used to allow the interviewer to become more familiar with the victim's communicative limitations and strengths (Milne & Bull, 2001).

Free Narrative

Psychological research has repeatedly demonstrated that people's most accurate recollections of what happened are those that are provided in their own words. Thus every effort must be made to assist victims to do this. Some young children and people with intellectual disabilities will be under the impression that the adult authority figure (i.e. the interviewer) already knows what happened (due to their inability to realize that what "is in their head" is not the same as in other people's – called "theory of mind" by psychologists). They will be under the impression that since the interviewer already knows what happened, their role is merely to confirm what the interviewer suggests. Therefore, the questioning of them must be delayed until every effort has been made to obtain free recall in their own words.

Compliance

A major reason why questioning, particularly any form of suggestive questioning, should be delayed is that children and people with intellectual disabilities are skilled at going along with what they believe authority adults want to hear. However, studies of real-life investigative interviews with such (alleged) victims have found that interviewers soon rush into questioning, without providing enough opportunity for free recall (Davies, Wilson, Mitchell & Milsom, 1995). Why do interviewers, even trained ones, do this? The answer to this question is that everyday conversations are full of questions and rarely is full, free recall asked for outside the investigative setting. Consequently, it takes a lot of practice and experience to obtain good free recall.

As stated above, interviewers must make it clear that they do not know what happened, that they were not there and that they may ask "silly" or "misguided" questions.

Acquiescence

This is somewhat similar to compliance but it specifically refers to saying "Yes" to yes/no questions (regardless of their content). Since to many questions in everyday conversations an acceptable answer is "Yes", vulnerable people acquiesce to get by in life. To yes/no questions on some topics, the "appropriate" answer is "No" and therefore some vulnerable interviewees will reply to questions regarding taboo topics (e.g. bodily touching) with "No", regardless of the wording of the question. Most yes/no questions can be reworded into either/or questions that are likely to be less affected by acquiescence.

Types of Questions

Once the first two phases of (i) rapport and (ii) obtain free narrative have been achieved to the best of the interviewer's and witness's ability, then and only then should questioning begin. Not every professional is aware that question types vary in how appropriate they are. A wealth of psychological research (Milne & Bull, 1999) supports the recommendations in official guidance documents that the questioning phase should always commence with open questions (if the interviewee has the communicative capacity to understand these and to reply to them).

Open questions "are ones that are worded in such a way as to enable the witness to provide an unrestricted response" (ABE, p. 74). This form of question reduces the likelihood that interviewers will let their expectations about what may have happened affect the victim. Of course, open questions can include information that the victim has already provided in the earlier free recall phase. For example, "A few minutes ago you told me that Robert hurt you. How did Robert hurt you?".

When some victims are responding to open questions, unskilled interviewers often interrupt them (i) when the victim seems (from the interviewer's point of view) to be going off the point or (ii) to seek clarification. This should be avoided, particularly since it may well convey to the victim that only short answers are acceptable. Interrupting also disempowers the witness, making them more compliant.

Though some people might label questions beginning with "Why" as open questions, these should be avoided with children and people with intellectual disabilities because they (i) could interpret this as attributing blame to them and (ii) they are particularly unlikely to have a good understanding of why other people (and, indeed, themselves) behave as they do.

It is imperative that it is fully explained to victims that replying "Don't know" (where appropriate) is a very welcome response (unlike in real life).

Specific-closed questions ask in a non-biasing, non-leading way for clarification/extension of what the (alleged) victim has earlier in the interview communicated. If worded skilfully they could also ask about matters not raised by the victim, but such questions run the grave risk of being suggestive (which ought to be avoided with child victims and those with intellectual disability).

Forced-choice (closed) questions "are ones that provide the interviewee with a limited number of alternative responses" (ABE, p. 76). Problems with this type of question are that: (i) they may not include the correct alternative; (ii) all the alternatives may not be equal from the victim's point of view so that one or two inappropriately "stand out"; and (iii) children and people with intellectual disability may only be able to "take in" the first or last alternative and so they choose that one.

Another form of closed question is one that offers only two alternatives (e.g. yes/no questions). These should be avoided unless they are the only type of question the witness can cope with (e.g. those with severe intellectual disability) and even then they should be either/or questions rather than yes/no questions. It must be emphasized to victims that replying "I can't remember" (where appropriate) is a welcome response that will not annoy the interviewer.

Leading questions imply the answer and/or assume matters not earlier revealed by the victim in the interview. Psychological research has revealed that even ordinary adults, who have not been victimized, readily go along with leading questions. People who have been victimized, especially children (Young, Powell & Dudgeon, 2003; Zalac, Gross & Hayne, 2003) and adults with intellectual disability are even more likely to go along with leading questions (Kebbell, Hatton & Johnson, 2004). One of the main problems with leading questions is that one cannot determine whether the answer is based on memory of the incident(s) or on compliance. This is why courts frown upon the use of leading questions during witnesses'/victims' evidence-in-chief.

If a leading question is asked that produces a response, interviewers should then refrain from asking another leading question but should revert back to open questions, or specific questions.

Closure

Once the questioning phase has been completed, a final and important phase remains. This closure phase has three main aims. The first involves the interviewer checking, in a non-suggestive way using language and communication that the victim can cope with, that the interviewer has correctly understood the witness. The second aim is to ensure that the victim leaves the interview in as positive a frame of mind as possible (which may well involve going back to some of the neutral topics conversed about in the rapport phase). The third aim is to try to ensure that if the victim subsequently has more to say, she/he will feel that the interview was conducted in a sensitive, professional yet supportive way and will be willing to experience a further interview. Psychological research and professional experience confirm that victims often are unable to remember everything in one interview (this may be especially so for children and people with intellectual disabilities). At present vulnerable witnesses' satisfaction with the investigative and other parts of the criminal justice system is less than that of ordinary witnesses (Hamlyn, Phelps & Sattar, 2004).

The above order of question types (i.e. open, specific-closed, forced-choice, leading) need not be rigidly stuck to regarding all the topics that may be focused on in the interview. A victim may have mentioned, say, three separate incidents in their free recall. The questioning on the first of these incidents could go through the above question types in the proper order, likewise the questioning on the second and then on the third incident, with some closure after each incident.

DISCUSSION

Victims and witnesses of all ages and vulnerabilities are pivotal to attaining justice. In order to achieve a correct solution to a crime all interviewees need to be interviewed appropriately, by fully trained interviewers. In addition, interviewers should be assessed regularly within the workplace to ensure that their skills are as high as possible. Furthermore, the recording of such interviews needs to be accurate and the interview process needs to be a transparent one. Thus it is recommended that: (i) witness/victim interviewing is put higher up on the agenda; (ii) interviews with witnesses and victims be electronically recorded; (iii) the training of interviewers to interview witnesses and victims is improved; (iv) such training should be assessed; and (v) regular supervision of witness and victim interviews should be carried out in the workplace as part of the interviewers' staff development.

To follow the recommendations mentioned above (and in official guidance documents) on the interviewing of vulnerable (alleged) victims does require proper understanding of the challenges interviewers face. However, these challenges are not that different from those relating to the interviewing of ordinary witnesses (Prosser & Bromley, 1998).

Kernan and Sabsay (1997) cite Turner (1984) who perceptively noted that "the retarded are just like us, only more so".

REFERENCES

Aarons, N. & Powell, M. (2003). Issues related to the professional's ability to elicit reports of abuse from children with intellectual disability: A review. *Current Issues in Criminal Justice, 14*, 257–268.

Ainsworth, P. (1995). *Psychology and policing in a changing world.* Chichester: John Wiley & Sons, Ltd.

Ask, K. & Granhag, P.A. (2005). Motivational sources of confirmation bias in criminal investigations: The need for cognitive closure. *Journal of Investigative Psychology and Offender Profiling, 2*, 43–63.

Clarke, C. & Milne, R. (2001). *National evaluation of the PEACE investigative interviewing course.* Police Research Award Scheme, PRAS/149. London: Home Office.

Clifford, B. & George, R. (1996). A field investigation of training in three methods of witness/victim investigative interviewing. *Psychology, Crime and Law, 2*, 231–248.

Crawford, E. & Bull, R. (2005). *Teenagers' difficulties with keywords regarding the criminal court process.* Paper presented at the Annual Conference of the European Association of Psychology and Law, Vilnius.

Davies, G., Wilson, C., Mitchell, R. & Milsom, J. (1995). *Videotaping children's evidence: An evaluation.* London: Home Office.

Ede, R. & Shepherd, E. (1997). *Active defence: A solicitor's guide to police and defence investigation and prosecution and defence disclosure in criminal cases.* London: The Law Society.

Fisher, R. & Geiselman, R. (1992). *Memory-enhancing techniques for investigative interviewing: The cognitive interview.* Springfield, IL: Thomas.

Fisher, R., Geiselman, R. & Raymond, D. (1987). Critical analysis of police interviewing techniques. *Journal of Police Science and Administration, 15*, 177–185.

Gudjonsson, G. (2003). *The psychology of interrogations and confessions.* Chichester: John Wiley & Sons, Ltd.

Hamlyn, B., Phelps, A. & Sattar, G. (2004). *Key findings from surveys of vulnerable and intimidated witnesses 2000/01 and 2003.* London: Home Office Research, Development and Statistics Directorate.

Heaton-Armstrong, A. (1995). Recording and disclosing statements by witnesses – law and practice. *Medicine, Science and the Law, 35*, 136–143.

Home Office. (1998). *Speaking Up For Justice.* London: Home Office.

Home Office and Department of Health. (1992). *Memorandum of good practice on video recorded interviews with child witnesses for criminal proceedings.* London: Her Majesty's Stationery Office.

Home Office and Department of Health. (2002). *Achieving best evidence: Guidance for vulnerable or intimidated witnesses, including children.* London: Her Majesty's Stationery Office.

Kebbell, M., Hatton, C. & Johnson, S. (2004). Witnesses with intellectual disabilities in court: What questions are asked and what influence do they have? *Legal and Criminological Psychology, 9*, 23–36.

Kebbell, M., Hurren, E. & Mazarolle, P. (2005). *Sex offenders' perceptions of police interviewing: Implications for improving the interviewing of suspected sex offenders.* Paper presented at the Annual Conference of the European Association of Psychology and Law, Vilnius.

Kebbell, M. & Milne, R. (1998). Police officers' perception of eyewitness factors in forensic investigations. *Journal of Social Psychology, 138,* 323–330.

Kebbell, M. & Wagstaff, G. (1999). *Face value? Evaluating the accuracy of eyewitness information.* Police Research Series Paper 102. London: Home Office.

Kernan, T. & Sabsay, S. (1997). Communication in social interactions: Aspects of an ethnography of communication of mildly mentally handicapped adults. In M. Beveridge and G. Conti-Ramsden (Eds), *Language and communication in people with learning disabilities.* London: Routledge.

Kernan, K., Sabsay, S. & Shinn, N. (1989). Lay people's judgements of storytellers as mentally retarded or not. *Journal of Mental Deficiency Research, 33,* 149–157.

Koehnken, G., Milne, R., Memon, A. & Bull, R. (1999). The cognitive interview: A meta-analysis. *Psychology, Crime and Law, 5,* 3–28.

Koehnken, G., Thurer, C. & Zoberbier, D. (1994). The cognitive interview: Are the interviewers' memories enhanced too? *Applied Cognitive Psychology, 8,* 13–24.

Lamb, M.E., Orbach, Y., Sternberg, K.J., Hershkowitz, I. & Horowitz, D. (2000). Accuracy of investigators' verbatim notes of their forensic interviews with alleged child abuse victims. *Law and Human Behavior, 24*(6), 699–708.

Macphearson, W., Cook, T., Sentamu, J. & Stone, R. (1999). *The Stephen Lawrence Inquiry report.* London: The Stationery Office.

McLean, M. (1995). Quality investigation? Police interviewing of witnesses. *Medicine, Science and the Law, 35,* 116–122.

Milne, R. & Bull, R. (1999). *Investigative interviewing: Psychology and practice.* Chichester: John Wiley & Sons, Ltd.

Milne, R. & Bull, R. (2001). Interviewing witnesses with learning disabilities for legal purposes. *British Journal of Learning Disabilities, 29,* 93–97.

Milne, R., Clare, I. & Bull, R. (1999). Interviewing adults with learning disability with the cognitive interview. *Psychology, Crime and Law, 5,* 81–100.

Milne, R. & Shaw, G. (1999). Obtaining witness statements: Best practice and proposals for innovation. *Medicine, Science and the Law, 39,* 127–138.

Mortimer, A. (1994a). *Cognitive processes underlying police investigative interviewing behaviour.* Unpublished PhD thesis, University of Portsmouth.

Mortimer, A. (1994b) Asking the right questions. *Policing, 10,* 111–123.

Mortimer, A. & Shepherd, E. (1999). Frames of mind: Schemata guiding cognition and conduct in the interviewing of suspected offenders. In A. Memon and R. Bull (Eds), *Handbook of the psychology of interviewing.* Chichester: John Wiley & Sons, Ltd.

Navon, D. & Gopher, D. (1979). On the economy of the human information processing system. *Psychological Review, 86,* 214–255.

Nurmoja, M. (2005). *Interrogative suggestibility, trait-related, and morphofeatural characteristics of human phenotype.* Unpublished Master's thesis, Department of Psychology, University of Tartu, Estonia.

Prosser, H. & Bromley, J. (1998). Interviewing people with intellectual disabilities. In E. Emerson, C. Hatton, J. Bromley & A. Caine (Eds), *Clinical psychology and people with intellectual disabilities.* Chichester: John Wiley & Sons, Ltd.

Rock, F. (2001). The genesis of a witness statement. *Forensic Linguistics, 8*, 44–72.

Sanders, G.S. (1986). The usefulness of eyewitness research from the perspective of police investigators. Unpublished manuscript, State University of New York. Cited in R. Fisher, R.E. Geiselman & M. Armador. (1989). Field test of the cognitive interview: Enhancing the recollection of actual victims and witnesses of crime. *Journal of Applied Psychology, 74*, 722–727.

Shepherd, E. & Milne, R. (1999). Full and faithful: Ensuring quality practice and integrity of outcome in witness interviews. In A. Heaton-Armstrong, D. Wolchover & E. Shepherd (Eds), *Analysing witness testimony*. London: Blackstone Press.

Turner, J. (1984). Workshop society: Ethnographic observations in a work setting. In K. Kernan, M. Begob & R. Edgerton (Eds), *Environments and behavior: The adaptation of mildly retarded persons*. Baltimore: University Park Press.

Wolchover, D. & Heaton-Armstrong, A. (1997a). Tape recording witness statements. *New Law Journal, June 6*, 855–857.

Wolchover, D. & Heaton-Armstrong, A. (1997b). Tape recording witness statements. *New Law Journal, June 13*, 894–896.

Young, K., Powell, M. & Dudgeon, P. (2003). Individual differences in children's suggestibility: A comparison between intellectually disabled and mainstream samples. *Personality and Individual Differences, 35*, 31–49.

Zalac, R., Gross, J. & Hayne, H. (2003). Asked and answered: Questioning children in the courtroom. *Psychiatry, Psychology and Law, 10*, 199–209.

CHAPTER 2

Procedural Recommendations to Increase the Reliability of Eyewitness Identifications

JENNIFER BEAUDRY, ROD LINDSAY AND PAUL DUPUIS

PROLOGUE

On 24 December 1981 a man in a cowboy hat entered a donut shop in Winnipeg, Manitoba, Canada. The only person in the shop was Barbara Stoppel, a 16-year-old employee. A short time later, Stoppel's body was found in a back room. Although no one witnessed the murder, many people saw the cowboy enter the shop, lock the door and later exit just before the body was found. One witness followed and confronted him. No one knew who he was. The witnesses assisted police in the construction of a composite picture. A police officer thought the composite showed a striking resemblance to a man he knew, Thomas Sophonow. Photos of Sophonow were obtained and shown to witnesses in a 10-person photo array. No one selected Sophonow. However, one witness suggested that seeing a live lineup would help. At the subsequent live lineup, again no one selected Sophonow – at first. A witness, after failing to choose anyone, asked to see the lineup again and selected Sophonow. When asked why he had selected that lineup member, the witness explained that he was the tallest. Based on this identification, striking similarity to the composite, lack of an alibi and the statement of a jailhouse informant, Sophonow was tried three times and eventually convicted of murder.

Practical Psychology for Forensic Investigations and Prosecutions.
Edited by Mark R. Kebbell and Graham M. Davies. © 2006 John Wiley & Sons, Ltd.

INTRODUCTION

In any criminal case, the role of the police officer is to interview potential witnesses to obtain as much information about the perpetrator as possible (for a detailed discussion of interviews of witnesses see Chapter 1). When the identity of the perpetrator is not known to the witness, police often rely on eyewitnesses to provide information that will lead them to suspects and then to confirm or disconfirm that the suspects are the perpetrator of the crimes. To do so, the witness is first asked to provide a description of the perpetrator. The identity of the perpetrator may subsequently be discovered through the creation (and identification) of a composite and/or through a search of mugshots.

Once a suspect has been located, the police officer may choose to present the witness with a lineup containing the suspect and other known-innocent lineup members or with only the suspect (a showup). Identification of the suspect is the ultimate goal of the lineup procedure; however, errors are common. DNA exoneration cases indicate that 80 to 90% of wrongful convictions occur when a false identification has been made by an eyewitness (Innocence Project, 2005). These numbers are staggering and spurred former US Attorney General Janet Reno to create, with the assistance of the Technical Working Group for Eyewitness Evidence, a National Institute of Justice guide for eyewitness procedures (Technical Working Group, 1999).

While eyewitness identification evidence has been implicated in numerous wrongful conviction cases, eyewitness evidence remains crucial to the administration of justice. The goal of this chapter is to help the police obtain the best identification evidence possible with the least risk of error. To this end, general recommendations will be made that are applicable regardless of the specific procedure employed. Then, the means police have to locate an unknown suspect – composites and mugshots – will be described. Finally, the procedures that are used to identify the perpetrator of a crime – lineups and showups – will be discussed. Current best practice recommendations, supported with brief reviews of the relevant research literature, are presented for each of these four eyewitness procedures. Detailed discussions of the eyewitness research literature associated with each of these topics can be found in the *Handbook of Eyewitness Psychology: Memory for People* (Lindsay, Ross, Read & Toglia, in press).

GENERAL RECOMMENDATIONS

The investigative process typically begins with one or more witnesses providing a description of the perpetrator to the police. The description is the starting point for all other procedures. While the description process is critical, it is not the focus of this chapter; therefore, we will presume that best practices are followed at the description stage. For a detailed consideration of descriptions of people see Schooler, Meissner & Sporer (in press).

Two general recommendations can be made that are applicable to investigations involving witnesses, regardless of the type of eyewitness procedure used in the case. The first involves situations in which multiple witnesses have viewed the same event. It is crucial to separate the witnesses as soon as possible – even before obtaining a description of the perpetrator – and this separation must be maintained throughout the identification phase to eliminate the potential influence of other witnesses (Luus & Wells, 1994).

The second general recommendation is to record all information before, during and after the identification phase (Technical Working Group, 1999). For example, a record must be kept of the description of the suspect, the statements made during the mugshot search and the witness's indication of their confidence in their identification of the suspect because this information may become critical at a later stage of the investigation or during trial.

These general recommendations should be followed for all procedures; however, further reference to them will be made in relation to specific procedures.

COMPOSITES

A composite is intended to be used in cases in which a witness to the crime is available, but the identity of the perpetrator is not known to the police or bystanders and cannot be determined through other means (e.g., video security footage). To produce a composite, witnesses are asked to render a likeness of the perpetrator of the crime with the assistance of a sketch artist or composite system operator. The creation of a composite is accomplished by interviewing the witness and leading him or her through the steps of describing the features of the perpetrator's face and judging the similarity of the composites to their memory of the perpetrator. If necessary, modifications may be made to the composite until a suitable likeness is achieved.

Frequently, composites are distributed in police stations in case the composite resembles a local person known by officers (Kitson, Darnbrough & Shields, 1978). Alternatively (or in addition), the composite may be released to the public to alert them to a dangerous individual and/or to elicit cooperation from the public in identifying and finding the individual.

The composite is always generated in an attempt to determine the identity of the perpetrator; however, the likeness can be created through the use of several different systems that are based on one of the following four methods: (i) sketch artist; (ii) mechanical systems; (iii) software systems; or (iv) genetic algorithms. These methods differ according to the manner by which the composite is constructed; that is, the sketch artist draws the composite, the operator of a mechanical system manually pieces together features of the face, and the operator of the software and genetic algorithm systems uses a computer to construct the composite. Rather than focus on the different methods, general guidelines will be provided that should be followed when creating a composite, regardless of which composite system is employed. For a detailed discussion of the various composite systems, see Davies and Valentine (in press).

Composite Recommendations

The composite production begins with an interview of the witness by a trained composite system operator or sketch artist (depending on the system). The recommendations made in this chapter will pertain to the function of the composite, the training of the operator, the interview process, the post-composite role of the witness and the special procedures for cases with multiple witnesses.

The first recommendation refers to the probative value of a composite. It is essential to understand that similarity to a composite is not strong evidence of guilt when presented in a court of law (Association of Chief Police Officers of England, Wales and Northern Ireland, 2003). Instead, a composite should be used as an investigative tool to locate potential suspects. Keeping this in mind reduces the probability that the investigation will focus on a single suspect without sufficient cause, a tendency referred to as "tunnel vision" (Cory, 2001).

The second recommendation is that the operator be appropriately trained on the system employed by the police force. Research has repeatedly demonstrated that, compared to a novice, experienced operators spend additional time in the description phase and obtain more elaborate descriptions from the witness (Davies, Milne & Shepherd, 1983). As well, experienced operators produce composites of better quality (e.g., Ellis, Davies & Shepherd, 1978) that are rated as better likenesses of the target's face (e.g., Davies et al., 1983).

The third recommendation is that the cognitive interview should be used to glean as much information as possible from the witness. The cognitive interview incorporates four techniques: (i) context reinstatement; (ii) recalling the events in different orders; (iii) mentally changing perspectives; and (iv) emphasizing the importance of reporting all information, even if it seems irrelevant to the witness (Geiselman et al., 1984). In addition, the witness is asked nonleading, open-ended questions that allow the witness to describe the event in his or her own words without constraint or direction (Geiselman, Fisher, MacKinnon & Holland, 1985). While studies have not yet been conducted to examine the impact of the combined elements of the cognitive interview on composite production, Davies and Milne (1985) have demonstrated that context reinstatement improves the quality of composites produced by eyewitnesses compared to control subjects. Furthermore, the potential benefits of the cognitive interview can be evident throughout the investigation. For instance, researchers have demonstrated increased identification accuracy from a lineup after context reinstatement (Krafka & Penrod, 1985) and upon employment of the entire cognitive interview technique (Finger & Pezdek, 1999).

The fourth recommendation pertains to the witness's role in the investigation after producing a composite. Involvement by a witness in the production of a composite may reduce the reliability of subsequent identification attempts. The main question here is: Should a witness involved in the production of a composite later be asked to identify the perpetrator from a lineup? Unfortunately, there are no hard and fast rules that can be applied in this situation; however, it has been strongly suggested that such a witness should not participate in a lineup procedure (e.g., Bruce, Ness, Hancock, Newman & Rarity, 2002; Wells, Charman & Olson, 2005).

Research findings regarding the impact of composite production on the accuracy of lineup identification has been inconsistent. Past research has demonstrated that a witness's ability to identify the perpetrator is not damaged by the process of composite construction (Davies, Ellis & Shepherd, 1978; Mauldin & Laughery, 1981). On the other hand, recent research has demonstrated that creating a composite, or even viewing a composite created by another participant, decreases the rate of correct identifications (with no effect on false identifications) compared to participants who did not partake in either activity (Wells et al., 2005). Until more consistent evidence emerges, the practice of using the same witness for composite and identification procedures should be approached with caution because producing a composite may reduce the reliability of subsequent identification attempts. If the same witness is used for both procedures, neither the composite nor description should be presented to the witness immediately before the identification procedure, as this information could be prejudicial to a suspect located based on such information. Moreover, this information could be detrimental to the witness's memory of the perpetrator (Sporer, 1996), particularly if the composite contains any misleading features (Jenkins & Davies, 1985).

The fifth recommendation is only applicable if multiple persons witnessed the crime. In this situation, it could be beneficial to have some witnesses involved in composite construction and to reserve the rest for subsequent identification procedures. However, if the officer decides to use all witnesses to construct composites, these witnesses should be separated as soon as possible, each witness should create their own composite, and all constructed composites should be released to police officers or the public. Multiple composites, regardless of whether they are presented together or digitally combined to form one composite (morphed), have been rated as better likenesses and have improved identification accuracy compared to any individual composite (Bruce et al., 2002; Hasel & Wells, in press). In addition, if feasible, different operators should be utilized to construct composites from multiple witnesses of the same crime to minimize the potential influence of other composites on the operator's construction decisions. When the use of different operators is not feasible, the operator should focus only on the current witness's description and incorporate only that information into the composite.

The above recommendations are applicable to all composite systems as they pertain to the preparation and distribution of the composite. There are no procedural recommendations regarding the construction of the composite itself, except to follow the advice and guidelines outlined in the system's training manual.

MUGSHOTS

Like a composite, mugshot searches are used in cases in which the police have a witness to the crime, but no suspect and no other way to determine the identity of the perpetrator. In this procedure, a witness is asked to look through, potentially, hundreds of mugshots in an attempt to locate possible suspects. In the past, witnesses manually flipped through mug books in search of suspects; however, mug books have become much more technologically advanced. Mugshots can now be presented to the witness in a computerized mug book. Regardless of whether photos are presented in albums or electronically, the witness's task remains unchanged. The impact of technology is evident, however, in the production of software that is designed to sort mugshots in an attempt to decrease the number of faces presented to a witness prior to encountering the perpetrator. These techniques are crucial because mugshot pools are often very large and research indicates that a witness's ability to identify the perpetrator is negatively impacted by exposure to a large number of mugshots (Laughery, Alexander & Lane, 1971; Pryke, Lindsay & Pozzulo, 2000).

Mugshots are generally sorted using one of two techniques that rely on different aspects of face processing, featural and holistic. The two methods rely upon different face-processing assumptions; the former, that humans process a face as an independent set of features, and the latter, that faces are processed in a holistic manner. Using the featural method, mugshots are sorted according to the degree of match between available mugshots and the witness's description of the perpetrator (e.g., Lee & Whalen, 1996; Lindsay, Nosworthy, Martin & Martynuck, 1994). Using the holistic method, mugshots are sorted according to the degree of similarity between each mugshot and the witness's overall visual memory of the perpetrator. In this technique, a witness begins with the standard mugshot search but is instructed to select a mugshot that is somewhat similar to their memory of the perpetrator to allow the computer (usually based on facial recognition or genetic algorithms) to select and present similar faces (e.g., Pentland, Picard & Sclaroff, 1996). At this time, a statement regarding the absolute advantage of one sorting technique over the other is not warranted because sufficient comparisons between the procedures have not yet been conducted (for a review, see McAllister, in press). Furthermore, this chapter is intended to be relevant to all agencies, regardless of the technological advancements that are available to them; as such, the following recommendations will be applicable to all mugshot search techniques.

Mugshot Recommendations

A mugshot search begins with the witness's description of the perpetrator. The mugshots are then sorted according to their relevance to the search parameters (again, may be done with different techniques), and the witness selects one or more mugshots of people he or she believes may be the perpetrator. The recommendations made in this chapter will pertain to the appearance of the mugshots, the investigative function of the mugshot search, the style of mugshot presentation, the post-mugshot role of the witness and the special procedures to be employed in cases with multiple witnesses.

The first (and perhaps most important) recommendation is that a mugshot should not stand out for any reason other than that it is recognized by the witness. Several corollaries follow from this recommendation. First, the mugshots should be presented in a uniform manner. The exact format of the mugshot is not the critical issue, as various formats (e.g., colour vs. black and white; profile vs. head-on vs. portrait) have been shown to have little effect on a witness's ability to select the perpetrator (e.g., Laughery et al., 1971). Rather, no single mugshot or small set of mugshots should stand out in comparison to the pool as a whole. Second, only one photograph of each individual should be contained in the mug book because a witness may be more likely to select a mugshot if they had previously seen the person during the mugshot search (Technical Working Group, 1999). Third, clothing matters such that identification of a person wearing clothing matching that described by the witness is of dubious validity. Even moderately similar people may be misidentified from mugshots if they are wearing clothing similar to that worn by the perpetrator during the crime (Lindsay et al., 1994). Ideally, mugshots should be restricted to facial photos (neck up) or taken wearing uniform clothing.

The second recommendation, as suggested by Lindsay et al. (1994), is that the mugshot search be treated as an investigative tool (to discover potential suspects) rather than as an identification procedure (to identify the perpetrator). Because mugshot pools are very large they are almost certain to contain many photos of people who could easily be confused with the person actually seen by the witness. As a result, selection from mugshots is, at best, very weak evidence and is better suited to advancing the case by indicating people worthy of further investigation. Again, two corollaries follow from this recommendation. First, to increase the utility of this investigative tool, witnesses could be allowed to provide *maybe* as well as *yes* or *no* responses to mugshots. Providing the witness with two positive response options increases the likelihood that the perpetrator will be selected, if present in the mug book (Lindsay et al., 1994). Also, the use of *maybe* responses reinforces the notion that the mugshot search is an investigative tool, not an identification task comparable to a lineup. Second, a witness who selects multiple photos should be allowed to view all selected photos after the search is completed and be invited to eliminate those individuals he or she no longer believes may be the perpetrator. This "second-pass" reduces the number of incorrect photos, while correct photos are rarely eliminated, from the final pool. As a result, the number of investigative leads is reduced to a more manageable number (Lindsay et al., 1994).

The third recommendation is that the mugshots be presented to the witness in a "grouped" display rather than individually. When multiple mugshots are presented together witnesses generally will scan the group of mugshots, find the individual most similar to their memory of the perpetrator, decide if that may be the person they saw, and move onto the next set of mugshots. Presenting individual photos takes more time and results in more incorrect selections compared to the grouped procedure (McAllister, in press; McAllister & Michel, 2002; Stewart & McAllister, 2001).

The fourth recommendation is that the value of subsequent lineup procedures must be assessed in light of participation in mugshot tasks. This issue is complex and depends on whether the witness selected anyone from the mug books and whether any individual seen in the mug books is in the subsequent lineup. Three scenarios are possible.

First, it is reasonable to ask a witness (after completion of a mugshot search) to attempt to identify a suspect from a lineup if he was *not* present in the mug book. A mugshot search that did not include the current suspect does not impair the witness's ability to identify the perpetrator from a subsequent lineup (e.g., Dysart, Lindsay, Hammond & Dupuis, 2001). Note that a corollary of this is that police need to record the identity of all people presented to the witness during a mugshot search, not just those selected by the witness. Failure to keep such records could leave subsequent lineup selections open to challenge.

Second, it is *not* reasonable to ask a witness to attempt to identify a suspect from a subsequent lineup if the witness already selected that suspect from the mug books. A witness who selects an innocent individual during the mugshot search is more likely to subsequently select that innocent individual from the lineup than a witness who was not exposed to or did not select the suspect from the mug books (Dysart et al., 2001). Once selected from the mugshots, innocent and guilty suspects are equally likely to be selected from a subsequent lineup. Repeating the choice of the suspect is likely to increase the witness's confidence in the identification but does not increase the probative value of the selection. Following such a procedure and presenting only the selection from the lineup in court misleads the judge and jury by suggesting that the evidence is more probative than it actually is.

Third, if the lineup contains a suspect presented in the mugshots who was not selected by the witness, police should *not* require this witness to participate in a lineup procedure containing the same suspect. The concern in this situation is that the witness will identify an innocent lineup member as the perpetrator as a result of exposure to the individual during the mugshot search. While this seems like a reasonable concern, tests of this hypothesis have produced inconsistent results (Brown, Deffenbacher & Sturgill, 1977; Dysart et al., 2001). However, the lineup identification evidence would be questionable at best as the witness failed to select the suspect during a previous opportunity.

The fifth recommendation is that in cases involving multiple witnesses, officers should try to preserve some witnesses who will not have been exposed to mugshots to provide untainted identification evidence from lineups. This recommendation follows the same logic from the fifth composite recommendation.

LINEUPS

Lineup procedures are required in cases where police have a suspect and one or more witnesses to the crime. The recommendations suggested in this chapter apply to lineups conducted live or with photographs (photo arrays). Police lineups contain the suspect (may be guilty or innocent) and fillers (non-suspects). The witness must decide if one of the lineup members is the person he or she saw. Three outcomes are possible: (i) the witness selects the suspect; (ii) the witness selects a filler; or (iii) the witness selects no one. If the suspect is the perpetrator, the correct decision is to select the suspect (correct identification). An incorrect decision is to select no one (a "miss" or incorrect rejection) or a filler (false positive). If the suspect is not the perpetrator, the correct decision is to select no one (correct rejection) and incorrect decisions are to select the suspect (false identification) or a filler (false positive). Because filler selections are "known errors" regardless of whether the criminal is in the lineup or not, they discredit the witness but do not tend to lead to wrongful convictions (provided that only a single suspect is in the lineup, Wells, 1984; Wells & Turtle, 1988).

Detailed discussion of the lineup literature and theory are available elsewhere (e.g., Charman & Wells, in press; Dupuis & Lindsay, in press). The following recommendations provide police with guidelines that are designed to increase the likelihood that the witness will avoid selecting innocent people while still selecting the culprit (if present) at a reasonably high rate. The following recommendations address factors that are within the control of the police (see Wells, 1978, for a discussion of system and estimator variables).

Lineup Recommendations

The lineup procedure begins with the witness's description of the perpetrator (which is used to construct the lineup) and ends once the witness attempts an identification from the lineup. The recommendations in this chapter pertain to the number of suspects in a single lineup, the number of fillers needed in a lineup, the criteria to be used for filler selection, how the lineup should be administered, the instructions provided to the witness, the witness's confidence statement, and the style of lineup presentation. The following recommendations are based on previous policy recommendation papers (e.g., Technical Working Group, 1999; Turtle, Lindsay & Wells, 2003; Wells et al., 1998).

The first recommendation is that each lineup must contain only one suspect (Wells & Turtle, 1988). Evidence of guilt is created by the witness's ability to select the suspect rather than another lineup member. Because witnesses are prone to guessing, the inclusion of more than one suspect in a lineup increases the likelihood that a witness will select a suspect by chance alone. A lineup containing only suspects is similar to a multiple-choice test with no wrong answer. If multiple suspects exist, it is best to reduce the number of plausible alternatives through investigative techniques and hold the lineup in reserve until a single suspect remains. If lineups must be used even when there is more than one suspect, a separate lineup must be conducted for each suspect.

The second recommendation is that the lineup must contain an "appropriate" number of fillers. Required numbers vary by country and jurisdiction (Nosworthy & Lindsay, 1990). Assuming the presence of only one suspect in the lineup, the larger the lineup, the less likely an identification of a suspect is to be false (Turtle et al., 2003; Wells & Turtle, 1988). Insufficient research data exists at this time to clearly state an optimal lineup size but, until further research is conducted, employing lineups smaller than six (Technical Working Group, 1999) or larger than 20 (Beaudry, Boyce, Dupuis & Lindsay, 2005) may be unwise.

The third recommendation pertains to the criteria used to select the filters. All lineup members should resemble the suspect on all features included in the witness's description of the criminal (Lindsay, 1999; Malpass, Tredoux & McQuiston, in press; Wells, Rydell & Seelau, 1993; Wells, Rydell, Seelau & Luus, 1994). It is crucial that the suspect not stand out in the lineup as being different from the fillers based on the witness's description. If the suspect could be selected based solely on the description, selection from the lineup provides no evidence of guilt beyond the fact that the suspect matches the description. If some of the lineup members fail to match the description, the lineup is effectively smaller than it appears to be with the attendant increase in the risk of false identification due to guessing and thus lineup fairness is reduced (Malpass et al., in press; Wells, Leippe & Ostrom, 1979). As lineups become less fair, they produce less probative evidence of guilt (Lindsay, Smith & Pryke, 1999). The objective is not to provide the witness with a lineup of clones, but instead to determine if the witness can select the perpetrator based on his or her memory of the person, not as a result of a biased lineup (Wells et al., 1998). Three corollaries follow from this recommendation.

First, when the suspect does not match the witness's description of a feature of the criminal, the fillers should match the suspect on the relevant feature. Thus, if the suspect is discrepant from the original description (e.g., criminal was described as having a beard, but when apprehended suspect is clean-shaven), then all fillers should match the suspect on this feature (in this case, all lineup members would be clean-shaven).

Second, when features cannot be matched, the relevant feature of all lineup members should be concealed. If the criminal was described as having an unusual facial scar, birthmark or tattoo that could not be matched, this feature should be concealed (e.g., by placing a piece of tape on the photos or bandage on the person) and the same area on all fillers must be treated similarly. Often, this may not be an issue because the presence of a unique scar or tattoo may be sufficient evidence of the perpetrator's identity.

Third, when there are multiple witnesses, it may be necessary to construct different lineups for each witness even though there is only a single suspect. To the extent that witnesses' descriptions vary, fillers must be selected as described by the particular witness that will view that lineup. This point emphasizes the fact that the description as well as the appearance of the suspect combine to determine the appropriateness of lineup fillers.

The fourth recommendation is that the police officer administering the lineup must not know the identity of the suspect and that the witness be made aware of this fact. This recommendation has been emphatically endorsed by researchers (e.g., Wells et al., 1998) and judges alike (e.g., Cory, 2001). Apparently, police officers are often insulted by this recommendation because of the insinuation that they are intentionally influencing the witness (Wells et al., 2000). However, the basis for this recommendation is the understanding that witnesses often assume that the guilty party must be in the lineup and that the police officer administering the lineup knows the "correct response". As a result, witnesses may look to the police officer for cues and may interpret unintentional behaviour as signals regarding which lineup member to choose. If the recommended procedure, known as double-blind testing, is used and known to be used, there will be no reason to look to the officer for guidance. Double-blind testing reduces unintentional bias and protects officers from accusations of intentional bias as well.

Double-blind testing requires the presence of a second officer, unfamiliar with the case, in order to conduct a lineup. This can be difficult in small departments and with highly publicized cases. Several alternatives exist if a second officer is not available. A "high tech" alternative uses computers programmed to present the lineup in the absence of the officer. In effect, the computer acts as the second officer in the double-blind testing procedure (Turtle et al., 2003). "Low tech" alternatives require that the officer simply not be in the room when the witness is exposed to the lineup or not be able to see the lineup while the witness is examining it. These alternatives will not always work. For example, witnesses can ask the officer questions or show the officer a photo they are considering and ask for his or her opinion. Clearly, double-blind testing is superior to these alternatives because an officer unaware of which lineup member is suspected cannot, either intentionally or inadvertently, direct the witness to choose the suspect.

The fifth recommendation pertains to the instructions provided to the witness before the lineup is presented. For step-by-step instructions the reader may refer to the report by the Technical Working Group (1999); only the two most important instructions will be highlighted here. First, as indicated above, a witness may look to the person administering the lineup for clues or hints. As such, it is important that the witness be told that the administrator does not know the identity of the suspect or what position he or she occupies in the lineup. This instruction is intended to make it clear to the witness that a double-blind procedure is in use and that it is inappropriate to search for or expect any "help" with the selection of a lineup member from the officer presenting the lineup. Second, to eliminate any pressure the witness may feel to make a selection, the witness must be told that the perpetrator may or may not be in the lineup. This instruction reduces the rate of false identifications without negatively impacting the rate of correct identifications (Steblay, 1997). An additional instruction stating that exonerating the innocent is as important as identifying the guilty is also recommended for the same reasons (Technical Working Group, 1999).

The sixth recommendation is that the witness should report, in his or her own words, how certain he or she is that the selected person is the perpetrator *before* receiving any feedback. Post-identification feedback may come from the police officer ("good you got him"), other witnesses ("I picked number two also"), the media ("police suspect identified by witness"), or from the courts (subpoena to testify). Any form of feedback can bolster the witness's confidence (e.g., Bradfield, Wells & Olson, 2002). Increased confidence normally strengthens the belief of the witness but does not help jurors to discriminate between accurate and inaccurate witnesses (e.g., Lindsay, Wells & O'Connor, 1989).

The seventh, and final, recommendation is that the officer considers presenting the lineup in a sequential rather than a simultaneous fashion. A simultaneous lineup follows the standard procedure: lineup members are presented to the witness all at once. This method encourages the witness to select the person that most resembles the perpetrator compared to other lineup members, regardless of whether that person is the actual perpetrator (Wells, 1984). The sequential lineup procedure, on the other hand, encourages witnesses to determine, for each lineup member, whether that person is or is not the perpetrator (Lindsay & Wells, 1985). Compared to the simultaneous lineup, the sequential lineup dramatically reduces the number of false identifications with little decrease in correct identifications (Steblay, Dysart, Fulero & Lindsay, 2001). In addition, sequential lineups are less damaged by lineup biases such as poor fillers, biased instructions and clothing bias (Lindsay et al., 1991).

Of particular importance is the ratio of correct to false identifications for each procedure (Wells & Lindsay, 1980). The odds that a suspect identification is accurate are approximately doubled by the use of a sequential lineup and thus the probative value of identification evidence from sequential lineups is much greater than from simultaneous lineups (Steblay et al., 2001; Turtle et al., 2003).

The following five elements are critical to the administration of a sequential lineup. First, the procedure must be double-blind. Failure to use proper, double-blind procedures eliminates the advantage of sequential lineup presentation (Phillips, McAuliff, Kovera & Cutler, 1999). If the procedure will not be performed double-blind, do not use a sequential lineup! Second, the witness must not know the number of photographs that will be presented in the lineup procedure. Awareness of the number of members in a sequential lineup increases pressure to choose as the lineup continues, which increases incorrect choices late in the procedure (Lindsay, Lea & Fulford, 1991). Third, the witness is presented with one lineup member at a time. This procedure encourages the witness to compare the individual presented to their memory of the criminal rather than to the other lineup members. Fourth, for each photograph, the witness must indicate *yes* or *no*, to the question, "Can you state that this is the person you saw?" before seeing the next photo. By far the most common procedural errors when using sequential lineups are violations of this principle (based on the second author's past consultations in Canadian cases). A witness must not put photos aside or simply not respond until after seeing further photos. If allowed to do this, the witness will compare the lineup members to each other rather than just to his or her memory of the criminal (Lindsay & Bellinger, 1999). Fifth, the witness cannot retract previous decisions. Witnesses will sometimes say "no" to each of the lineup members but when told the lineup is over ask to see one of them again or state "It was number two". This indicates the use of relative judgements and is dangerous. Little is to be gained from allowing this as the witness has already failed to state that the person was the criminal.

SHOWUPS

A showup is an identification technique in which the witness is presented only with a suspect, or a photo of a suspect, and is asked to determine if this is the person he or she saw commit the crime. This procedure is generally used when the police find a person fitting the witness's description of the criminal in the immediate vicinity and shortly after the crime occurred.

Showups are a controversial identification procedure. The general opinion of eyewitness researchers is that the use of a showup, compared to a lineup, increases the risk of false identification (Kassin, Tubb,

Hosch & Memon, 2001). A major concern is that witnesses are more likely to select an innocent suspect from a showup, perhaps because the procedure itself implies that the person is guilty (Wells et al., 1998). However, there is disagreement in the courts surrounding whether showups should ever be used, and if so, under what circumstances (e.g., *State* v. *Dubose*, 2005).

Inconsistent results regarding the accuracy of showup identifications have been produced by individual studies (e.g., Beal, Schmitt & Dekle, 1995; Yarmey, Yarmey & Yarmey, 1996). A recent meta-analysis comparing lineups to showups has supported researchers' concerns. Correct identification rates from showups and lineups were comparable; however, showups doubled the false identification rate of simultaneous lineups (Steblay, Dysart, Fulero & Lindsay, 2003). Witnesses are less likely to make a choice from a showup than from a lineup when the culprit is absent. Since choosing no one is the correct decision in this situation, absolute accuracy is actually greater using showups than lineups. Unfortunately, the only choice available in a showup is the suspect, whereas in a lineup the options include the suspect and fillers. Thus, all choices from a culprit-absent showup are false identifications while only a fraction of the choices from culprit-absent lineups are false identifications, the remainder being false positive filler selections. Taking this factor into account, lineups do produce more errors but ironically will lead to fewer false identifications (selections of innocent suspects) and thus fewer wrongful convictions (Dysart & Lindsay, in press; Steblay et al., 2003). Despite warnings from researchers, police still employ the showup procedure frequently (e.g., Flowe, Ebbesen, Burke & Chivabunditt, 2001) and will likely continue to do so.

Showup Recommendations

As with the other eyewitness procedures, the showup is based on the witness's description of the perpetrator. If the officers find someone in the immediate vicinity of the crime, they often conduct a showup to immediately determine if they have the culprit in custody or if they should continue the search. The following recommendations regarding the investigative function, construction and administration of the showup, as well as the post-showup role of the witness are designed to reduce the suggestive nature of the procedure as much as possible.

The first recommendation is that a showup should only be used when it is *impossible* to present the witness with a lineup. Due to the potential for false identifications, showups should be avoided unless absolutely necessary; for example, if it is unknown whether the witness will survive long enough to conduct a lineup (*Stovall* v. *Denno*, 1967). Without adherence to this regulation the police risk having the identification evidence suppressed at trial (*State* v. *Dubose,* 2005).

The second recommendation is to eliminate the impact of clothing bias through the concealment of the suspect's clothing from the witness. This practice has no effect on the witness's ability to correctly identify the perpetrator, if present, but significantly reduces the chances that an innocent (similar looking) suspect will be identified (Dysart, Lindsay & Dupuis, in press). Concealment may be by way of tape over a photo or spreading a jacket or blanket over the actual suspect from the neck down. Clothing bias is particularly problematic for showups because police often will have been drawn to the suspect by the fact that his or her clothes match the description provided by the witness. If the suspect happens to resemble the criminal, a clothing biased showup may generate false identifications at a rate as much as eight times the rate for a fair simultaneous lineup. Even if the suspect is only slightly similar to the actual perpetrator, very large increases in false identifications occur (Dysart et al., in press).

The third recommendation is that the police officer must instruct the witness that the suspect may or may not be the perpetrator. This recommendation was previously discussed as a lineup recommendation, and as such will only be touched upon briefly. The negative impact of instruction bias in lineups may be more pronounced in a showup because the witness may feel increased pressure to choose. False identification rates in showups decreased as a result of the "may or may not" instruction, while the correct identification of the culprit was unaffected (Dysart et al., in press).

The fourth recommendation is to present the suspect to the witness only once. Upon identification of the suspect, the witness should not be asked to select the suspect from a subsequent lineup (*State* v. *Dubose,* 2005). Research with both showups (Behrman & Vayder, 1994) and mugshots (e.g., Dysart et al., 2001) indicates that a witness is likely to select an innocent suspect from a lineup if he or she was previously selected. If the suspect was not identified from the showup, it makes no sense to expose the witness to the same suspect in a subsequent lineup since the witness has already failed to identify the suspect once and selection from the lineup could be based on memory from the irrelevant prior exposure (e.g., Ross, Ceci, Dunning & Toglia, 1994).

While the authors do not endorse the use of showups by police, we understand that circumstances exist in which it is imperative to immediately present the suspect to the witness without the safeguard of a complete and unbiased lineup. If followed, the showup recommendations increase the likelihood that the identified suspect is in fact the perpetrator.

CONCLUSION

The above recommendations are based on research designed to improve eyewitness procedures. There will always be elements of the crime, witness and witnessing conditions that are specific to each case and beyond the control of the investigating officers. However, the recommendations made here address factors that are within the officer's control. Following the recommended procedures will increase the probability that suspects found and identified by eyewitnesses did in fact commit the crimes with which they are charged. Because the eyewitness evidence obtained from such procedures has greater probative value, adhering to these recommendations improves the identification evidence. As a result, the evidence will be more difficult to challenge in court.

EPILOGUE

Eventually, after he had spent almost four years in prison, Thomas Sophonow's conviction was overturned (Cory, 2001). The Winnipeg police are now convinced that Sophonow is innocent and that they know who committed the crime. The "new" suspect did not closely resemble Sophonow in 1981 but, ironically, he did bear a striking resemblance to the composite.

REFERENCES

Association of Chief Police Officers of England, Wales and Northern Ireland. (2003). *National Working Practices in Facial Imaging*. Retrieved April 12, 2005 from http://www.acpo.police.uk//asp/policies/Data/garvin _facial_imaging_guidelines.doc.

Beal, C.R., Schmitt, K.L. & Dekle, D.J. (1995). Eyewitness identification of children: Effects of absolute judgments, nonverbal response options, and event encoding. *Law and Human Behavior, 19*, 197–216.

Beaudry, J.L., Boyce, M.A., Dupuis, P.R. & Lindsay, R.C.L. (2005, March). *An assessment of the multiple-choice, sequential, large lineup*. Poster session presented at the annual meeting of the American Psychology–Law Society, La Jolla, CA.

Behrman, B.W. & Vayder, L.T. (1994). The biasing influence of a police showup: Does the observation of a single suspect taint later identification? *Perceptual and Motor Skills, 79*, 1239–1248.

Bradfield, A.L., Wells, G.L. & Olson, E.A. (2002). The damaging effect of confirming feedback on the relation between eyewitness certainty and identification accuracy. *Journal of Applied Psychology, 87*, 112–120.

Brown, E., Deffenbacher, K. & Sturgill, W. (1977). Memory for faces and the circumstances of encounter. *Journal of Applied Psychology, 62*, 311–318.

Bruce, V., Ness, H., Hancock, P.J.B., Newman, C. & Rarity, J. (2002). Four heads are better than one: Combining face composites yields improvements in face likeness. *Journal of Applied Psychology, 87*, 894–902.

Charman, S. & Wells, G.L. (in press). Applied lineup theory. In R. Lindsay, D. Ross, D. Read & M. Toglia (Eds), *Handbook of eyewitness psychology: Memory for people.* Hillsdale, NJ: Erlbaum Associates.

Cory, P.E. (2001). *The inquiry regarding Thomas Sophonow: The investigation, prosecution and consideration of entitlement to compensation.* Winnipeg, MB: Department of Justice. Retrieved August 12, 2005 from http://www.gov.mb.ca/justice/sophonow/toc.html.

Davies, G., Ellis, H. & Shepherd, J. (1978). Face identification: The influence of delay upon accuracy of Photofit construction. *Journal of Police Science and Administration, 6*, 35–42.

Davies, G. & Milne, A. (1985). Eyewitness composite production: A function of mental or physical reinstatement of context. *Criminal Justice and Behavior, 12*, 209–220.

Davies, G., Milne, A. & Shepherd, J. (1983). Searching for operator skills in face composition reproduction. *Journal of Police Science and Administration, 11*, 405–409.

Davies, G.M. & Valentine, T. (in press). Facial composites: Forensic utility and psychological research. In R. Lindsay, D. Ross, D. Read & M. Toglia (Eds), *Handbook of eyewitness psychology: Memory for people.* Hillsdale, NJ: Erlbaum Associates.

Dupuis, P. & Lindsay, R.C.L. (in press). Radical alternatives to traditional lineup procedures. In R. Lindsay, D. Ross, D. Read & M. Toglia (Eds), *Handbook of eyewitness psychology: Memory for people.* Hillsdale, NJ: Erlbaum Associates.

Dysart, J.E., Lindsay, R.C.L., Hammond, R. & Dupuis, P. (2001). Mug shot exposure prior to lineup identification: Interference, transference and commitment effects. *Journal of Applied Psychology, 86*, 1280–1284.

Dysart, J.E. & Lindsay, R.C.L. (in press). Suggestive technique or reliable method: What do we really know about show-up identifications? In R. Lindsay, D. Ross, D. Read & M. Toglia (Eds), *Handbook of eyewitness psychology: Memory for people.* Hillsdale, NJ: Erlbaum Associates.

Dysart, J.E., Lindsay, R.C.L. & Dupuis, P.R. (in press). Clothing matters: The effects of clothing bias on identification accuracy from show-ups. *Applied Cognitive Psychology.*

Ellis, H., Davies, G.M. & Shepherd, J.W. (1978). A critical examination of the Photofit system for recalling faces. *Ergonomics, 21*, 297–307.

Finger, K. & Pezdek, K. (1999). The effect of the cognitive interview on face identification accuracy: Release from verbal overshadowing. *Journal of Applied Psychology, 84*, 340–348.

Flowe, H., Ebbesen, E., Burke, C. & Chivabunditt, P. (2001, June). *At the scene of the crime: An examination of the external validity of published studies on line-up identification accuracy.* Paper presented at the annual meeting of the American Psychological Society, Toronto, Ontario, Canada.

Geiselman, R.E., Fisher, R.P., Firstenberg, L., Hutton, L.A., Sullivan, S.J., Avetissian, I.V., et al. (1984). Enhancement of eyewitness memory: An empirical evaluation of the cognitive interview. *Journal of Police Science and Administration, 12*, 74–80.

Geiselman, R.E., Fisher, R.P., MacKinnon, D.P. & Holland, H.L. (1985). Eyewitness memory enhancement in the police interview: Cognitive retrieval mnemonics versus hypnosis. *Journal of Applied Psychology, 70,* 401–412.

Hasel, L.G. & Wells, G.L. (in press). Catching the bad guy: Morphing composite faces helps. *Law and Human Behavior.*

Innocence Project (2005). *Innocence Project: Latest news.* Retrieved August 13, 2005, from http://www.innocenceproject.org/index.php

Jenkins, F. & Davies, G. (1985). Contamination of facial memory through exposure to misleading composite pictures. *Journal of Applied Psychology, 70,* 164–176.

Kassin, S.M., Tubb, V.A., Hosch, H.M. & Memon, A. (2001). On the general acceptance of eyewitness testimony research: A new survey of the experts. *American Psychologist, 56,* 405–416.

Kitson, A., Darnbrough, M. & Shields, E. (1978). Let's face it. *Police Research Bulletin,* no. 30, 7–13.

Krafka, C. & Penrod, S. (1985). Reinstatement of context in a field experiment on eyewitness identification. *Journal of Personality and Social Psychology, 49,* 58–69.

Laughery, K.R., Alexander, J.F. & Lane, A.B. (1971). Recognition of human faces: Effects of target exposure time, target position, pose position and type of photograph. *Journal of Applied Psychology, 55,* 477–483.

Lee, E. & Whalen, T. (1996). Feature approaches to suspect identification: Effect of multiple raters on system performance. *Ergonomics, 39,* 17–34.

Lindsay, R.C.L. (1999). Eyewitness evidence. In G. Chayko and E.D. Gulliver (Eds), *Forensic evidence in Canada* (2nd ed., pp. 157–211). Toronto: Canada Law Book.

Lindsay, R.C.L. & Bellinger, K. (1999). Alternatives to the sequential lineup: The importance of controlling the pictures. *Journal of Applied Psychology, 84,* 315–321.

Lindsay, R.C.L., Lea, J. & Fulford, J. (1991). Sequential lineup presentation: Technique matters. *Journal of Applied Psychology, 76,* 741–745.

Lindsay, R.C.L., Lea, J.A., Nosworthy, G.J., Fulford, J.A., Hector, J., LeVan, V., et al. (1991). Biased lineups: Sequential presentation reduces the problem. *Journal of Applied Psychology, 76,* 796–802.

Lindsay, R.C.L., Nosworthy, G.J., Martin, R. & Martynuck, C. (1994). Using mug shots to find suspects. *Journal of Applied Psychology, 1994,* 121–130.

Lindsay, R.C.L., Ross, D.F., Read, J.D. and Toglia, M.P. (Eds), (in press). *Handbook of eyewitness psychology: Memory for people.* Hillsdale, NJ: Erlbaum Associates.

Lindsay, R.C.L., Smith, S.M. & Pryke, S. (1999). Measures of lineup fairness: Do they postdict identification accuracy? *Applied Cognitive Psychology, 13*(SI), S93–S107.

Lindsay, R.C.L. & Wells, G.L. (1985). Improving eyewitness identifications from lineups: Simultaneous versus sequential lineup presentation. *Journal of Applied Psychology, 70,* 556–564.

Lindsay, R.C.L., Wells, G.L. & O'Connor, F.J. (1989). Mock-juror belief of accurate and inaccurate eyewitnesses: A replication and extension. *Law and Human Behavior, 13,* 333–339.

Luus, C.A.E. & Wells, G.L. (1994). The malleability of eyewitness confidence: Co-witness and perseverance effects. *Journal of Applied Psychology, 79,* 714–723.

Malpass, R.S., Tredoux, C. & McQuiston, D. (in press). Lineup construction and measuring lineup fairness. In R. Lindsay, D. Ross, D. Read & M. Toglia

(Eds), *Handbook of eyewitness psychology: Memory for people*. Hillsdale, NJ: Erlbaum Associates.

Mauldin, M.A. & Laughery, K.R. (1981). Composite production effects on subsequent facial recognition. *Journal of Applied Psychology, 66*, 351–357.

McAllister, H.A. (in press). Mug books: More than just large photospreads. In R. Lindsay, D. Ross, D. Read & M. Toglia (Eds), *Handbook of eyewitness psychology: Memory for people*. Hillsdale, NJ: Erlbaum Associates.

McAllister, H.A. & Michel, L. (2002). *Simultaneous and sequential procedures in lineups and mug books: Implications for a hybrid lineup procedure*. Unpublished manuscript.

Nosworthy, G.J. & Lindsay, R.C.L. (1990). Does nominal lineup size matter? *Journal of Applied Psychology, 75*, 358–361.

Pentland, A., Picard, R. & Scarloff, S. (1996). Photobook: Content-based manipulation of image databases. *International Journal of Computer Vision, 18*, 233–254.

Phillips, M.R., McAuliff, B.D., Kovera, M.B. & Cutler, B.L. (1999). Double-blind photoarray administration as a safeguard against investigator bias. *Journal of Applied Psychology, 84*, 940–951.

Pryke, S., Lindsay, R.C.L. & Pozzulo, J.D. (2000). Sorting mug shots: Methodological issues. *Applied Cognitive Psychology, 14*, 81–96.

Ross, D.F., Ceci, S.J., Dunning, D. & Toglia, M.P. (1994). Unconscious transference and lineup identification: Toward a memory blending approach. In D. Ross, J. Read & M. Toglia, (Eds), *Adult eyewitness testimony: Current trends and developments*. New York: Cambridge University Press.

Schooler, J., Meissner, C. & Sporer, S.L. (in press). Person descriptions as eyewitness evidence. In R. Lindsay, D. Ross, D. Read & M. Toglia (Eds), *Handbook of eyewitness psychology: Memory for people*. Hillsdale, NJ: Erlbaum Associates.

Sporer, S.L. (1996). Experimentally-induced person mix-ups through media exposure and ways to avoid them. In G. Davies, S. Lloyd-Bostock, M. McMurran & C. Wilson (Eds), *Psychology, law, and criminal justice: International developments in research and practice*. Oxford: Walter De Gruyter.

State *v*. Dubose, 272 Wis. 2d 856, 679 N.W.2d 927 (2005).

Steblay, N.M. (1997). Social influence in eyewitness recall: A meta-analytic review of lineup instruction effects. *Law and Human Behavior, 21*, 283–297.

Steblay, N., Dysart, J., Fulero, S. & Lindsay, R.C.L. (2001). Eyewitness accuracy rates in sequential and simultaneous lineup presentations: A meta-analytic comparison. *Law and Human Behavior, 25*, 459–473.

Steblay, N., Dysart, J., Fulero, S. & Lindsay, R.C.L. (2003). Eyewitness accuracy rates in police showup and lineup presentations: A meta-analytic comparison. *Law and Human Behavior, 27*, 523–540.

Stewart, H.A. & McAllister, H.A. (2001). One-at-a-time versus grouped presentation of mug book pictures: Some surprising results. *Journal of Applied Psychology, 86*, 1300–1305.

Stovall *v*. Denno, 388 U.S. 293 (1967).

Technical Working Group for Eyewitness Evidence. (1999). *Eyewitness evidence: A guide for law enforcement*. Office of Justice Programs Document No. NCJ-178240. Washington, DC: United States Department of Justice.

Turtle, J., Lindsay, R.C.L. & Wells, G.L. (2003). Best practice recommendations for eyewitness evidence procedures: New ideas for the oldest way to solve a case. *Canadian Journal of Police and Security Services, 1*, 5–18.

Wells, G.L. (1978). Applied eyewitness-testimony research: System variables and estimator variables. *Journal of Personality and Social Psychology, 36,* 1546–1557.

Wells, G.L. (1984). The psychology of lineup identifications. *Journal of Applied Social Psychology, 14,* 89–103.

Wells, G.L., Charman, S.D. & Olson, E.A. (2005). Building face composites can harm lineup identification performance. *Journal of Experimental Psychology: Applied, 11,* 147–157.

Wells, G.L., Leippe, M.R. & Ostrom, T.M. (1979). Guidelines for empirically assessing the fairness of a lineup. *Law and Human Behavior, 3,* 285–293.

Wells, G.L. & Lindsay, R.C.L. (1980). On estimating the diagnosticity of eyewitness nonidentifications. *Psychological Bulletin, 88,* 776–784.

Wells, G.L., Malpass, R.S., Lindsay, R.C.L., Fisher, R.P., Turtle, J.W. & Fulero, S.M. (2000). From the lab to the police station: A successful application of eyewitness research. *American Psychologist, 55,* 581–598.

Wells, G.L., Rydell, S.M. & Seelau, E.P. (1993). On the selection of distractors for eyewitness lineups. *Journal of Applied Psychology, 78,* 835–844.

Wells, G.L., Rydell, S.M., Seelau, E.P. & Luus, C.A.E. (1994). Recommendations for constructing lineups. In D. Ross, D. Read & M. Toglia (Eds), *Adult eyewitness testimony: Current trends and developments.* New York: Cambridge University Press.

Wells, G.L., Small, M., Penrod, S., Malpass, R.S., Fulero, S.M. & Brimacombe, C.A.E. (1998). Eyewitness identification procedures: Recommendations for lineups and photospreads. *Law and Human Behavior, 22,* 603–647.

Wells, G.L. & Turtle, J.W. (1988). Eyewitness identification: The importance of lineup models. *Psychological Bulletin, 99,* 320–329.

Yarmey, A.D., Yarmey, A.L. & Yarmey, M.J. (1996). Accuracy of eyewitness identification in showups and lineups. *Law and Human Behavior, 20,* 459–477.

CHAPTER 3

Investigating Criminal Cases of Delayed Reports of Sexual Abuse

LAURENCE ALISON AND MARK R. KEBBELL

Recovered memories of sexual abuse are reported by some theorists to represent cases where individuals who initially had no memory of being sexually abused later come to believe that they were. In this respect they differ from cases in which complainants always knew they were abused as children (Lindsay & Read, 1995). However, in reality, cases are not so clear-cut. Instead, claims more often involve complex and uncertain processes of remembering, and greater subtlety in the complainants' claims of how and what they remembered. Despite this, heated controversy still surrounds the debate, with many experts apparently treating cases as if the process of remembering involves either complete fabrication or unequivocal fact. In doing so, many experts retain a firmly entrenched perspective either in favour of a "post-trauma global amnesia followed by spontaneous or gradual full remembering" (and therefore "true") or a "false, iatrogenic process of recovery" (and therefore "false") argument. These extreme views emerge from an incomplete consideration of the way in which complainants' claim to have remembered, and may misrepresent the complexity of the case in court where due consideration may not be given to the range of factors and subtleties that inform the decision to admit evidence.

This chapter reviews the origins of the memory recovery debate and outlines contemporary literature on the process of remembering. We

Practical Psychology for Forensic Investigations and Prosecutions.
Edited by Mark R. Kebbell and Graham M. Davies. © 2006 John Wiley & Sons, Ltd.

suggest that, in practice, actual cases rarely provide clear-cut examples of either full global amnesia followed by spontaneous recovery, or relatively uncontroversial cases of clear-cut, well-remembered accounts. Instead, such cases are mired in the complexities of how a person remembered, what they remembered and what processes may have distorted and shaped their memory. We conclude with an analysis of how academics and the courts should approach the issue of credibility of delayed reports of sexual abuse.

INTERPRETING COMPLAINANTS' ACCOUNTS OF HOW THEY REMEMBERED ABUSE

Many of the principles underpinning the recovered memory debate originate in Freud's argument that traumatic memories are repressed to the unconscious mind (Freud, 1962). The consequence of this is that the memory is prevented from having a deleterious influence over the individual's capacity to function. Although the memories are "hidden", they can be "cued" in response to contexts that approximate the conditions of the original encoding event (DelMonte, 2000). Several researchers assert that they have established supporting evidence for this model through many examples of partial or complete amnesia for traumatic events (Andrews, Brewin, Ochera, Morton, Bekerian, Davies & Mollon, 1999; Andrews, Brewin, Ochera, Morton, Bekerian, Davies & Mollon, 2000; Briere & Conte, 1993; Feldman-Summers & Pope, 1994; Herman & Schatzow, 1987; Loftus, Polonsky, Fullivore & Thompson, 1994; Read & Lindsay, 2000; Whitfield & Stock, 1996 and Williams, 1995).

For example, Herman and Schatzow (1987) found 63% of 53 adults in a treatment programme for victims of child sexual abuse (CSA) claimed to have experienced partial or complete amnesia, with 74% of the amnesic sample reporting corroborative evidence of the abuse. Feldman-Summers and Pope (1994) found that 40.5% of 79 adults who had been sexually or physically abused as children experienced periods of amnesia. They found that "the rates of corroboration for abuse memories are unrelated to whether there had ever been a period of forgetting" (Cossins, 1997, p. 11). However, they used a small and potentially biased sample, thereby raising questions about the generalizability of the findings (Epstein & Bottoms, 2002). Loftus, Polonsky, Fullilove and Thompson (1994) conducted a clinical, retrospective study of 52 patients who reported CSA while attending an outpatient clinic for substance abuse. They found that 19% reported having experienced complete amnesia for the event and 12% reported partial amnesia.

This study, as well as many others, presents a consistent problem with retrospective studies because there is evidence that extended retrieval attempts can lead individuals to believe that, at a previous period of their life, they were more amnesic than they in fact were. With increasing effort invested in remembering, comes increased overestimation of previous forgetting. Read and Lindsay (2000) found in their study that retrieval efforts could bias retrospective judgements about autobiographical memory. The authors examined autobiographical memories for nontraumatic, but, nevertheless, potentially consequential (i.e., significant unusual events that are likely to prove memorable) childhood events such as summer camps and graduations. The participants were asked whether there was a period of time in which they had "less or no memory" for the event. Prior to any sustained attempts to retrieve, 16% ("less memory") and 5% ("no memory") claimed amnesia for specific events. After prolonged retrieval attempts the rate of perceived partial amnesia rose from 16% to 70%.

Similarly, Belli, Winkielman, Read, Schwartz and Lynn (1998) established that the more childhood events participants tried to remember the more likely they were to report amnesia for these events. Joslyn, Loftus, McNoughton and Powers (2001) suggest that as increased effort is required in recalling the memories, the individual assumes their memory must have been incomplete, leading to the perception that the event must have been forgotten. That extended retrieval attempts can bias judgements of amnesia raises serious questions about the validity of retrospective studies (Read & Lindsay, 2000). The implication of this is that complainants may believe that they did *not* have a continuous memory for what happened and that they recovered a memory, when in fact they remembered all along.

A number of other studies also suggest that individuals appear to have a poor understanding of the way in which they remember events. For example, Parks (1999) found that individuals claim to forget recalling a childhood event that they thought about only minutes earlier (Joslyn et al., 2001). Further, Schooler, Bendiksen and Ambadar (1997) established that two of their four interviewees claimed complete amnesia for abuse prior to disclosure despite the fact they had previously told others about the abuse during the period of claimed "amnesia".

Williams' (1995) study is one of the few prospective studies to have used a community sample of 129 adults with a history of CSA. Williams interviewed participants several years later but failed to directly ask about incidents of abuse. Of those that mentioned the abuse, 16% reported a period of amnesia in which they had less memory of the event and when asked to give details, their reports reflected an extremely accurate account of the original details of the documented abuse. Though frequently cited as evidence that memories can be recovered accurately after a period of amnesia, the study suffers from similar reporting problems as highlighted in Read and Lindsay (2000) as well as the associated problem of not asking direct questions about the abuse.

Whitfield and Stock (1996) found similar results to Williams (1995) in their community sample of 100 adults with histories of CSA. They found that 32% reported a period of complete amnesia and 38% a period of partial amnesia. Further, only 3% of the 59 individuals who recovered memories did so while in therapy and for 63% there was external corroboration (Cossins, 1997). An important feature of Williams' (1995) study lies in her point that "children who have never reported may have a different pattern of remembering and forgetting the abuse" (p. 669). Thus, those reporting the event at an early stage and having the opportunity to consolidate the account, may remember differently from those that have not been able or willing to report such events. This argument is a central feature of the Andrews et al. (1999, 2000) studies. They have conducted research into the timing, triggers, qualities and characteristics of memories of traumatic events by surveying 108 therapists. Therapists provided accounts of 690 patients with apparent amnesia for traumatic events. Of these 65% involved CSA cases and the remaining were classified as other traumas. Further, they claimed that evidence was available to corroborate these memories in 41% of cases. Therapists reported that 32% began recovering traumatic memories before entering therapy, and that in 78% of cases the memories recalled preceded the use of therapeutic techniques. Andrews et al. (1999, 2000) suggest this provides evidence that the vast majority of recovered memories are not iatrogenic.

The characteristic features of the memories in their sample are similar to those found in Van der Kolk and Fisler's study (1995), beginning with flashbacks – emotional, fragmented highly detailed images as if the patient were reliving the experience. Roe and Schwarz (1996) also claim that recovered memories of CSA are retrieved in a fragmentary form. Andrews et al. (1999) acknowledge that the reliability of the participants considered in the study was "unknown" because of the second-hand nature of the accounts. Further, one cannot be assured that the therapists in the sample knew the definitional criteria for amnesia because Andrews et al. failed to provide an operational definition. For example, a question such as "Was there ever a period of time when you remembered less or had no memory for this event?" fails to differentiate between patients who have partially forgotten details and those that claim to have no memory for the event. Consequently, therapists may overestimate the occurrence of complete forgetting and subsequent "recovery". Of the original 180 therapists who reported having at least 1 client with recovered memories, 16 subsequently reported being mistaken and 9% could not later recall the client in question. This suggests that there is reason to question therapists' interpretation of the question.

Epstein and Bottoms (2002) demonstrated that when patients are asked a less ambiguously worded question, fewer than 1% reported complete amnesia. The varying base rates of amnesia for CSA found in previous studies ranging from around 16% in Williams (1995) to 63% in Herman and Schatzow (1987) could simply be a function of the wording and interpretation of the question. Thus, the question, "Have you ever encountered a client who has had less memory for an event of sexual abuse at some stage in his/her life than he/she appears to now?" and, "Have you ever encountered a client who states they had (for at least a period of 1 year or more) no memory whatsoever for a proven (by forensic evidence and conviction in court) case of sexual abuse that involved penetrative rape, who subsequently has been able to recall this event in detail?" may generate very different answers.

An additional definitional problem in the Andrews et al. study is the lack of differentiation between the type and frequency of the sexual abuse reported. For example, the consequentiality of a single incident of groping may be less available to memory than serial, full penetrative rape, with the former proving less consequential for the victim than the latter. Another crucial area that the study fails to address is whether any of the individuals in the sample had any organic damage or co-morbid symptoms that may account for the forgetting of traumatic events rather than psychogenic amnesia.

ASSESSING THE ORIGINS OF "SUGGESTIONS" OF ABUSE

The issue of recovered memories as a product of therapy and inappropriate memory work techniques is, of course, controversial. Several researchers have argued that memories recovered after long periods of apparent forgetting can emerge in response to poorly conducted therapeutic intervention that either consciously or unconsciously employ suggestive techniques (Berliner & Williams, 1994; Holmes, 1990; Loftus, 1993; Loftus & Ketcham, 1994; Mulhern, 1991; Ofshe & Watters, 1994; Spanos, 1996). Another issue in the iatrogenic debate is the increase in the number of cases of recovered memories. Many argue this is due to overdiagnosis by therapists who believe that a patient is revealing signs of a hidden abuse history (DSM-IV, APA, 1994). In light of this the American Psychiatric Association (APA) has been keen to point out the attendant caveats in diagnosing such issues. Others have argued that many patients in therapy are searching for reasons and solutions for their unhappiness. Consequently, they are highly suggestible to the views of an authoritative figure like a therapist (Gudjonsson, 1992; Lindsay & Read, 1994; Loftus, 1993; Mulhern, 1991; Spanos, 1996).

In contrast, many therapists argue that the increase in the numbers of reported cases of recovered memories is due to a greater awareness among clinicians that abuse is prolific and reflects the "identification of cases that were previously undiagnosed" (APA, 1994. DSM-IV: The diagnosis of dissociative amnesia, p. 479). Kristiansen, Felton and Hovdestad (1996) found that 84% of those in their study who recovered memories stated that, "the therapist had never even asked if they had an abuse history" (Cossins, 1997, p. 21). In addition, 40% recovered memories outside of therapy. In Elliott and Briere's (1995) study 22% of 116 participants reported partial amnesia and 20% complete amnesia for CSA. Only 8% of those with recovered memories had undergone therapy. In Whitfield and Stock's (1996) study only 3% of 59 individuals recovered their memories in a therapeutic setting.

However, one particular concern involves the over-representation of recovered memories among clients of particular therapists (Van Koppen & Crombag, 1999) as well as the over-representation of recovered memories of CSA among psychiatric patients (Orr, 1999). It is unclear whether the latter concern reflects a causal relationship between abuse and mental disorders or whether such illness makes this population particularly vulnerable to suggestion.

A variety of processes have been thought to influence the production of false memories. Coercion or compliance can occur in instances where the therapist is perceived as an authoritative figure. Research indicates that clients will admit to claiming pseudo memories they knew were false in order to comply with the experimenter (Barnier & McConkey, 1992). Similarly, Hoelscher, Rosenthal and Lichstein (1986) established that patients sometimes misdescribe their behaviors in order to conform and comply with the views and beliefs of their therapist. This reveals that compliance can occur in clinical settings as well as under laboratory conditions. Spanos, Burgess, Burgess, Samuels and Blois (1999) have also discovered that merely having an authoritative person suggest a certain body sensation (in this case, umbilical itching) is sufficient to generate such memories. Thirty-two per cent of age regression hypnotized participants and 38% of the control group reported experiencing umbilical itching. (See also Chapter 1 concerning interviewing witnesses).

Bottoms, Shaver and Goodman (1991) and Mulhern (1991) suggest that the procedures used by certain therapists are important determinants of "memories" generated. For example, Loftus and Pickrell (1995) asked participants to provide imaginary details of events that had occurred in childhood. The research team provided the to-be-imagined event, in this case, being lost in a shopping mall. Participants gave detailed, confident descriptions of what they "remembered" about an event that never actually happened and that they had been provided with. Similarly, Loftus and Coan (1994) led 5 participants to believe they were lost in a shopping mall when they were 5 years old. Four of the participants recounted very detailed narratives of this imaginary event and refused to believe it was false when they were reminded of the imaginary nature of the experiment. Crombag, Wagenaar and Van Koppen (1996) and Ost, Vrij, Costall and Bull (2002) have also demonstrated that individuals are willing to report that they have witnessed an event that they could not have done (an aeroplane crash in Crombag et al.'s study and the car crash that killed Princess Diana in Ost et al.'s study). Crombag et al. (1996) found that 55% reported having seen an aeroplane crash (on TV) when there was no such footage of this event.

Porter, Yuille and Lehman (1999) asked participants to provide details of emotional childhood events. Some of these were real events as corroborated by the participants' relatives while other events had never happened. The research team asked some participants to deliberately fabricate events that never actually happened to them. They found that participants reported highly detailed accounts of the "created" events and, after 3 interviews, 25% had developed false memories and 30% had developed partial false memories.

However, some have criticized this study on the grounds that the "false" memories could have been imported from actual memories and were merely distortions of those genuine events (Conte, 1999). Pezdek, Finger and Hodge (1997) demonstrated this by using less plausible events unlikely to have occurred in the participant's childhood and found significantly fewer false memories. In their first experiment (in which the participants were either Jewish or Catholic) the false possible scenarios were Communion or Jewish prayer. The event was considered less plausible if it was incongruent with their respective religious ideology. Although all 10 accepted the plausible suggestion, only one accepted the implausible event. The second experiment involved a plausible event of getting lost in a mall or an implausible event of receiving an enema after suffering from constipation. In this study, 3 out of 20 participants accepted the plausible suggestion while none accepted the implausible event. They concluded that only plausible events could be implanted.

Suengas and Johnson (1988) have established that in asking individuals to imagine events, therapists may inhibit the client's ability to distinguish fact from fiction. The inability to identify the origin of the memory (imagined or genuine) is known as source attribution error. Spanos et al. (1999) tested the hypothesis that hypnotized participants would be more prone than non-hypnotized participants to generating and accepting false memories in an "age-regression" experiment in which they were told that this process would increase their remembering of the suggested event. A memory from the day after their birth was suggested to them. This study provided evidence that by shaping expectations (i.e. by suggesting that age regression is a credible method for enhancing memory) one can encourage false memories. Spanos et al. (1999) suggest that procedures such as age regression "provide patients with the expectation that they have been abused, encourage them to generate imaginings that are consistent with this idea and then legitimate these imaginings as actual memories of early abuse" (p. 201). A perceived authority figure, such as a therapist, is particularly likely to be seen as a credible and reliable source (Lindsay & Read, 1994; Mulhern, 1991; Van Koppen & Crombag, 1999). Repetitive questioning can also influence individuals' readiness to accept prior amnesia for events. Extended efforts to remember give the illusion of prior amnesia (Read & Lindsay, 2000) and repeated retrieval techniques can also contribute to enhance individuals' commitment to errors. In summary, Lindsay and Read (1995) conclude that the perceived authority and trustworthiness of the source of suggestion, repetition of the suggestion, the plausibility of the event being suggested, imagibility and lowering of memory-monitoring response criteria, all contribute to producing memories that may either be distortions or complete fabrications that are subsequently held with great conviction by those who have "remembered" such events.

DelMonte (2000) suggests that if "psychotherapists would follow recommended clinical practice, for example by not being forcibly directive, avoiding strongly suggestive comments, monitoring their own countertransferences, and not imposing ideologically motivated 'explanations' and 'interpretations', some of this confusion might abate" (p. 10).

While it is important that potential "interference" from therapists should be considered carefully by the courts, it is neither a necessary nor sufficient condition for false accounts. In the first author's view, it is misguided for an expert to take the view that a case is either false or true based on whether a therapist was involved. For example, in one case that the first author was involved in, the expert for the prosecution discounted the possibility that the claims for abuse should be treated with caution because there had been only minimal correspondence with a therapist (though no case notes were provided as to the extent of the therapist's involvement). In another case the expert for the defence claimed that because a therapist had used hypnosis, the claims of abuse had "the smell of false memories". This was despite evidence that the overwhelming bulk of the complainant's reporting of the abuse had occurred prior to any involvement with the therapist. When challenged on the time frame within which the reporting of the abuse had occurred the expert had failed to check any of the dates at which the reports had been made. "Knee-jerk" reactions to the realization that a complainant has been in therapy could seriously misguide the courts unless such assumptions are seriously challenged. Nevertheless, a clear implication of this body of work is that the fact that a memory could have been induced by a therapist must always be borne in mind.

THE DIFFICULTY OF GENERALIZING FROM EMPIRICAL RESEARCH TO THE INDIVIDUAL CASE

According to MacMartin and Yarmey (1998), many sceptics of the recovered memory phenomenon "draw on positivist standards of scientific rigor and reliability to undermine claims of recovered memory" (p. 203). Indeed, many challenges to the recovered memory phenomenon have focused on the inadequacy of the necessary conditions to experimentally control studies supporting memory recovery. Thus, while some experimental psychologists concede that case studies may be instructive, they agree that case studies are inadequate as evidence to satisfy the courts. One of Van der Kolk and Fisler's (1995) rebuttals to this argument centres on the notion that many of the individuals in the sceptical camp include individuals, "who have not studied trauma and who have a hard time understanding that memories of having been raped are qualitatively different from remembering nonsense words in a laboratory" (Cossins, 1997, p. 31).

Even beyond the argument of the validity of transferring conclusions from the laboratory to the real world are arguments about the fundamental question of whether trauma enhances or inhibits memory. The trauma superiority argument contends that trauma enhances memory for events rather than inhibits it (especially the central details) (Shobe & Kihlstrom, 1997; Thompson, Morton & Fraser, 1997; Wagenaar & Groenweg, 1990; Yuille & Cutshall, 1986). In contrast, the traumatic memory argument asserts that traumatic events result in different encoding, storage and retrieval processes and can easily be forgotten for long periods until particular cues facilitate retrieval (Van der Kolk & Fisler, 1995; Van der Kolk, Hopper & Osterman, 2001).

A major challenge to the latter view is the very large corpus of research from human and animal studies that reveals how trauma and stress enhance the memory of the experience. Berntsen (2001) explains how the brain releases a stress hormone that aids in the consolidation of memory during high arousal states. Indeed, Alvarez (1992) asserts that a common problem for trauma survivors is an inability to forget the event. As long ago as 1890 James (cited in Porter & Birt, 2001) claimed that a highly traumatic event could be so stressful and emotional that it would almost "leave a scar upon the cerebral tissues" (p. 102). Several studies have supported this basic principle. For example, Yuille and Cutshall (1986) found memory to be intact for witnesses to murder; Thompson et al. (1997) found the same in survivors of a ferry disaster; Wagenaar and Groenweg (1990) found that concentration camp survivors retained intact memories of their experiences and Porter and Birt (2001) found that the individuals in their study had intrusive and repetitive memories that were rich, coherent and detailed. However, Chapman and Underwood (2000) suggested that memories of a traumatic event vary contingent on the level of stress associated with the event. They found that moderately stressful events such as a near-accident in a car, resulted in memory impairment with 80% of incidents forgotten within two weeks, however, higher levels of arousal, involving actual collisions rather than near misses, led to detailed memories.

Joslyn, Carlin and Loftus (1997) established a strong positive relationship between comprehensively understanding an event and its perceived significance, as well as a positive relationship between the number of self-reported incidents of thinking about an event and the probability of being able to accurately recall it. Easterbrook (1959) argues that trauma can both inhibit and enhance memory depending on the level of arousal and stress involved, with moderate arousal enhancing memory but extreme arousal causing interference with encoding due to a narrowing of attention (Byrne, Hyman & Scott, 2001). However, Shobe and Kihlstrom (1997) point out that there are no laboratory studies to support the hypothesis that central details of an event can be entirely forgotten.

Van der Kolk and Fisler (1995) argue that in order to demonstrate the "special" nature of traumatic memories, studies need to measure the characteristics and content of traumatic memories over time and in comparison to nontraumatic memories. They assert that the many experimental studies of memory are of little significance since such studies do not involve highly stressful and traumatic stimuli. Van der Kolk and Fisler (1995) state:

> If trauma is defined as the experience of an inescapable stressful event that overwhelms one's existing coping mechanisms, it is questionable whether findings of memory distortions in normal subjects exposed to videotaped stresses in the laboratory can serve as meaningful guides to understanding traumatic memory (p. 506).

Hopper and Van der Kolk (2001) claim to have been able to resolve many of these issues in their studies of patients waking up from anaesthesia during surgery. In a semi-structured interview they asked participants how they remembered the traumatic experience across various stages; from when they initially remembered, to the peak of the memory and then presently at the time of the study. Although this method helps establish the changing nature of the memory over time it is still essentially a retrospective design in which the patients are asked to remember what they remembered (Van der Kolk et al., 2001).

However, there are some instructive findings in their studies and in their original work using the TMI traumatic memory inventory (TMI) procedure. For example, Van der Kolk and Fisler (1995) and Van der Kolk, Burbridge and Suzuki (1997) found that, in contrast to non-traumatic memories, traumatic experiences are initially retrieved as loosely connected "chunks" of sensory information and "flashbacks" in a fragmentary and confusing form. The sensations include visual images, smells, sounds, affective states and bodily sensations that are associated with the traumatic experience intruding into consciousness. Van der Kolk et al. (2001) argue that these fragments of sensory information represent implicit memories of the experiences encoded in place of explicit, narrative memories. The latter is less available to consciousness because of the individual's dissociative state at encoding. The suggestion is that the stress of the event interferes with consolidation of explicit memories, though the inhibition of explicit memory formation fails to influence implicit memory. Over the course of a professionally conducted therapeutic intervention the flashbacks and fragmentary pieces of information can be constructed into a verbal account. However, Van der Kolk and Fisler's (1995) study has been criticized more recently by Gray and Lombardo (2001), who observe that there was no control group and that the traumatic and nontraumatic events chosen were not matched for age of occurrence, with the traumatic memories generally being from childhood and the nontraumatic memories from adulthood. Therefore the differences found could have been due to conventional processes of decay of the childhood trauma or due to infantile amnesia. Further, the advertisement for participants required individuals "haunted" by a traumatic memory. This may have selectively biased the participant group by discouraging individuals with explicit memories of traumatic experience (Shobe & Kihlstrom, 1997). Finally, the researchers failed to corroborate individuals' accounts.

Van der Kolk et al. (2001) tried to overcome these criticisms in a more recent study using the TMI procedure. In this study, they found mixed support for their views of trauma and memory. For example, individuals who suffered from post-traumatic stress disorder (PTSD) were less able to verbalize a narrative account of the experience compared to the non-PTSD group. However, both PTSD sufferers and the non-PTSD control group reported sensory and affective memory components. Hopper and Van der Kolk (2001) contend that this result could be an artefact of a small sample size and the fact that coding is constrained by dichotomous evaluations (did "X" occur or not). They recommend that the reporting of sensations should be coded according to intensity rather than occurrence.

Brewin, Dalgleish and Joseph's (1996) dual representation theory of forgetting of traumatic memories postulates that memories have two representations. One is the explicit or verbally accessible memory of the trauma that can be consciously recollected and articulated. The other is the implicit or situationally accessible memory of trauma that cannot consciously be recollected unless appropriate cues are present. It remains as a nonverbal, somatosensory store of the experience. The memories of trauma remain dissociated from conscious awareness, although they cause intrusive feelings and panic. With time and repeated activation from cues, they can be slowly integrated into normal explicit and verbalizable memory.

Brewin and Andrews (1998) believe that this theory can be used alongside a more narrowly defined concept of repression to explain the mechanism behind recovered memories as "a decrease in the level of activation and hence of the accessibility of a specific representation in memory, produced by an active inhibitory process" (p. 966).

Van der Kolk et al. (2001) also propose a neurological justification for differences in traumatic and nontraumatic memories. They found that positron emission tomography (PET) scans of PTSD sufferers revealed increased activation in the right hemisphere during a traumatic memory, an area considered dominant in evaluating the emotional significance of sensory information. They propose that narrative verbal accounts of traumatic memories are difficult to recall because the hippocampal memory system fails under extreme stress. Van der Kolk et al. (2001) have concluded that "both interviews and brain imaging of traumatized people confirm that traumatic memories come back as emotional and sensory states, with limited capacity for verbal representation" (p. 28).

Alongside Van der Kolk et al.'s argument that trauma memories are distinct from conventional memories is the more recent proposal that CSA memories are qualitatively different from other trauma memories. A study by Mechanic, Resick and Griffin (1998) appears to support Van der Kolk and Fisler (1995) and Van der Kolk et al.'s work (1997) in establishing that rape victims' memories improved over time, with 37% reporting significant amnesia for the experience two weeks afterwards, and 16% reporting similar levels three months after. Roe and Schwartz

(1996) established that 60% of the clients in their sample reported initially recovering memories of abuse in the form of flashbacks and sensations. Clients were only able to put the traumatic experience into a continuous verbal narrative after time. In a study comparing individuals who had experienced amnesia for abuse with individuals with continuous memories of the abuse, Cameron (1996) established that the former were more likely to report sensory and fragmented memories and less able to articulate the experience. In Burgess, Hartman and Baker's (1995) prospective study of 34 abused children they established that, although at the time clients had both implicit and narrative memories for the abuse, 5–10 years later many had lost the narrative aspects of the memory but retained implicit aspects of the memory (i.e. flashbacks). Many authors have cited these studies as evidence of dissociation, despite the many limitations of self-report measures (see the arguments outlined in the opening section of this chapter). However, a key feature of all these studies is that they include clients' efforts at mental rehearsal of the event, with those individuals verbalizing the account being more likely to consolidate the memory.

More recently, Gray and Lombardo (2001) failed to find support for Van der Kolk and Fisler (1995) or Van der Kolk et al.'s (2001) view that traumatic memories are "special". In Gray and Lombardo's work nontraumatic memories also initially occurred as sensations and subsequently in narrative form. Thus nontraumatic memories evolved in much the same way as traumatic events, with fragmentation and disorganization in the early stages and more detailed narratives emerging over time. Koss, Figueredo, Bell, Tharan and Tromp (1996) suggest that the reason memories evolve in this way is due to lack of rehearsal at the early stages with increasing rehearsal and consolidation over time.

Similarly, Porter and Birt (2001) found that traumatic and nontraumatic memories were comparable in vividness, coherence and overall quality even though clients spent more time ruminating over nontraumatic events. Porter and Birt (2001) argue that although their study involved students, the results can be generalized to clinical samples since the traumas were extremely frightening, painful and distressing as revealed by high stress ratings and high scores on the impact of events scale (IES).

Berntsen (2001) has established that involuntary memories involving emotional, behavioral and physiological reliving are not just limited to traumatic experiences. Berntsen found that flashbacks could occur for "peak" events as well as traumatic ones. Further, Read and Lindsay (2000) found that nontraumatic memories could be forgotten and triggered in the same way as traumatic ones and Shobe and Kihlstrom

(1997) argue that the evidence presented for traumatic memories being "special" is anecdotal and comes from clinical evidence drawn from poorly controlled and confounded investigations.

A central difficulty for the expert wishing to provide evidence for the courts involves the need to be able to counter arguments based on poorly conducted studies or inconsistent findings. The sheer volume of material that has been devoted to arguing for and against recovered memories makes it extremely difficult to devote sufficient time to explaining the limitations of the variety of studies in support of or against false/recovered memories. Indeed, the first author has experienced many occasions on which counsel have stated that they could not hope to adequately cross-examine an expert witness promoting a particular view of the debate because the barrister him/herself would be ill equipped to cross-examine the expert with regard to all the necessary aspects of scientific rigor, and the jury may have difficulty comprehending the intricacies of the arguments. For example, it would be relatively easy for an expert to quote the Brewin and Andrews study to claim that a significant proportion of therapists provided evidence for clients developing amnesia in response to traumatic events. It would be more difficult for opposing counsel to go through the variety of explanations as to why such a statement might be misrepresenting the evidence. For example, there are a variety of terms to explain the processes of remembering and forgetting that, while common parlance in the psychological literature, could present problems in court. The variety of terms used to describe these processes, and the disagreement as to legitimacy of each of them as a recognizable psychological process, could lead to a great deal of confusion in court, even where experts can advise counsel with regard to formulating cross-examination questions.

SUMMARY OF THE PSYCHOLOGICAL ISSUES

In reviewing the psychological evidence, it is clear that considerable debate persists with regard to the proposed processes of recovering memories. Several researchers claim evidence for a special and discrete mechanism for forgetting and recovering memories. Others argue that conventional memory processes can account for this process, while others argue that the contemporary view of memory presents compelling evidence that such events cannot be easily forgotten. As well as the diversity of opinion, this chapter has argued that there are several other difficulties in assessing the credibility of any given account. These include establishing how the complainant claims to have remembered, establishing the extent to which other individuals may have shaped the account and the difficultly of applying general research findings to specific cases. While it may be possible for experts to advise on general processes of how memory operates, this chapter advocates extreme caution with regard to advising on the credibility of the complainant's account. In the next section we map out the implications for investigations and prosecutions taking into account the lack of agreement in the scientific community.

IMPLICATIONS FOR INVESTIGATORS AND PROSECUTORS

To date there has been no scientific evidence to support complete global amnesia for multiple events of sexual abuse over an extended period of time. Nor has there been any irrefutable empirical research evidence that proves beyond doubt the existence of recovered memories. This appears to show that although there may be a historical truth behind a recovered memory, there are limitations surrounding the measurement of the forgetting and recovery experiences (Read, 1999). It would appear therefore, that loose generalizations about the credibility of a particular witness based on polarized views of recovered/false memories is inappropriate for investigators. As such, experts must restrain from applying the broad to the particular, and must recognize that little is known about how individuals report remembering or forgetting events.

This chapter has highlighted a number of difficulties for psychologists who become immersed in such debates, and flags up the important caveat that close attention must be paid to the interpretation placed upon the complainant's or defendant's account of how they remembered or forgot the event, before conclusions can be made as to the credibility or otherwise of the account. This has clear implications for investigators and prosecutors who must make a decision about how much reliance should be placed on a complainant's testimony using a systematic approach (Haber & Haber, 1998).

The first step in determining how much reliance should be placed on an account is to determine if a memory is genuinely independent. To find out if the account is genuinely independent it is important to determine if the complainant was influenced or pressurized into their account by a third party, which may include a therapist. Similarly, information may have been acquired from a third party that tainted the complainant's account, for example from a newspaper report. Importantly, consideration must also be given to the fact that the witness might be lying. If there is explicit evidence that the memory was produced in an untainted and independent fashion, then the evidence is likely to have evidential weight.

If the evidence appears to be tainted by any of the factors that have been previously mentioned in this chapter, or it is not clear how the memories were produced, then caution should be exercised. In these cases consideration must be given to why the complainant did not immediately report the crime but came forward later (Haber & Haber, 1998). Any considerable delay in reporting raises the suspicion that the reported memory may not be independent. Importantly though, reasons for a delay in reporting may well be sound. For example, a child may have been scared of the consequences of saying what his or her father had done. If there are no credible reasons for the delayed report, however, additional caution is warranted, as unsubstantiated eyewitness evidence may result in a false conviction. In these instances the eyewitness cannot be relied upon unless there is additional evidence. This may take the form of an additional independent eyewitness to the event. If there is an independent witness then this clearly strengthens the likelihood of the complainant's evidence being accurate. Similarly, other corroborative forensic evidence will strengthen the likelihood of the eyewitness evidence being accurate. For example in one case of child murder an autopsy showed the body had wounds consistent with a child's account of a murder (Haber & Haber, 1998).

Throughout the investigation and prosecution it is important to minimize the ability of complainants to change accounts so that they appear more credible. While a complainant's memory may not be accurate, the witness may firmly believe that it is accurate. Consequently, if an eyewitness becomes aware that his or her evidence may be treated with more caution if it was elicited in a particular way, the witness may not be honest about how an account was elicited. For example, if an account of abuse was elicited with hypnosis and the witness subsequently finds out that hypnotic evidence is likely to be less credible than nonhypnotically elicited evidence. In this case the witness might deny or simply not mention that they had been hypnotized. Thus, police officers should be very careful about suggesting how witnesses can give the most credible answers.

CONCLUSIONS

In this chapter the ways in which accurate and inaccurate memories may be formed have been outlined. In addition, a systematic approach to looking at how complainants came to their memories and reports has been given so that investigators and prosecutors can evaluate the veracity of these memories. This is no easy task given that some complainants may have false memories of abuse that they confidently and genuinely believe. It is to be hoped that from the divisive debate over historical memories will eventually emerge some consensus on the distinction between those memories that are historically accurate and those that are not. However, until that time, in many instances we simply do not know if a memory is accurate or inaccurate. Therefore, we must be cautious, particularly in order to avoid the conviction of innocent people.

REFERENCES

Alvarez, A. (1992). *Live company*. London: Routledge.
American Psychiatric Association. (1994). *Diagnostic and statistic manual of mental disorders* (4th edn). Washington, DC: American Psychiatric Association.
Andrews, B., Brewin, C.R., Ochera, J., Morton, J., Bekerian, D.A., Davies, G.M. & Mollon, P. (1999). The characteristics, context and consequences of memory recovery among adults in therapy. *British Journal of Psychiatry, 175*, 141–146.
Andrews, B., Brewin, C.R., Ochera, J., Morton, J., Bekerian, D.A., Davies, G.M. & Mollon, P. (2000). The timing, triggers and qualities of recovered memories in therapy. *British Journal of Clinical Psychology, 39*, 11–26.
Barnier, A.J. & McConkey, K.M. (1992). Reports of real and false memories: The relevance of hypnosis, hypnotizability and context of memory test. *Journal of Abnormal Psychology, 101*, 521–527.
Belli, R.F., Winkielman, P., Read, J.D., Schwartz, N. & Lynn, S.J. (1998). Recalling more childhood events leads to judgments of poorer memory: Implications for the recovered/false memory debate. *Psychonomic Bulletin and Review, 5*, 318–323.
Berliner, L. & Williams, L.M. (1994). Memories of child sexual abuse: A response to Lindsay and Read. *Journal of Applied Cognitive Psychology, 8*(3), 379–387.
Berntsen, D. (2001). Involuntary memories of emotional events: Do memories of traumas and extremely happy events differ? *Applied Cognitive Psychology, 15*, 135–158.
Bottoms, B., Shaver, P. & Goodman, G. (1991). *Profile of ritualistic and religion-related abuse allegations in the United States*. Paper presented at the ninety-ninth annual convention of the American Psychological Association, San Francisco, August.
Brewin, C.R. & Andrews, B. (1998). Recovered memories of trauma: Phenomenology and cognitive mechanisms. *Clinical Psychology Review, 18*, 949–970.
Brewin, C.R., Dalgleish, T. & Joseph, S. (1996). A dual representation theory of post traumatic stress disorder. *Psychology Review, 103*, 670–686.
Briere, J. & Conte, J. (1993). Self-reported amnesia for abuse in adults molested as children. *Journal of Traumatic Stress, 6*, 21–31.

Burgess, A.W., Hartman, C.R. & Baker, T. (1995). Memory presentations of childhood sexual abuse. *Journal of Psychosocial Nursing, 33*(9), 9–16.

Byrne, C.A., Hyman, I.E. & Scott, K.L. (2001). Comparisons of memories for traumatic events and other experiences. Special issue: Trauma, stress and autobiographical memory. *Applied Cognitive Psychology, 15,* S119–S133.

Cameron, A. (1996). Comparing amnesic and non-amnesic survivors of childhood sexual abuse: A longitudinal study. In K. Pezdek & W. P. Banks (Eds), *The recovered memory / false memory debate* (pp. 41–68). New York: Academic Press.

Chapman, P. & Underwood, G. (2000). Forgetting near-accidents: The roles of severity, culpability and experience in the poor recall of dangerous driving situations. *Applied Cognitive Psychology, 14,* 31–44.

Conte, J.R. (1999). Memory, research and the law: Future directions. In Williams, L.M. & Banyard, V.L. (Eds), *Trauma and memory* (pp. 77–92). Thousand Oaks, CA: Sage Publications.

Cossins, A. (1997). Recovered memories of child sexual abuse: Fact or fantasy? *Judicial Review,* 163–199.

Crombag, H.F.M., Wagenaar, W.A. & Van Koppen, P.J. (1996). Crashing memories and the problem of source monitoring. *Applied Cognitive Psychology, 10,* 95–104.

DelMonte, M.M. (2000). Retrieved memories of childhood sexual abuse. *British Journal of Medical Psychology, 73,* 1–13.

Easterbrook, J.A. (1959). The effect of emotion on cue utilization and the organization of behavior. *Psychological Review, 66,* 183–201.

Elliot, D.M. & Briere, J. (1995) Post-traumatic stress associated with delayed recall of sexual abuse: A general population study. *Journal of Trauma Stress, 8,* 629–647.

Epstein, M.A. & Bottoms, B.L. (2002). Explaining the forgetting and recovery of abuse and trauma memories: Possible mechanisms. *Child Maltreatment, 7,* 210–25.

Feldman-Summers, S. & Pope, K.S. (1994). The experience of forgetting childhood abuse: A national survey of psychologists. *Journal of Consulting and Clinical Psychology, 62,* 636–639.

Freud, S. (1962). The aetiology of hysteria. In J. Strachey (Ed. and Trans.), *The standard edition of the complete works of Sigmund Freud* (Vol. 3, pp. 191–221). Toronto: Clark, Irwin. (Original work published in 1896).

Gray, M.J. & Lombardo, T.W. (2001). Complexity of trauma narratives as an index of fragmented memory in PTSD: A critical analysis. *Applied Cognitive Psychology, 15,* 171–186.

Gudjonsson, G. (1992). *The psychology of interrogations, confessions and testimony.* Chichester: John Wiley & Sons, Ltd.

Haber, L. & Haber, R.N. (1998). Criteria for judging the admissibility of eyewitness testimony of long past events. *Psychology, Public Policy, and Law, 4,* 1135–1159.

Herman, J. & Schatzow, E. (1987). Recovery and verification of memories of childhood sexual trauma. *Psychoanalytic Psychology, 4,* 1–14.

Hoelscher, T.L., Rosenthal, T.L. & Lichstein, K.L. (1986). Home relaxation practice in hypertension treatment: Objective assessment and compliance induction. *Journal of Consulting and Clinical Psychology, 54,* 217–221.

Holmes, D.S. (1990). The evidence for repression: An examination of sixty years of research. In J.L. Singer (Ed.), *Repression and dissociation: Implications for personality theory, psychopathology and health.* Chicago: University of Chicago Press.

Hopper, J.W. & Van der Kolk, B.A. (2001). Retrieving, assessing and classifying traumatic memories: A preliminary report on three case studies of a new standardized method. *Journal of Aggression, Maltreatment, and Trauma, 4*, 33–71; and Freyd, J.F. and DePrince, A.P. (Eds), *Trauma and cognitive science* (pp. 33–71). Binghamton, NY: Haworth Press.

Joslyn, S., Carlin, L. & Loftus, E.F. (1997). Remembering and forgetting childhood sexual abuse. *Memory, 5*(6), 703–724.

Joslyn, S., Loftus, E.F., McNoughton, A. & Powers, J. (2001) Memory for memory. *Memory and Cognition, 29*(6), 789–797.

Koss, M.P., Figueredo, A.J., Bell, I., Tharan, M. & Tromp, S. (1996). Traumatic memory characteristics: A cross-validated mediational model of response to rape among employed women. *Journal of Abnormal Psychology, 105*, 421–432.

Kristiansen, C.M., Felton, K.A. & Hovdestad, W.E. (1996). Recovered memory of child abuse: Fact, fantasy or fancy? *Women and Therapy, 19*(1), 47–59.

Lindsay, D.S. & Read, J.D. (1994). Psychotherapy and memories of child sexual abuse: A cognitive perspective. *Applied Cognitive Psychology, 8*, 281–338.

Lindsay, S. & Read, D. (1995). Memory work and recovered memories of childhood sexual abuse: Scientific evidence and public, professional and personal issue. *Psychology, Public Policy, and Law, 1*(4), 846–908.

Loftus, E.F. (1993). The reality of repressed memories. *American Psychologist, 48*, 518–537.

Loftus, E.F. & Coan, D. (1994). The construction of childhood memories. In D. Peters (Ed.), *The child witness in context: Cognitive, social and legal perspectives.* New York: Kluwer.

Loftus, E. & Ketcham, K. (1994). *The myth of repressed memory.* New York: St Martins Press.

Loftus, E.F. & Pickrell, J.E. (1995). The formation of false memories. *Psychiatric Annals, 25*, 720–725.

Loftus, E.F., Polonsky, S., Fullilove & Thompson, M. (1994). Memories of childhood sexual abuse: Remembering and repressing. *Psychology of Women Quarterly, 18*(1), 67–84.

MacMartin, C. & Yarmey, A.D. (1998). Repression, dissociation, and the recovered memory debate: Constructing scientific evidence and expertise. *Expert Evidence, 6*(3), 203–226.

Mechanic, M.B., Resick, P.A. & Griffin, M.G. (1998). A comparison of normal forgetting, psychopathology, and information-processing models of reported amnesia for recent sexual trauma. *Journal of Consulting and Clinical Psychology, 66*, 948–957.

Mulhern, S. (1991). Satanism and psychotherapy. A rumor in search of an inquisition. In J. T. Richardson, J. Best & D. G. Bromley (Eds), *The satanism scare* (pp. 145–172). New York: Aldine.

Ofshe, R. & Watters, E. (1994). *Making monsters: False memories, psychotherapy and sexual hysteria.* New York: Scribner.

Orr, M. (1999). Believing patients. In C. Feltham (Ed.), *Controversies in psychotherapy.* London: Sage.

Ost, J., Vrij, A., Costall, A. & Bull, R. (2002). Crashing memories and reality monitoring: Distinguishing between perceptions, imaginings and false memories. *Applied Cognitive Psychology, 16*, 125–134.

Parks, T.E. (1999). On one aspect of the evidence for recovered memories. *American Journal of Psychology, 112*, 365–370.

Pezdek, K., Finger, K. & Hodge, D. (1997). Planting false childhood memories: The role of event plausibility. *Psychological Science, 8*, 437–441.

Porter, S. & Birt, A.R. (2001). Is traumatic memory special? A comparison of traumatic memory characteristics with memory for other emotional life experiences. *Applied Cognitive Psychology, 15*, 101–117.

Porter, S., Yuille, J.C. & Lehman, D.R. (1999). The nature of real, implanted and fabricated memories for emotional childhood events: Implications for the recovered memory debate. *Law and Human Behavior, 23*, 517–537.

Read, J.D. (1999). The recovered/false memory debate: Three steps forward, two steps back? *Expert Evidence, 7*, 1–24.

Read, J.D. & Lindsay, D.S. (2000). Amnesia for summer camps and high school graduation: Memory work increases reports of prior periods of remembering less. *Journal of Traumatic Stress, 13*, 129–147.

Roe, C.M. & Schwarz, M.F. (1996). Characteristics of previously forgotten memories of sexual abuse: A descriptive study. *Journal of Psychiatry and Law, 24*, 189–206.

Schooler, J.W. Bendiksen, M. & Ambadar, Z. (1997). Taking the middle line: Can we accommodate both fabricated and recovered memories of sexual abuse? In M. Conway (Ed.), *False and recovered memories* (pp. 251–292). Oxford: Oxford University Press.

Shobe, K.K. & Kihlstrom, J.F. (1997). Is traumatic memory special? *Current Directions in Psychological Science, 6*, 70–74.

Spanos, N.P. (1996). *Multiple identities and false memories*. Washington, DC: American Psychological Association.

Spanos, N.P., Burgess, C.A., Burgess, M.F., Samuels, C. & Blois, W.O. (1999). Creating false memories of infancy with hypnotic and non-hypnotic procedures. *Applied Cognitive Psychology, 13*, 201–218.

Suengas, P.W. & Johnson, M.K. (1988). Qualitative effects of rehearsal on memories for perceived and imagined events. *Journal of Experimental Psychology General, 117*, 377–389.

Thompson, J., Morton, J. & Fraser, L. (1997). Memories for the marchioness. *Memory, 5*, 615–638.

Van der Kolk, B.A., Burbridge, J.A. & Suzuki, J. (1997). The psychobiology of traumatic memories: Clinical implications of neuroimaging studies. In R. Yehuda & A.C. McFarlane (Eds), *Annals of the New York Academy of Sciences: Psychobiology of post-traumatic stress disorder, 821.* (pp. 99–113). New York: New York Academy of Sciences.

Van der Kolk, B. & Fisler, R. (1995). Dissociation and the fragmentary nature of traumatic memories: Overview and exploratory study. *Journal of Traumatic Stress, 8*, 505–525.

Van der Kolk, B.A., Hopper, J.W. & Osterman, J.E. (2001). Exploring the nature of traumatic memory: Combining clinical knowledge with lab methods. *Journal of Aggression, Maltreatment, and Trauma, 4*, 9–31; and Freyd, J.F. & DePrince, A.P. (Eds), *Trauma and cognitive science* (pp. 9–31). Binghamton, NY: Haworth Press.

Van Koppen, P.J. & Crombag, H.F.M. (1999). Claims of early sexual abuse: Guidelines for investigating cases with allegedly recovered memories. *Expert Evidence, 7*, 187–208

Wagenaar, W.A. & Groenweg, J. (1990). The memory of concentration camp survivors. *Applied Cognitive Psychology, 4*, 77–87.

Whitfield, C.L. & Stock, W.E. (1996). *Traumatic amnesia in 100 survivors of childhood sexual abuse*. Presented at the national conference on trauma and memory, University of New Hampshire.

Williams, L.M., (1995). Recovered memories of abuse in women with documented child sexual victimization histories. *Journal of Traumatic Stress, 8,* 649–673.

Yuille, J.C. & Cutshall, J.D. (1986). A case study of eyewitness memory of a crime. *Journal of Applied Psychology, 71*(2), 291–301.

CHAPTER 4

Psychological Characteristics of Offenders

KEVIN HOWELLS AND JACQUELINE STACEY

Understanding the psychology of offending and offenders is an important task for a range of professionals working in the criminal justice system. Police investigators, lawyers, judges, psychologists, correctional officers and others, share the experience of encountering an individual offender and needing to understand why this person has committed the offence. Typically, over time, the professional deals with a series of offenders and may begin to perceive patterns, coming to believe, for example, that most offenders have been abused in childhood, that sex offenders are lonely and socially isolated or that violent offenders are heavy users of alcohol. These perceptions and inferences amount to hypotheses (often implicit rather than explicit) that such factors are more common in offenders, or particular categories of offenders, than in non-offenders, and that these factors have a causal role in offending. (See also Chapter 11 concerning how individuals' characteristics influence risk.)

While inductive thinking of this sort is important, it has its limitations. Human judgements are fallible. The professional may have little opportunity to gather similar information from non-offenders (many of whom have been abused, are lonely and are abusers of alcohol). Additionally, the fact that offenders may disproportionately have a particular psychological characteristic does not necessarily mean that this characteristic is causal of their offending. Engaging in offending behaviour and being deemed to be an offender may cause social difficulties

Practical Psychology for Forensic Investigations and Prosecutions.
Edited by Mark R. Kebbell and Graham M. Davies. © 2006 John Wiley & Sons, Ltd.

such as social isolation and substance abuse. Alternatively, the offending behaviour and the social difficulties may both be caused by some third factor (family disruption or personality factors, for example).

The individual psychological level of analysis is only one approach to explaining offending (McGuire, 2000). Nevertheless it is an important one and has been particularly influential in terms of shaping the assessment, treatment and rehabilitation of offenders in the criminal justice system. Individual psychological theories are not necessarily incompatible with broader sociological and even historical analyses. This was brought home to the first author during a period in which he was assessing and planning rehabilitation programmes for offenders in the Australian correctional system. When asked to assess the factors that had contributed to a homicide by a middle-aged, male offender who was an indigenous (aboriginal) Australian, the usual categories of individual causal factors (as outlined below) were highly relevant (poor attachments, inconsistent parenting, substance abuse, associating with other offenders, cognitive and problem-solving limitations, hostile beliefs and anger) but such factors need to be viewed in the context of the fact that indigenous people are vastly over-represented in the Australian criminal justice system (as they are in many other societies). Part of the explanation of why this person offended would have to make reference to the collective trauma, family disruption, social exclusion and marginalization, poverty, poor health and stigma suffered by this group, historically (following European colonization) and contemporaneously. Such historical and sociological factors do not preclude trying to determine how these factors manifest themselves in this individual's current psychological problems, and planning an intervention to reduce the probability of future offending.

DEVELOPMENTAL FACTORS

There is a long tradition of examining the childhood and adolescence of offenders in order to find out whether their early development is significantly different from that of non-offenders. The ideal way to do this is through prospective studies, where children at risk for criminality are identified early in their lives, their behaviour and environments are assessed in childhood and then they are followed through to ascertain who does and does not become an offender in adulthood. Such studies are difficult, laborious and expensive but when accomplished (as in the famous Cambridge study, Farrington, 1995) they have proven useful and influential. Farrington (1996) in a review of such work identified

Table 4.1 Individual and family factors in the developmental histories of offenders (Farrington, 1996)

Factor
High impulsivity
Lower intelligence
Poor conceptual thinking
Egocentricity/low empathy
Poor parental supervision
Harsh and erratic parental discipline
Cold and rejecting parental attitude
Separation from a parent
Large family size
Having a criminal parent

the developmental factors listed in Table 4.1 as ones with considerable evidence for a correlation with offending in adulthood.

To these individual and family influences we would need to add factors of a more social sort, including school factors (academic failure, low commitment and drop-out) and the peer group (having social support for antisocial attitudes, antisocial peers, Andrews & Bonta, 2003).

It is important to remember, however, that these are statistical correlates of offending and they do not establish that the relationship is causal nor do they indicate what the mediating mechanism is. One example serves to illustrate this. A large number of studies have demonstrated that offenders have IQs that are between 5 and 10 points lower than those of non-offenders. Is this finding to be explained in terms of: (a) Low IQ offenders being more likely to be caught? (b) Low IQ leading to low academic achievement, the latter being the crucial variable? (c) The behavioural and personality correlates of offending causing lower IQ? (For a discussion of these possibilities see Andrews & Bonta, 2003, Chapter 5.) In any event, measures of general intelligence are relatively crude and it may be that the intellectual deficits associated with offending, are specific, involving, for example difficulties in dealing with abstract and verbal tasks. Such deficits may be the product of parenting styles and of individual differences in neurophysiological processes.

Psychologists' concerns about identifying the mediating factor, is more than academic fastidiousness. It is having knowledge about mediating or causal factors that allows us to identify the appropriate target for intervention. Low academic achievement or failure at school, for example, may be more remediable than low IQ per se.

It is common in such research (see Andrews & Bonta, 2003) to distinguish adolescence-limited offenders whose offending begins and ends within the adolescence phase from persistent, "life-course" offenders whose antisocial behaviours become chronic and who turn out to have had extensive antisocial behaviour problems earlier in childhood. It is the persistent offender that typically attracts most attention from professionals in the criminal justice system and for whom questions of rehabilitation and treatment arise.

COGNITIVE AND SELF-REGULATION DEFICITS

Some researchers have suggested that chronic offenders have pervasive cognitive deficits and that these deficits affect their capacity for self-regulation. Such problems are believed by some (Barkley, 1997) to have a neurophysiological basis and to be strongly associated with the trait of impulsivity. There are indications that the most severe and repetitive adult offenders are particularly likely to share the cognitive and self-regulatory deficiencies of children with developmental disorders related to impulsivity. Johansson, Kerr and Andershed (2005), for example, compared adult offenders with diagnoses of psychopathy, with those who were nonpsychopathic. The psychopathic group was more likely to have conduct disorders before the age of 15 and problems of hyperactivity, impulsivity and poor attention before the age of 10.

Self-regulation problems may be one component of what have been termed deficient "social cognitive skills". The latter refers to the internal factors that influence how the environment impinges on the emotions and behaviours of the person. Such factors include perceptions, beliefs, appraisals of meaning, attributions of causation and the use of *cognitive scripts* that guide behaviour and social problem solving (Dodge & Crick, 1990; Ross & Fabiano, 1985). There is now considerable evidence that offenders often lack skills and are prone to biases in these aspects of thinking. Neurophysiological factors and poor intellectual functioning probably contribute to these deficits in social cognition. An intriguing hypothesis, recently advanced (Bennett, Farrington & Huesmann, 2005), is that gender differences in social cognitive skills may account for the large gender difference in offending behaviour. Girls are less likely to develop disorders of the attention deficit hyperactivity disorder (ADHD) type and are less at risk for the various developmental behavioural and brain disorders associated with subsequent criminality.

One consequence of the acquisition of this knowledge about offenders has been the development of rehabilitation programmes in many jurisdictions to remediate such deficits. These are often referred to as *cognitive skills programmes*.

MORAL DEVELOPMENT

Kohlberg's theory (Kohlberg, 1976) of moral development highlights the importance of possessing abstract reasoning ability. Without abstract reasoning, according to Kohlberg, an individual cannot progress successfully through the stages of cognitive moral development. Instead, the individual remains at a concrete thinking stage. Kohlberg hypothesized that moral actions were dependent upon moral reasoning; suggesting that if moral reasoning was underdeveloped in an individual then he/she would be unable to control or resist temptation when the opportunity arose. Current research tends to support this hypothesis, with moral reasoning being particularly associated with the criminal behaviour of the young. Although the strength of the relationship may vary depending on the type of crime, offenders have shown lower levels of moral reasoning than non-offenders (Palmer, 2004).

AFFECTIVE AND EMOTIONAL FACTORS

Over the past decade, within psychology in general, and within criminological psychology in particular, there has been increasing interest in affective and emotional *states* (particular affects and emotions experienced at a particular moment, for example immediately prior to a violent offence) and affective and emotional *traits* (the general disposition of the person to experience these affects and emotions in a frequent and intense way). The role of emotions has been investigated in both violent and sexual offenders in particular and it is on these groups that we shall focus here.

The emotion most commonly seen as important in violent offending has been anger. It is important to emphasize that the emotion of anger is neither a necessary nor a sufficient condition for human aggression and violence. Anger is not necessary in the sense that some violent offences occur without anger being a significant antecedent. Violence in the "psychopathic" offender (see below), for example, may be entirely *instrumental* (to obtain a particular goal) and dispassionate. It is also clear that the vast majority of episodes of anger do not culminate in violence. Anger is, after all, a common experience for most people in the community and can stimulate a broad range of constructive and destructive behaviours. We might, therefore label anger as a *contributing factor*, one that may affect the probability of violence, typically when it co-occurs with a number of other conditions.

There is evidence that anger is an important antecedent for many forms of violent offending, including homicide, violence between

Table 4.2 Components of anger assessment

Component

Triggering events for anger episodes
Cognitive appraisals and evaluations of these events, including cognitive
    biases and underlying cognitive structures or schemas
Physiological activation, particularly of the autonomic nervous system
The subjective experience of angry feelings
Action tendencies (impulses) evoked by angry emotion (for example to
    strike out)
Self-regulation strategies for anger
Behavioural reactions (what the person actually does in response to anger)
The functions of angry behaviour (social or environmental consequences of the
    form of behavioural expression that occurs)

(From Howells, 2004)

partners in long-term relationships, child abuse (physical violence) and
sex offending. There exists a range of psychological theories about the
nature of anger and its component processes. While there are differences of detail between such theories there is also much in common.
Most identify components such as those listed in Table 4.2 as important theoretically and also as foci for assessment and interventions.

The most common assumption in the assessment of offenders,
particularly violent offenders, is that it is individuals high in trait anger
(they experience anger with a high frequency and intensity) who are
most at risk for violent offending. However, the class of serious violent
offenders also includes individuals with very low levels of anger experience and expression – sometimes labelled as anger-inhibited or over-
controlled offenders. Typically such offenders rarely express anger, but
when they do it may be with a low frequency but very high intensity, for
example involving repeated stabbing or violent acts disproportionate to
the intention to hurt or even to kill (Davey, Day & Howells, 2005).

AFFECT AND EMOTION IN SEX OFFENDERS

It may seem intuitively obvious that anger problems are important
characteristics of some violent offenders. It is rather less obvious that
anger and other emotions might be important for sexual offending.
Howells, Day and Wright (2004) recently reviewed evidence relating
to the question of whether negative emotions are common antecedents
for sexual offences such as rape and sexual abuse of children. The research evidence did support the hypothesis that negative emotional
states have an influence.

Negative emotions also appear to have an influence on sexual recidivism. Thus when sex offenders are released to the community the probability of them offending again may depend in part on their emotional state. Two Canadian researchers (Hanson & Harris, 1998) studied 400 recidivists and non-recidivists during community supervision, based on interviews with supervising officers and case notes. An important finding was that the two groups did not differ on trait level mood and emotion that is in their general disposition to experience particular negative emotions. But the recidivists showed an increase in negative mood, anger and general psychiatric symptoms just prior to reoffending. Interestingly, the recidivists were also more disengaged and uncooperative in supervision. It is not clear whether negative mood causes disengagement though this would be consistent with more general findings on the effects of negative mood. Anger was one of the three best overall predictors of recidivism in this study.

Explaining exactly *how* negative emotions influence sexual offending (the causal *mechanism*) is not straightforward. A variety of mechanisms have been proposed but it is not yet clear which is correct (Howells et al., 2004). Among the hypotheses put forward are suggestions that sex offenders have learned in their developmental histories to cope with negative emotions (reducing them) by engaging in deviant sexual fantasy and behaviour. Others have proposed that the process called "cognitive deconstruction" is important (Baumeister, 1990). This involves the person responding to stress by "disengaging from the self system". A mental shift occurs to a state which has a number of important features including:

- less integrated and meaningful awareness of self;
- guilt is therefore diminished;
- focus on immediate, short-term concerns;
- proximal rather than distal goals dominate;
- concreteness;
- lessened influence of self-standards;
- passivity;
- diminished inhibitions;
- fantasy proneness.

It is not difficult to see how such a state would influence the likelihood of a sexual offence occurring.

Whatever the explanation of how negative emotions influence sexual offending, it is clearly important that emotions need to be investigated by any professional who is concerned to understand why a sexual offence occurred. Such an investigation would need to include attention to the long-term emotional dispositions (emotional traits) the offender or suspect might have. This would need to be supplemented by an assessment of the emotional state of the person in the weeks and days leading up to the actual offence. The emotional state of the offender immediately prior to the offence would be vital to know. In an investigative context, the characteristics of the offence itself, for example details suggesting that the motive was to harm rather than purely to obtain sexual gratification (see above), may throw some light on the most likely offence pathway (see below) for this particular offence.

CONTROL, DOMINANCE AND OTHER MOTIVATIONS IN SEX OFFENDERS

Feminist theorists and researchers were the first to draw attention to the importance of sex- and gender-related ideological beliefs both in sexual offenders and in the broader society of which they form a part. Notions of high and uncontrollable male sexual drive, ignoring lack of consent to sex and motivation to control and dominate sexual relationships are common in sex offenders and, undoubtedly, more widely in society (Field, 1978). Many sex offenders, particularly those with child victims, have also been shown to have problems in establishing intimacy in adult relationships and to hold a number of distorted beliefs about potential victims and their own sexual behaviour which contribute to and appear to justify their sexual offending (Marshall, Anderson & Fernandez, 1999).

A wide range of cognitive distortions exist which are consistently employed by offenders in order to evade responsibility for their actions. Offenders use cognitive distortions to deny, minimize, rationalize and justify their behaviour (Ward, Hudson, Johnston & Marshall, 1997). Beliefs such as "men get overpowered by their sexual urges and cannot control their feelings" have been observed in rapists and "sex is good for children" in offenders against children.

PATHWAYS TO SEXUAL OFFENDING

It can be seen from the above that the antecedents to sex offending are multifaceted, involving interplay of cognitive, affective and behavioural factors. The same is likely to be true for violent and other forms of offending. In recent years there have been attempts to weave such elements together by identifying "pathways" to offending. New Zealand psychologists (Hudson, Ward & McCormack, 1999) have demonstrated a number of different pathways to sexual offences. Two pathways from Hudson et al.'s account are as follows.

PATHWAY 1

Positive affect -◊ explicit plan →◊ positive affect →◊ perceived mutuality →◊ positive evaluation →◊ persistence

Men on this pathway showed positive mood at the outset, were "appetitively driven" (that is, actively seeking sexual satisfaction) and typically explicitly planned their offence. They perceived a mutual relationship with the victim and positively evaluated their offending sexual behaviour. Subsequent to this there was a commitment to continue offending.

PATHWAY 2

Negative affect →◊ explicit plan →◊ ± affect →◊ self focused →◊ negative evaluation →◊ avoidance

This pathway begins with negative affect (typically depression, feeling down or lonely for child molesters) and involves explicit planning of the offence. The affect involved in the high-risk situation (proximal planning) is either energizing but negative "used my position of power to get her to do what I wanted" or positive and integrated with the offending itself ("I enjoyed it – felt loved") Post-offence evaluations in this case are typically negative about the offence and the intention is to avoid offending subsequently.

Empathy

Empathy has many component parts. To be empathic requires a *cognitive/perceptual ability* (recognizing, for example, that someone is distressed), an *affective reaction* (sharing their distress) and *behavioural expression* (acting towards the distressed person in a way which takes account of their distress). The lay and professional viewpoint is likely to be that offenders are unempathic and even that lack of empathy plays a part in the causation of offending. It is plausible that empathy with the potential victim of an antisocial act (violence or sexual offending) serves as an inhibitor of the impulse. Media accounts of serious offenders often stress their apparent callousness, and lack of feeling and concern for the victim. Treatment programmes for offenders may include "empathy training" in an attempt to remedy such deficits.

There is a research literature investigating whether such beliefs have any factual basis. This literature was subjected to a rigorous review and meta-analysis by Jollife and Farrington in 2004 and we shall summarize some of their findings. Meta-analysis refers to an important statistical tool in contemporary social science which allows for the aggregation of findings from a large number of studies to produce an overarching conclusion on whether the two factors (for example low empathy and offending) are related and an estimate of "effect size" (the extent of their relationship).

Jollife and Farrington analysed 35 studies, involving more than 5 000 research participants. They concluded that, broadly speaking, there was a significant relationship between low empathy and offending, but that the cognitive aspect (see above), which includes the capacity to take the perspective of others, was more strongly related to offending than was the affective aspect (sharing the distress). A complication in understanding the various interrelationships was that low intelligence correlated with low empathy. It is possible, therefore, that the empathy differences between offenders and non-offenders can be accounted for by the known association (see above) between low intelligence and offending. Moreover, low empathy was more strongly associated with general offending than with sex offending. There was an association between low empathy and violent offending.

Such studies would seem to support the provision of empathy treatment programmes for offenders in general, with a particular focus on developing the cognitive and perceptual skills involved in the perceptions of others in distress. There is support too for providing such treatment for violent offenders but less for providing it to sex offenders. Clinician researchers in the sex offender field have suggested for some time that the empathy deficits in sex offenders are not general but may be specific to the victim. It may also be the case that particular events and states of mind serve to diminish empathy in offence situations. In this circumstance, an offender who usually has reasonable levels of empathy may find empathy diminished in a particular situation. It is reasonable to conclude that the professional wishing to understand the individual offender does indeed need to consider the role of empathy deficits in the offence situation. In particular clinical groups, such as those with psychopathic personalities (below), empathy deficits are severe and central to the disorder.

MENTAL DISORDER IN OFFENDERS

The previous discussion of negative emotions in relation to offenders alerts us to the potential importance of psychological and psychiatric disorders in offenders. This is a vast and controversial area of research and theory. It is possible to discuss only some broad themes and issues within this chapter. It is clear that offenders, particularly imprisoned offenders, have high prevalence rates for mental disorder, when assessed in terms of criteria specified by recognized diagnostic systems such as the DSM-IV (Diagnostic and Statistical Manual of the American Psychiatric Association) and the ICD (International Classification of Diseases). Rates of schizophrenia, mood disorders and substance abuse, for example, are high. Diagnostic systems such as the DSM typically distinguish Axis 1 disorders (well-recognized clinical syndromes such as schizophrenia, bipolar disorder, anxiety disorders) which may be time limited, from Axis II disorders which reflect long-term traits. The personality disorders (PDs) are located within Axis II. They are particularly relevant to this chapter in that PD prevalence is very high indeed in offender populations, particularly antisocial personality disorder (APD), the diagnostic criteria for which include a history of conduct disorder, dishonesty, lack of responsibility, breaking the law and an absence of remorse. In some studies, more than half of the offenders studied have met the criteria for APD.

A particular personality disorder – psychopathic disorder (psychopathy) – though not yet included in the DSM system – has attracted considerable attention in the criminal justice field in the past decade. Based largely on the work of Robert Hare (1999), psychopathy has become important for two reasons. First, it can now be measured in a rigorous and reliable manner using the psychopathy checklist (PCL-R). Such assessments are now routinely administered in many correctional systems. Secondly, psychopathy has proven to be a reliable predictor of future risk of offending, particularly violent and sexual offending. A number of controversies surround the concept of psychopathy and its measurement. Should it be conceived, for example, as a dimension from high to low on which we can all be placed, or is it a discrete category – a *taxon* – implying that psychopaths are a separate group, different in quality from nonpsychopaths? Paradoxically, in the past the diagnosis of psychopathy has often been a reason for *not* referring the offender for treatment, on the assumption that "psychopaths are untreatable".

The evidence for this latter assertion has started to be questioned in recent years, with many researchers concluding that there have been too few scientific treatment outcome studies to know whether psychopaths are treatable or not. Given that the prevalence of psychopathy is high in populations of serious violent offenders, many policy makers and professionals in the criminal justice system are concerned to develop treatment interventions which might lower the risk of serious violence in this group. In England and Wales, the Home Office and the Department of Health have recently developed intensive assessment and treatment programmes for those with dangerous and severe personality disorders (DSPD) in both psychiatric hospital and prison settings. Admission to these programmes is largely determined by having a high psychopathy score in combination with a very high level of risk. It remains to be seen whether such treatments are effective but psychopathy is likely to remain an important attribute for assessment in a variety of criminal justice settings.

When we are considering an individual offender with a serious mental disorder, important issues arise, once again, as to the issue of causality. It is easy, but often wrong, to assume that the mental disorder in such cases causes the offending behaviour. The presence of Axis 1 mental disorders, in general, contributes only modestly to the probability of violent offending. If we look at schizophrenia in relation to violent offending, for example, we find that in some offenders the pattern of violent behaviour commenced prior to the diagnosis of schizophrenia, while in others it followed the diagnosis. It is obvious that only in the second case could schizophrenia have a causal influence. It is also the case that the same factors predict the probability of future offending in mentally disordered offenders as in nonmentally disordered offenders (Bonta, Law & Hanson, 1998), tending to suggest that the causal role of psychiatric symptoms may be limited.

ALCOHOL USE AND OFFENDING

There is little doubt that alcohol use and criminal behaviour are closely associated. Not only are alcoholics more likely than nonalcoholics to have a history of violent behaviour, but also many prisoners experience ongoing problems with alcohol use. Research with convicted prisoners has also suggested that many offenders are under the influence of alcohol when they offend. Pernanen, Cousineau, Brochu and Sun (2002) reported that just over one-third (38%) of their sample of Canadian federal prison inmates committed their most serious crime while under the influence of alcohol. A number of other studies have also consistently reported that both perpetrators and victims of violent crimes are likely to have consumed alcohol prior to certain aggressive acts, such as rape, domestic violence and murder.

Zamble and Quinsey (2001) in their detailed study of recidivism found consumption of alcohol was a distinguishing feature of the preoffence period. In the six months preceding arrest, most of the recidivists in their sample not only used alcohol, but also used it regularly and in high amounts. In the 24-hour period preceding the offence, a majority reported drinking heavily before offending, leading Zamble and Quinsey to conclude that even the most experienced heavy drinkers were likely to have been intoxicated at the time of their offence.

In short, there appears to be strong evidence supporting a close epidemiological association between alcohol use, intoxication and offending. It is important to distinguish between alcohol use at the time of the offence (alcohol as a proximal state antecedent), and habitual alcohol use (alcohol as a trait or distal antecedent). This distinction is particularly important given that there is evidence to suggest that the correlation between trait alcohol use and crime disappears once drinking immediately prior to the offence is controlled for.

UNDERSTANDING THE INDIVIDUAL OFFENDER

Our discussion so far has stressed the heterogeneity of offenders and the wide range of factors that may play a causal role in the development of offending behaviour. An important consequence of these points is that two offenders could engage in criminal acts which were identical *topographically*, that is, for example, both had committed a serious violent assault such as a very serious stabbing, nevertheless the acts could be *functionally* entirely different. By functionally we mean here the antecedents (contributing factors) and the functions the behaviour serves for the person. Offender A's assault for example may have been influenced by an episode of depression and binge drinking which reduced his usual level of self-control of angry impulses. Offender B's assault, on the other hand was a consequence of paranoid thinking, chronic hostility to others and very high levels of physical tension. The terminology used in the criminological literature on offenders is that A and B have different *criminogenic needs*. Criminogenic needs, therefore, are characteristics of the individual that are functionally related to his or her offending behaviour.

A core task for the criminal justice system and health professionals who wish to understand, manage, treat or rehabilitate offenders is to conduct, or at least be cognizant of, a *criminogenic needs analysis* of the individual. Such an analysis not only seeks to establish what causes the person to offend, but also it simultaneously describes risk factors for future offending. Even more importantly, the criminogenic needs identified are crucial in deciding rehabilitation or treatment targets for change. Improvement for an individual would also be measured by the extent of change that has occurred for each area of criminogenic need. This approach may sound entirely "commonsense" at a first hearing, which, in some ways it is. However, it is only in the past decade that systematic criminogenic needs analyses have become part of the assessment process in the criminal justice systems around the world.

Commonsense and less rigorous criminogenic needs analysis (the actual term was not used) in the past have often been characterized by unifactorial rather than multifactorial thinking about the causation of offending. An offender's behaviour may be seen as caused by his "drink problem", for example, without acknowledgement that a number of characteristics, events and circumstances need to come together for an offence to occur. A second problem with informal analyses in the past has been that such analyses have not always been based on knowledge about studies which have empirically investigated what the common causes of crime actually are. An example often used by criminogenic needs analysts has been "self-esteem". "Low self-esteem" is very often ascribed to offenders by lay and professional groups alike and is seen as a cause of offending that needs remediation. Unfortunately, the evidence that offenders in general have low self-esteem is minimal. There is even some evidence that they have an above-average level of self-esteem. Thus it is not a criminogenic need. It is possible, of course, that low self-esteem *is* criminogenic for particular individual offenders. Anxiety problems may provide another example of a factor which is criminogenic for relatively few offenders.

We suggest that an adequate criminogenic needs analysis should be based on three types of knowledge: (i) Knowledge about the many causes of general offending. A professional's competence at criminogenic needs assessment might be viewed as suspect if he or she regularly identified criminogenic needs which did not show up as important in the many empirical studies that have been conducted. (ii) Knowledge about causal influences in specific offence types. Sexual offenders, for example, are likely to have some criminogenic needs which are not found in general offenders (deviant sexual fantasies, loneliness etc.). The professional needs, therefore, to be knowledgeable about the sex offender literature. This is not to say that some sex offenders do not share some criminogenic needs with general offenders (impulsivity and hostility in some rapists, for example). (iii) Knowledge about, and a method to assess, criminogenic needs which are idiosyncratic to a particular individual offender. Some offenders have criminogenic needs which do not feature in any of the "lists" we might derive from empirical studies of general offenders or specialist offenders such as sex offenders.

THE FUNCTIONAL ANALYSIS APPROACH

A method for assessing the causes of an individual's problems has been developed in clinical psychology, with the description "functional analysis" (Daffern & Howells, 2002; Sturmey, 1996). Functional analysis involves assessment of the antecedents and functions of the particular presenting problem for the individual. A functional analysis of smoking, for example, would involve analysing for the individual smoker antecedents such as the situations that elicit smoking and the emotions and thoughts that occur. This would be complemented by an analysis of the functions of smoking for the person, for example to become more relaxed, to become more alert or to look "cool" in social situations. Functional analysis would involve intensive study of the particular occasions on which the individual smoked. An important principle in functional analysis is that the factors important in the onset of the problem ("distal factors") may differ from those that maintain it in the present ("proximal factors"). Thus people typically commence smoking for social reasons (social image) but maintain smoking for pharmacological reasons (the negative feelings associated with nicotine withdrawal).

A functional analysis can be conducted in relation to criminal and antisocial behaviours along similar lines (Daffern & Howells, 2002). A sex offender may have distal antecedents for his offending in the form of his being sexually abused in childhood, but functional analysis of his current offending requires that we translate such a distal factor into a proximal one. How exactly does his experience of sexual abuse in childhood influence his propensity to sexually offend in the here and now? It may be, for example, that his abuse led him to believe now that "sex with children is normal" or that "sex abusers can get away with it because abuse is not reported by the child". It is the identification of maintenance factors, both antecedent and functional, that is critical in criminogenic needs analysis because such factors are likely to be amenable to change whereas purely distal factors (the abuse in childhood) are not.

In practice, functional analysis of offending is a demanding, time-consuming and skilled task, requiring a detailed analysis of current and previous offences, using records, the offender's account and the observations of others. The days and weeks leading to the offences will receive the most scrutiny. Detailed assessments of the individual are most likely to be conducted where the offence is particularly serious or where less intensive assessments have failed to reveal what the important criminogenic needs are. Some broad areas that would need attention in a functional analysis of an offence, or series of offences are described in Table 4.3.

A functional analysis involves the following steps:

1. Specifying the "A"s (antecedents) for a particular offence or series of offences.
2. Specifying the "B"s (behaviour) in detail. In this case the B is the offence itself (the murder, the sexual assault).
3. Specifying the "C"s (consequences) or functions of the offence for the offender.

Table 4.3 Areas requiring assessment in functional analysis of offences

Assessment area
Frequency, intensity, form of criminal behaviour
Environmental triggers (including stressors)
Cognitive (attitudinal) factors
Emotional antecedents
Physiological antecedents
Coping/problem-solving skills
Personality dispositions, e.g. anger proneness, impulsivity, psychopathy
Mental disorders, e.g. mood disorders, brain impairment, delusions, hallucinations, personality disorders
Consequences or functions of offence – for self, others, short and long term
Opportunity factors, e.g. weapons, victim availability, restrictions
Disinhibitors, e.g. substance abuse, criminal associates
Buffers, e.g. employment, attachments, achievement

4. Distinguishing proximal and distal antecedents (see above).
5. From the above, deriving a statement of the individual's criminogenic needs.

We shall illustrate this process with a case example. Brandon was aged 32 and had convictions for a series of violent offences, usually against strangers in public settings such as bars and clubs. The offence being analysed here involved a serious stabbing of someone he had just met in a bar. Addressing the areas outlined in Table 4.3, it became clear from the information available, that his violence usually took the form of stabbings – an intense form of violence which was relatively infrequent – about four occasions in all. Analysis of these offences indicated that they occurred at times when there were many negative events and stresses in his life. He had characteristic cognitions and thoughts at these times, being preoccupied with ideas that he was unfairly treated and a victim of the malevolence of others. His emotional state was one of angry resentment at the time. His stress took the form of tension

Table 4.4 Functional analysis for "Brandon"

Antecedents	Behaviours	Consequences/Functions
Stressful and frustrating life events	Stabbings	Relief from stress
Anger and frustration		Restoration of dominance
Hostile/paranoid appraisals/beliefs		
Anger-proneness		
Substance abuse		
Carrying a weapon		

and physiological arousal. He had few skills for coping with negative events and what he saw as the provocative behaviour of others. He had long-term personality traits of anger proneness. He showed a moderate degree of impulsivity. Often he could exert self-control but this was impaired after heavy drinking. He had been drinking heavily on all 4 occasions on which he stabbed someone.

His personality problems did not amount to psychopathy. He did not suffer from any formal mental disorder, though his negative thoughts had a "paranoid" flavour, seeing the worst in others and their intentions. The consequences/functions of his stabbings were not clear-cut but he reported a sense of relief and satisfaction at having "cut someone down to size". The major opportunity factor was that he routinely carried a knife. Although disinhibited by alcohol, he did not have criminal associates who might support and reinforce his antisocial beliefs and behaviours. He had one buffer (protective factor) against offending, a long-term relationship, but had few achievements or satisfactions in employment. The analysis for Brandon could be summarized as in Table 4.4:

Note the antecedents listed are proximal. Distal antecedents (childhood events) are not discussed here. Both the As and Cs above point to Brandon's criminogenic needs – exposure to stressors, hostile beliefs, high anger, substance abuse etc. and these would form the basis for any rehabilitative or treatment programme. Ideally sentencing would ensure that such needs could be addressed.

CRIMINOGENIC VERSUS NONCRIMINOGENIC NEEDS

Offenders have noncriminogenic as well as criminogenic needs. The former, by definition, are unrelated to the propensity to offend, but may nevertheless be vitally important in understanding, managing and humanely treating offenders in the criminal justice system. An offender may be distressed, anxious, depressed and suicidal. Such attributes need to be assessed and managed for duty-of-care reasons rather than because of a direct link to offending. Consideration of such noncriminogenic features may also be important because they are likely to affect the individual's readiness for, and capacity to benefit from, therapeutic programmes designed to diminish criminogenic needs.

SUMMARY AND CONCLUSIONS

It is clear that offenders and non-offenders differ substantially on a number of attributes, though questions of causality are far from being answered. Offenders are heterogeneous, and one-factor explanations of crime, even of specific types of crime, are inappropriate. A broad array of causal factors needs to be considered, as discussed in this chapter. Proper understanding of offenders and of their rehabilitation needs by criminal justice professionals requires individualized assessment. Psychology undoubtedly has a significant part to play in such work.

REFERENCES

Andrews, D.A. & Bonta, J. (2003). *The psychology of criminal conduct*, 3rd edn. Oklahoma: Anderson.

Barkley, R.A. (1997). *ADHD and the nature of self control*. New York: Guilford Press.

Baumeister, R.F. (1990). Suicide as escape from self. *Psychological Review, 97*, 90–113.

Bennett, S., Farrington, D.P. & Huesmann, L.R. (2005). Explaining gender differences in crime and violence: The importance of social cognitive skills. *Aggression and Violent Behavior, 10*, 263–288.

Bonta, J., Law, M. & Hanson, K. (1998). The prediction of criminal and violent recidivism among mentally disordered offenders. *Psychological Bulletin, 123*, 123–142.

Daffern, M. & Howells, K. (2002). Psychiatric inpatient aggression: A review of structural and functional assessment approaches. *Aggression and Violent Behavior, 7*, 477–497.

Davey, L., Day, A. & Howells, K. (2005). Anger, overcontrol and violent offending. *Aggression and Violent Behavior, 10*, 624–635.

Dodge, K.A. & Crick, N.R. (1990). Social information-processing biases of aggressive behavior in children. *Personality and Social Psychology Bulletin, 16*, 8–22.

Farrington, D.P. (1995). The development of offending and antisocial behavior from childhood: Key findings from the Cambridge study in delinquent development. *Journal of Child Psychology and Psychiatry, 36*, 929–964.

Farrington, D.P. (1996). Criminological psychology: Individual and family factors in the explanation and prevention of offending. In C.R. Hollin (Ed.), *Working with offenders: Psychological practice in offender rehabilitation* (pp. 3–39). Chichester: John Wiley & Sons, Ltd.

Field, H.S. (1978). Attitudes towards rape: A comparative analysis of police, rapists, crisis counsellors and citizens. *Journal of Personality and Social Psychology, 36*, 156–179.

Hanson, R.K. & Harris, A.J.R. (1998). Where should we intervene? Dynamic predictors of sexual offence recidivism. *Criminal Justice and Behavior, 27*, 6–35.

Hare, R.D. (1999). *Without conscience: The disturbing world of the psychopaths among us*. New York: Guilford Press.

Howells, K. (2004). Anger and its links to violence. *Psychiatry, Psychology and Law, 11*, 189–196.

Howells, K., Day, A. & Wright, S. (2004). Affect, emotions and sex offending. *Psychology, Crime and Law, 10*, 179–195.

Hudson, S.M., Ward, T. & McCormack, J.C. (1999). Offence pathways in sexual offenders. *Journal of Interpersonal Violence, 14*, 779–798.

Johansson, P., Kerr, M. & Andershed, H. (2005). Linking adult psychopathy with childhood hyperactivity–impulsivity–attention problems and conduct problems through retrospective self-reports. *Journal of Personality Disorders, 19*, 94–101.

Jolliffe, D. & Farrington, D.P. (2004). Empathy and offending: A systematic review and meta-analysis. *Aggression and Violent Behavior, 9*, 441–476.

Kohlberg, L. (1976). Moral stages and moralisation: The cognitive-developmental approach. In T. Lickona (Ed.), *Moral development and behavior*. New York: Holt, Rhinehart & Winston.

Marshall, W.L., Anderson, D. & Fernandez, Y. (1999). *Cognitive behavioural treatment of sex offenders*. Chichester: John Wiley & Sons, Ltd.

McGuire, J. (2000). Explanations of offence behaviour. In J. McGuire, T. Mason & A. O'Kane (Eds), *Behaviour, crime and legal processes* (pp. 135–159). Chichester: John Wiley & Sons, Ltd.

Palmer, E. (2004). *Offending behaviour: Moral reasoning, criminal conduct and the rehabilitation of offenders*. Cullompton: Willan Publishing.

Pernanen, K., Cousineau, M., Brochu, S. & Sun, F. (2002). Proportions of crimes associated with alcohol and other drugs in Canada. Available online from Solicitor General Canada website: http://www.sgc.gc.ca/releases/e20020430.htm.

Ross, R.R. & Fabiano, E.A. (1985). *Time to think: A cognitive model of delinquency prevention and offender rehabilitation*. Johnson City, TN: Institute of Social Sciences and Arts.

Sturmey, P. (1996). *Functional analysis in clinical psychology*, Chichester: John Wiley & Sons, Ltd.

Ward, T., Hudson, S.M., Johnston, L. & Marshall, W.L. (1997). Cognitive distortions in sex offenders: An integrative review. *Clinical Psychology Review, 17*, 479–507.

Zamble, E. & Quinsey, V.L. (2001). *The criminal recidivism process*. Cambridge: Cambridge University Press.

CHAPTER 5

Detecting Deception

ALDERT VRIJ

INTRODUCTION

Preventing and solving crime are important issues, both to the general public and politicians, and having the ability to detect deceit would help in achieving these aims. Hopes are raised that these aims could be accomplished by: (i) commercial companies promoting and selling lie-detector equipment such as "voice-stress analysers" (VSA); (ii) pilot studies in the United Kingdom (and probably in other countries) where the traditional lie detector, the polygraph, is tested; and (iii) researchers testing and promoting new methodologies such as thermal imaging (Pavlidis, Eberhardt & Levine, 2002). These initiatives receive substantial media attention. The question is, how well informed are the claims that are made in these initiatives? For example, the then Home Secretary, David Blunkett, approved a scheme in the United Kingdom where sex offenders face traditional lie-detector tests before and after being freed from prison. He said of this scheme: "We are all a bit sceptical because we've all been brought up with the spy films and the way in which the KGB are allegedly able to train people to avoid them [polygraph]", but, he continued, "We are talking about really modern technology in the 21st century and we are testing it" (*The Independent*, 29 May 2004, p. 4). This seems at odds with the conclusion of the National Research Council (2003, p. 102) that "Research on the polygraph has not progressed over time in the manner of a typical scientific field", and with research findings showing that people's ability to beat polygraph tests once they know how such tests work, is a serious problem

Practical Psychology for Forensic Investigations and Prosecutions.
Edited by Mark R. Kebbell and Graham M. Davies. © 2006 John Wiley & Sons, Ltd.

in polygraph lie detection (Honts & Amato, 2002).[1] (See also Chapter 11 for a discussion of the use of the polygraph in assessing risk.)

Perhaps most importantly, traditional polygraph tests, as well as VSA and thermal imaging, are unreliable lie-detection tools. The main problem with such methods is that they are based on the assumption that liars are more aroused than truth tellers, due to liars' fear of getting caught. As I will demonstrate, there are serious problems with relying on this premise, and I therefore argue that lie-detection methods that rely on this premise should not be used. Instead, I will introduce alternative methods. I will commence this chapter with discussing theoretical reasons why we can expect liars and truth tellers to sometimes react differently, and with discussing several arousal-based lie-detection techniques, such as the traditional polygraph test, VSA, thermal imaging and techniques based on observations of arousal-based behaviours.

THEORY BEHIND DECEPTION

A main problem lie detectors face is that the mere fact that people lie will not result in any specific verbal, nonverbal or physiological response. In other words, a cue akin to Pinocchio's growing nose does not exist. Lie detectors thus have no other choice but to detect deceit in an indirect way. Deception theory (Vrij, 2000; Zuckerman, DePaulo & Rosenthal, 1981) suggests that three factors may affect people when they lie: emotions, content complexity and attempted behavioural control. If one or more of these factors are present when people deceive, lies could be indirectly detected by measuring the responses associated with these factors.

Regarding emotions, liars may be afraid of getting caught. The strength of this fear depends, among other factors, on the circumstances under which the lie takes place (Ekman, 1985/2001; Vrij, 2000). In high-stakes situations, where getting away with the lie is really important to the liar, the fear is typically higher than in low-stakes situations. Emotions may influence a liar's response. For example, they may result in overt signs of stress such as gaze aversion, an increase in movements, an increase in speech hesitations (mm's and er's) and speech errors (stutters, repetition of words, omission of words) or a higher pitched voice. They may also result in physiological reactions, such as increased palmar sweating, heightened blood pressure and an increased heart rate.

In order to convince others, liars need to provide plausible answers while avoiding contradicting themselves. They must tell a lie that is consistent with everything the observer knows or may find out. Liars also need to remember what they have said, so that they can say the same things again when asked to repeat their story. They may also feel an urge to control their demeanour so that they will appear honest (as emphasized in the attempted control process below), and may wish to observe the target person's reactions carefully in order to assess whether they are getting away with their lie. The task liars face may therefore be cognitively demanding. The extent to which lying is cognitively demanding often depends on the type of lie. Telling an outright lie may be more cognitively challenging than concealing information, and telling an elaborate lie may be more demanding than providing short yes or no answers. Lying may also be more demanding when the lie is not well prepared or rehearsed. People engaged in cognitively complex tasks make more speech hesitations (e.g., stutters) and speech errors, speak slower, pause more and wait longer before giving an answer. Cognitive complexity also leads to fewer hand and arm movements and to more gaze aversion, because looking the conversation partner in the eye can be distracting.

Liars may well realize that observers look at their behavioural reactions to judge whether they are lying, and may therefore attempt to control their behaviour in order to appear credible. To be successful, liars must suppress their nervousness while masking evidence of having to think hard. They should also be able to show honest-looking behaviours and avoid dishonest-looking behaviours (Hocking & Leathers, 1980). It effectively means that liars need to act. This may easily lead to behaviour that appears planned and rehearsed, or lacks spontaneity, similarly to how some people react when they realize that their photo will be taken. Liars' motivation and efforts to control their behaviour will probably increase when the stakes increase.

TRADITIONAL POLYGRAPH TESTS, VSA, THERMAL IMAGING AND OBSERVING BEHAVIOUR

Observing Behaviour

Despite the fact that "fear of detection" is thus only one of a number of factors that could affect liars' responses, many lie-detecting methods (including the traditional polygraph test, VSA and thermal imaging) focus exclusively on this factor. It is also popular among lie detectors who observe people's behaviour. For example, the vast majority of police officers believe that people look away and fidget when they lie (Strömwall, Granhag & Hartwig, 2004; Vrij & Semin, 1996), and such views are also promoted in police manuals (Inbau, Reid, Buckley & Jayne, 2001). However, there is no evidence that suspects predominantly show nervous behaviours during their police interviews. On the contrary, Mann, Vrij and Bull's (2002) analysis of the behaviours shown by suspects during their police interviews, revealed that compared to when they told the truth, the suspects exhibited more pauses, fewer eye blinks and fewer arm, hand and finger movements (by male suspects) when they lied. These are all indicators of cognitive load. Indicators of being tense (such as fidgeting and gaze aversion) did not emerge. Unsurprisingly, when Mann and Vrij (2005) showed police officers a selection of the truthful and deceptive clips of Mann et al.'s (2002) study, and asked them to indicate to what extent each suspect (i) seemed tense, (ii) gave the impression that he or she had to think hard and (iii) appeared to be controlling him/herself. The police officers were not told when the suspects were lying and when they were telling the truth. Results revealed that the suspects appeared to be thinking harder and trying to control themselves more when they lied than when they told the truth. However, in contrast to popular beliefs, the suspects appeared more tense when they told the truth than when they lied.

These findings could be explained in several ways. First, many of the suspects included in Mann et al.'s (2002) study had previously had regular contact with the police and were probably familiar with the police interview situation. Perhaps they were therefore not nervous when they lied. Second, the suspects may not only have been nervous when they lied, they also may have been nervous when they told the truth, making it less likely that nerves will differentiate between truths and lies. Third, suspects in police interviews are typically of below average intelligence (Gudjonsson, 2003), and less intelligent people may have particular difficulty in inventing plausible and convincing stories (Ekman & Frank, 1993). There is evidence that having to think hard results in an automatic and momentary suppression of arousal (Jennings, 1992; Leal, 2005). Fourth, it may be that the suspects actively (and successfully) tried to suppress showing signs of nervousness when they lied.

The third reason (momentary suppression of arousal due to cognitive demand) suggests that the suspects did not show signs of nervousness because these signs were overshadowed by the signs of cognitive demand. This suggests that signs of nervousness may arise when lies are not cognitively demanding. Cognitive demand is unlikely to play a major role in traditional polygraph testing, particularly because the questions are discussed with the examinee prior to the polygraph test in order to prevent possible confusion about the exact meaning of the questions. However, as we will see, during traditional polygraph tests, liars do not necessarily show the increased arousal that polygraph examiners expect them to show.

Traditional Polygraph Tests

During traditional polygraph tests, examinees are hooked up to a machine, the polygraph, and their palmar sweating, heart rate and blood pressure are measured. All of these indicators measure arousal. In its most simplistic form, examinees are asked *relevant* questions such as "On March 12, did you shoot your wife?" and *control* questions such as "Are you sitting down?" Control questions are necessary to ask because people's individual physiological responses differ in intensity, just as people differ in their tone of voice, speech rate, the number of movements they make, how talkative they are and so on. Control questions are therefore asked in an attempt to control for such individual differences. The examiner compares the physiological responses to control and relevant questions. It is assumed that truth tellers will show a similar response to both types of questions, as they will be truthful while answering both types of questions. Liars, however, will show a stronger response to the relevant questions than to the control questions, because they answer those questions deceptively and experience fear of getting caught.

This assumption is theoretically flawed. First, liars are not necessarily more aroused when answering the relevant questions, because they do not necessarily experience fear of not being believed when answering the relevant questions, or because they may successfully influence their own arousal levels during the test. (People who are trained to do this can successfully do so, without the examiner noticing, Honts & Amoto, 2002). Second, truth tellers may show increased arousal when answering the relevant questions. They may well be afraid of not being believed when answering the relevant questions, because being judged as deceptive in a polygraph test has negative consequences for innocent people. At the very least, it makes them a suspect in the crime with all its negative consequences, such as being interviewed by the police about the crime, fear that the truth about their innocence may not come out and perhaps negative reactions from family members, colleagues, neighbours, etc. For these reasons, this simplistic form of polygraph testing has been criticized by the scientific community, including those who are in favour of polygraph testing (Raskin & Honts, 2002; Vrij, 2000). However, I suspect that the simplistic form of polygraph testing frequently takes place, as I will discuss below.

The test promoted by traditional polygraph supporters (Raskin & Honts, 2002) is different in the sense that different control questions are asked. Rather than asking "Are you sitting down?", questions such as "Have you ever tried to hurt someone to get revenge?" are asked, where the examiner believes or, even better, has evidence that the examinee has indeed hurt someone at some point previously in his life. Under normal circumstances, some examinees might admit this wrong-doing. However, during a polygraph examination they will not, because the examiner will give the examinee the impression that admitting this would cause the examiner to conclude that the examinee is the type of person who would commit the crime in question and is therefore considered guilty. The rationale is that innocent examinees will show stronger responses to these control questions than to the relevant questions, because they are very concerned about the control questions and are lying when answering these questions. Guilty examinees, however, will show stronger responses when answering the relevant questions, because those questions contain the immediate threat of being accused of committing the crime. Opponents of traditional polygraph testing argue that this rationale is still flawed for the same reasons as mentioned above: guilty suspects do not necessarily show stronger responses to the relevant questions, and innocent suspects may well show stronger responses to relevant questions. Opponents have research findings on their side. Research where the accuracy of the type of polygraph tests promoted by polygraph supporters has been tested, revealed that errors are frequently made, especially when classifying innocent suspects. Reviews examining the accuracy of traditional polygraph testing in real-life cases show different findings, but, in the worst-case scenario, it was found that 47% of innocent suspects were incorrectly classified as guilty, and 17% of guilty suspects were incorrectly classified as innocent (BPS Working Party, 2004).

Voice-Stress Analysers

Voice-stress analysers differ from traditional polygraph tests because arousal is measured in a different way. Voice-stress analysis measures arousal non-intrusively by measuring people's pitch of voice (another indicator of arousal). A possible benefit is that lie-detection tests can be carried out without the examinee's awareness. This is how I suspect VSA tests are typically conducted, for example, by insurance companies when they assess claims made during telephone calls. They probably use the test in its simplistic form, discussed above, because this is the test that could most easily be carried out without the examinee being aware of being tested. In the test promoted by traditional polygraph supporters, also discussed above, examinees must be subtly guided to lie to the control questions. It is difficult to see how this can be achieved without raising suspicions by the examinee. A further complication of such tests is that background information about the examinees is needed, because the examiner must be certain that the examinee actually lies while answering the control questions. As already noted, the polygraph test in its simplistic form has been criticized even by academics who support polygraph testing. Given the problems with this simplistic way of testing, it is not surprising that the National Research Council (2003, p. 167) concluded that "although proponents of voice-stress analysis claim high levels of accuracy, empirical research on the validity of the technique has been far from encouraging".

Thermal Imaging

The thermal-imaging technique involves measuring instantaneous warming around the eyes. This is another measure of arousal and is recorded non-intrusively with a camera. Pavlidis et al. (2002, p. 35), who published a study about thermal imaging, claim that it "has potential for application in remote and rapid screening, without the need for skilled staff or physical contact" and "it could be used for instantaneous lie detection without the subject even being aware of the test". Although they do not discuss how these tests should be conducted (that is, what questions should be asked) it may well be that they are inclined to use the test in its most simplistic form, as discussed above, because this test can be carried out without the examinee being aware of it. Alternatively, just single questions could be asked (i.e., "Are you smuggling any goods?"). The latter test is certainly the quickest test that can be conducted, and it can also be carried out without the examinee's awareness. However, it is also the least reliable test, and even less reliable than the test in its most simplistic form, because, since control questions are lacking, such a test does not control for individual differences in physiological responses (see above). In other words, the tests that are probably proposed in thermal-image testing are not reliable. Unsurprisingly, the National Research Council (2003, p. 157) concluded that Pavlidis et al.'s (2002) study "does not provide acceptable scientific evidence for the use of facial thermography in the detection of deception".

Pavladis et al.'s (2002) view that thermal imaging could be used for screening creates another problem. Screening, for example at airports, means that thousands of people will be tested. Suppose that thermal imaging would be able to correctly classify 90% of the truth tellers and 90% of the liars. As mentioned above, this is a huge exaggeration of its accuracy, but let's suppose these are accurate figures. The vast majority of travellers will be truth tellers who do not smuggle any goods or have any intention of hijacking an airplane. This means that if 1 000 people are screened, 100 of them will be classified as "deceptive". Although this is a huge reduction of potential wrongdoers, it is still a substantial number and all these travellers need to be further checked. More importantly, it is not certain that the single person among the thousand travellers who has bad intentions will be in the sample of 100, because some wrongdoers will pass the test. The likelihood that a wrongdoer will pass the test will become higher if terrorist organizations or organizations dealing with smuggling, come to know that thermal-imaging procedures are used. They can simply recruit terrorists and smugglers who they know are likely to pass thermal-imaging screening tests.[2]

ALTERNATIVE LIE-DETECTION METHODS

The alternative methods, discussed below, all have in common that they do not rely on the premise that liars will be more afraid of being believed than truth tellers. I will commence by discussing an alternative polygraph test.

Guilty Knowledge Test

The guilty knowledge test (GKT) is based upon the principle that an orienting response occurs in response to personally significant stimuli. Thus, people can be unaware of the conversations around them, yet notice when their name is mentioned in one of these conversations. Such an orienting response is associated with increased arousal (Lykken, 1998). This premise has strong support in psychophysiological research (Fiedler, Schmidt & Stahl, 2002).

The aim of the GKT is to examine whether examinees possess knowledge about a particular crime which they do not want to reveal. If they do possess such knowledge, it will trigger an orienting response that will be picked up by the polygraph. Similar to traditional polygraph testing, during a GKT test, examinees are hooked up to the polygraph machine and their palmar sweating, heart rate and blood pressure are measured. Lykken (1998) described how the GKT could have been used in the O.J. Simpson murder case. Questions that could have been asked in a GKT immediately after the body of Simpson's wife was found, included: (i) "You know that Nicole has been found murdered, Mr Simpson. How was she killed? – Was she drowned? Was she hit on the head with something? Was she shot? Was she beaten to death? Was she stabbed? Was she strangled?" and (ii) "Where did we find her body? Was it – In the living room? In the driveway? By the side gate? In the kitchen? In the bedroom? By the pool?" (Lykken, 1998, p. 298). Only a guilty examinee would know the correct answer and a heightened response to this correct answer is likely due to the orienting response.[3]

The GKT is not without criticism either, and this is largely related to its assumed limited applicability. The problem with the GKT is that only questions can be asked to which *only the person who designed the test and the guilty examinee* know the answers. The person who designs the test should know the correct answer, otherwise he runs the risk that the correct answer is not in the set of alternatives. Moreover, the GKT only works when questions are asked about details that are actually known to the culprit, otherwise there is no guilty knowledge to detect. This is not always the case. The guilty suspect may not have perceived the details the examiner is asking about, or may have forgotten them by the time the test takes place. The longer the period between the crime and the polygraph test, the more likely it is that the suspect has forgotten certain details. The problem is that the person who designs the test can never be sure that the culprit knows the answer to the crucial questions.

Finally, only questions can be asked about items to which innocent suspects do not know the answers (otherwise they will also have guilty knowledge). In many cases the salient details of the crime are made available by the media, investigators or lawyers.[4] In order to minimize this problem, a decision could be made to ask questions about minor details that are not widely known. However, this increases the likelihood that the guilty suspect does not know the answers either. The result is that the number of cases where the GKT can be used is limited.

Encourage Suspects to Elaborate

Mann et al.'s (2002) examination of real-life police interviews, discussed earlier, suggested that suspects experience high cognitive demand when they lie. Police interviewers could exploit this by employing interview techniques that further increase cognitive demand in lying suspects. There are several ways in which this could be established.

Rather than accusing a suspect (e.g., "We know that you have done it"), interviewers could employ an information-gathering approach (e.g., "Tell me in as much detail as possible what you did last night"). An accusation approach has three problems. First, it is likely to result in short replies from the suspect (e.g., "I am not lying", "I didn't do it", etc.) which are cognitively easier to formulate than extensive answers (Vrij, Mann & Fisher, 2005). Second, short replies typically result in fewer speech differences between truth tellers and liars than longer statements (Vrij, 2005). Third, truth tellers and liars may well show similar behavioural responses after being accused, because the behaviour caused by the accusation may overshadow possible differences in behaviour caused by lying (Vrij, in press). That is, after being accused both liars and truth tellers may panic and show signs of distress (Ekman, 1985/2001).

An open-ended information-gathering question is thus preferable. Cognitive load could be increased in such interviews by asking specific follow-up questions about the information provided by the suspect in response to the initial open-ended question (e.g., "You mentioned that you went to the gym last night, could you please describe who else was there?"). Answering such questions may be more difficult for liars than for truth tellers. The liar's strategy might be to prepare a fabricated alibi. Asking more questions forces the suspect to provide more details about the alibi, and this may well include details not previously prepared. In that case the suspect needs to elaborate spontaneously which is cognitively demanding. Obviously, the suspect could always decide just to stick to his or her prepared alibi and not to provide any further information (e.g., "Sorry, I don't know who else was at the gym"). This is unlikely to happen, because not being able to elaborate on a previous statement looks suspicious, which is something liars normally attempt to avoid.

A sophisticated alibi would be to describe an event that the suspect has actually experienced before, albeit not at the time he claims. Thus, the gym example mentioned above would be particularly useful if the suspect indeed has been to that gym before. The interviewer should be aware of this. Questions such as "What equipment did you use at the gym?" are then easy to answer for the suspect. Instead, the interviewer should ask time-specific questions (e.g., "Could you please describe who else was there?") as this is the only aspect of the event the suspect lies about.

Strategic Use of Evidence

Police officers could strategically use the evidence they have against a suspect. Inbau et al. (2001) advise the police to present such evidence at the beginning of the interview (e.g., "Our CCTV footage shows that you were in Commercial Road on Saturday evening at 8 p.m."). The task the lying suspect then faces is to fabricate an alibi that is consistent with this factual evidence. This may be an awkward task, particularly if the suspect is taken by surprise by the fact that the police have this evidence. However, the task could easily be made more difficult when the police do not initially reveal the evidence, but first let the suspect talk about his whereabouts on Saturday night. A lying suspect may face a considerable problem if his alibi does not include him being in Commercial Road on Saturday night when he is confronted with this CCTV evidence after he has presented his alibi. Indeed, an experiment where the timing of presenting the evidence was manipulated (it was presented either before or after the interviewee was given the opportunity to present his false alibi) showed that lies were more readily detected by observers when the evidence was presented at a later stage (62% accuracy) compared to at an earlier stage (43% accuracy). Accuracy in detecting truths did not differ from chance in both conditions (Hartwig, Granhag, Strömwall & Vrij, in press).

This method could be further expanded. For example, if the suspect did not mention the evidence in his initial answer, the police could ask several questions about this evidence, rather than simply presenting it. This could be done when the evidence is multi-interpretable (Van den Adel, 1997). Presenting evidence too early may give the suspect the opportunity to "escape" by providing alternative explanations. For example, suppose that the suspect's car was noticed near the scene of crime just after the crime took place but that the suspect does not refer to his car in his alibi. After being confronted with this piece of evidence, the suspect may then reply that his girlfriend may have used his car on that particular day. However, the suspect has fewer opportunities to escape when, before the evidence is presented, he has told the interviewer (after being asked about this) that he did not use the car that particular day, that he never lends his car to anyone else and that nobody else has keys to his car. A recent lie-detection experiment, where half of the police officers were trained how to use this technique, revealed that the trained officers obtained a considerably higher deception detection accuracy rate (85.4%) than untrained interviewers (56.1%) (Hartwig, Granhag, Strömwall & Kronkvist, 2005).

AVOID PAYING ATTENTION TO NONDIAGNOSTIC CUES: IMPLICIT LIE DETECTION

A popular belief is that lie detection is easiest when the lie detector has access to the full picture of the potential liar and that just reading a textual version of a statement, or just listening to someone's voice, hampers lie detection. However, research has shown that this is not the case. People become better lie detectors when they pay attention to speech content cues (plausibility, contradictions, etc.) and vocal aspects (tone of voice, etc.) (Vrij, 2004a, 2004b). Furthermore, people become better lie detectors when they cannot see the person's face (Vrij, 2004a, 2004b). The reason for this is that lie detectors are inclined to look at someone's eye movements when available to them, whereas in fact eye movements are quite easy to control and not related to deception.

There is a subtle way of encouraging lie detectors to pay attention to more diagnostic cues to deception, for example, by asking them to look for signs of cognitive load rather than for signs of deceit (Vrij, Edward & Bull (2001). When people are asked to detect deceit, they tend to pay attention to cues such as gaze aversion and fidgeting, which are unreliable cues to deceit. However, when observers are asked to detect cognitive load, they tend to pay attention to cues that are more diagnostic cues to deceit, such as a decrease in movements (Vrij et al., 2001).

CONCLUSION

Many lie-detection techniques are based upon the theoretical premise that liars are more aroused than truth tellers due to the fear of getting caught. I have argued that this is a flawed premise. Instead, I propose several interview methods that all have in common that they are not related to this premise. Focusing on such alternative methods is a relatively new direction in lie detection. I hope that this contribution will encourage practitioners to use and test these, and perhaps other, alternative methods.

NOTES

1 It is further proposed in this scheme to force sex offenders to undergo lie detector tests (*The Times*, 29 May 2004, p. 7). This seems at odds with the fact that cooperation of examinees is required during polygraph testing, both when formulating the questions that will be asked during the test and during the actual test (see Raskin & Honts, 2002, and Vrij, 2000, for detailed descriptions of traditional polygraph tests).
2 In that respect, Pavlidis et al.'s (2002, p. 602) erratum stating that the error rate in their study "*might* preclude large-scale application" probably does not go far enough.
3 When employing a GKT test, examiners should make sure that the correct questions are asked. For example, it could be that the correct multiple choice alternative (i.e., "gun") is a more arousal-evoking option than the other alternatives (i.e., "rope") or that the innocent suspect can guess what the correct alternative is. This may result in innocent examinees showing increased arousal when the correct alternative is mentioned. Whether this is the case could easily be checked by conducting mock tests with known innocent persons. The test is unfair when these mock suspects show stronger responses to the correct alternatives.
4 Making details about the crime available to suspects, so-called information leakage, is according to Ben-Shakhar, Bar-Hillel & Kremnitzer (2002) the main problem with GKT testing. It is common practice to disclose details of crimes to suspects in police interviews as it is seen as a possible way to make suspects confess (Inbau, Reid, Buckley & Jayne, 2001). Many suspects, including those who are innocent, therefore might have guilty knowledge after being interviewed. Ben-Shakhar et al. (2002) point out that this might not be problematic as long as innocent suspects are aware of having acquired the guilty knowledge in this way and can account for it. However, if

guilty knowledge is leaked without the innocent suspects' awareness, they may incriminate themselves. Also, that crime-relevant details were leaked to the suspect in the police interview may be used as an excuse by guilty suspects, because they then can point out that they obtained this guilty knowledge during the interview rather than through their involvement in the crime.

REFERENCES

Ben-Shakhar, G., Bar-Hillel, M. & Kremnitzer, M. (2002). Trial by polygraph: Reconsidering the use of the guilty knowledge technique in court. *Law and Human Behavior*, 26, 527–541.

BPS Working Party (2004). *A review of the current scientific status and fields of application of polygraphic deception detection*. Leicester: BPS.

Ekman, P. (1985/2001). *Telling lies*. New York: W. W. Norton.

Ekman, P. & Frank, M.G. (1993). Lies that fail. In M. Lewis & C. Saarni (Eds), *Lying and deception in everyday life* (pp. 184–200). New York: Guilford Press.

Fiedler, K., Schmidt, J. & Stahl, T. (2002). What is the current truth about polygraph lie detection? *Basic and Applied Social Psychology*, 24, 313–324.

Gudjonsson, G.H. (2003). *The psychology of interrogations and confessions: A handbook*. Chichester: John Wiley & Sons, Ltd.

Hartwig, M., Granhag, P.A., Strömwall, L.A. & Kronkvist, O. (2005). *Strategic use of evidence during police interrogations: When training to detect deception works*. Manuscript submitted for publication.

Hartwig, M., Granhag, P.A., Strömwall, L.A. & Vrij, A. (in press). The strategic use of disclosing evidence. *Law and Human Behavior*.

Hocking, J.E. & Leathers, D.G. (1980). Nonverbal indicators of deception: A new theoretical perspective. *Communication Monographs*, 47, 119–131.

Honts, C.R. & Amato, S.L. (2002). Countermeasures. In M. Kleiner (Ed.), *Handbook of polygraph testing* (pp. 251–264). London: Academic Press.

Inbau, F.E., Reid, J.E., Buckley, J.P. & Jayne, B.C. (2001). *Criminal interrogation and confessions, 4th edition*. Gaithersburg, MD: Aspen Publishers.

Jennings, J.R. (1992). Is it important that the mind is in a body? Inhibition and the heart. *Psychophysiology*, 29, 369–383.

Leal, S., (2005). *Central and peripheral physiology of attention and cognitive demand: understanding how brain and body work together*. PhD thesis, University of Portsmouth.

Lykken, D.T. (1998). *A tremor in the blood: Use and abuses of lie detection*. New York: Plenum Trade.

Mann, S. & Vrij, A. (2005). *Police officers' judgements of veracity, tenseness, cognitive load and impression management in real-life police interviews*. Manuscript submitted for publication.

Mann, S., Vrij, A. & Bull, R. (2002). Suspects, lies and videotape: An analysis of authentic high-stakes liars. *Law and Human Behavior*, 26, 365–376.

National Research Council (2003). *The polygraph and lie detection*. Committee to Review the Scientific Evidence on the Polygraph (2003). Washington, DC: The National Academic Press.

Pavlidis, J., Eberhardt, N.L. & Levine, J.A. (2002). Erratum: Seeing through the face of deception. *Nature*, 415, 602.

Pavlidis, J., Eberhardt, N.L. & Levine, J.A. (2002). Seeing through the face of deception. *Nature, 415*, 35.

Raskin, D.C. & Honts, C.R. (2002). The comparison question test. In M. Kleiner (Ed.), *Handbook of polygraph testing* (pp. 1–47). London: Academic Press.

Strömwall, L.A., Granhag, P.A. & Hartwig, M. (2004). Practitioners' beliefs about deception. In P. A. Granhag & L.A. Strömwall (Eds), *Deception detection in forensic contexts* (pp. 229–250). Cambridge: Cambridge University Press.

Van den Adel, H.M. (1997). *Handleiding verdachtenverhoor*. Den Haag: VUGA-Uitgeverij.

Vrij, A. (2000). *Detecting lies and deceit: The psychology of lying and its implications for professional practice*. Chichester: John Wiley and Sons, Ltd.

Vrij, A. (2004a). Guidelines to catch a liar. In P.A. Granhag and L.A. Strömwall (Eds), *Deception detection in forensic contexts* (pp. 287–314). Cambridge: Cambridge University Press.

Vrij, A. (2004b). Invited article: Why professionals fail to catch liars and how they can improve. *Legal and Criminological Psychology, 9*, 159–181.

Vrij, A. (2005). Criteria-based content analysis: A qualitative review of the first 37 studies. *Psychology, Public Policy, and Law, 11*, 3–41.

Vrij, A. (2006). Challenging interviewees during interviews: The potential effects on lie detection. *Psychology, Crime, and Law, 12*, 193–206.

Vrij, A., Edward, K. & Bull, R. (2001). Police officers' ability to detect deceit: The benefit of indirect deception detection measures. *Legal and Criminological Psychology, 6*, 185–197.

Vrij, A., Mann, S. & Fisher, R. (2005). *Information-gathering vs accusatory interview style: Individual differences in respondents' experiences*. Manuscript submitted for publication.

Vrij, A. & Semin, G.R. (1996). Lie experts' beliefs about nonverbal indicators of deception. *Journal of Nonverbal Behavior, 20*, 65–80.

Zuckerman, M., DePaulo, B.M. & Rosenthal, R. (1981). Verbal and nonverbal communication of deception. In L. Berkowitz (Ed.), *Advances in experimental social psychology, volume 14* (pp. 1–57). New York: Academic Press.

CHAPTER 6

Improving the Interviewing of Suspected Offenders

MARK R. KEBBELL AND EMILY HURREN

INTRODUCTION

In this chapter, we will summarize the state of our knowledge concerning interviewing suspected offenders in order to increase the rates of confession from guilty suspects, while concomitantly, not increasing false confessions from innocent suspects. We will also aim to critically assess the strengths and weaknesses of past research.

To begin this chapter, we will identify the main benefits associated with an offender confessing, and will also present a brief overview of theoretical models that seek to explain why and how suspects decide to confess or deny an alleged crime. Next, we will review and present available literature regarding the importance of evidence in a suspect's decision to confess, and the impact of police interviewing techniques. Finally, we will present ethical considerations relevant to the area of suspect interviewing. (See also Chapter 7 for the importance of ensuring interviews do not create false confessions.)

THE BENEFITS ASSOCIATED WITH AN OFFENDER CONFESSING

Before presenting and summarizing the literature regarding improving rates of confessions, it is useful to justify why this area deserves

Practical Psychology for Forensic Investigations and Prosecutions.
Edited by Mark R. Kebbell and Graham M. Davies. © 2006 John Wiley & Sons, Ltd.

attention. Generally, there are three important advantages associated with an offender confessing to an investigator. First, the likelihood of a conviction being secured is greatly increased. As Justice Byron White has commented,

> The defendant's own confession is probably the most probative and dam-aging evidence that can be admitted against him.... [T]he admissions of a defendant come from the actor himself, the most knowledgeable and unimpeachable source of information about his past conduct. Certainly, confessions have profound impact on the jury, so much so that we may justifiably doubt its ability to put them out of mind even if told to do so.
> *Bruton* v. *United States*, 123–140.

Kassin and Neumann (1997) have confirmed this assertion experi-mentally. They conducted three mock-juror studies that compared the impact of confessions on mock jurors, compared with eyewitness iden-tifications and character testimony in trials for murder, rape, assault and theft. Results indicated that confessions had a greater impact on mock jurors than the other types of evidence.

Secondly, if an offender confesses the likelihood of the victim hav-ing to give evidence in court is reduced, as is the negative impact on the victim from testifying about their abuse (Eastwood & Patton, 2002; Lipovsky, 1994). This is particularly pertinent for cases involving sexual offences or vulnerable and intimidated witnesses. For example, testifying in a trial is one of four significant predictors of post-traumatic stress disorder (PTSD) symptoms in adult survivors of child rape, and having a civil lawsuit pending is one of three predictors of de-pression among adult victims (Epstein, Saunders & Kilpatrick, 1997; Mackey, Sereika, Weissfeld, Hacker, Zender & Heard, 1992). Thirdly, an advantage of an offender confessing early in the investigation, is that a lengthy trial can be avoided, thereby reducing the finan-cial burden and resource expenditure associated with prosecuting offenders.

Taken as a whole, the above literature suggests the great importance of securing confessions from offenders. Despite this argument though, to date, most psychological research has focused on the issue of identi-fying personality factors and situational influences that lead innocent individuals to falsely confess to crimes they have not committed (for a comprehensive review, see Chapter 7), rather than focusing on increas-ing confessions from guilty suspects. In light of the above, the focus of this chapter will remain on understanding offenders' decisions to con-fess or deny alleged criminal offences, as well as on police interviewing techniques associated with increased rates of confessions.

THEORETICAL MODELS

Before we can begin to understand why certain interviewing techniques are effective in increasing rates of confession, we need to first understand why an offender would choose to confess or deny a crime, and what factors might influence this decision. In previous literature, researchers have proposed a variety of different theories or models in an attempt to explain the decisions of suspects to confess or deny, and these models can be used to influence police interviewing or interrogation approaches. We will present the most prominent of these theoretical models here.

The Decision-Making Model

Higendorf and Irving (1981) proposed a theoretical model based on decision-making theory. They suggest that when offenders decide to admit or deny their offence, they first have to consider the likely consequences of each alternative decision, including whether they will be convicted even if they deny an offence. Next they have to estimate the subjective probability of each possible alternative actually occurring (see also Larrick, 1993). For offenders, the most obvious consequence of confessing to an offence is the increased likelihood of a conviction and subsequent punishment. However, if they deny a crime and are convicted they are likely to receive a higher punishment, and so, if it is probable that they will be convicted, their best choice is to confess.

Less obvious consequences may also be associated with an offender confessing. For example, the suspect may believe the interviewing police officer would be disgusted by the offender if they confessed and this may increase the consequences of confessing and in turn reduce the likelihood of a decision to confess.

The "Reid" Model

Inbau, Reid and Buckley (1986) describe the "Reid" model, which can be construed as a psychological manipulation that seeks to increase the likelihood of a suspect confessing through making decisions to confess more appealing and decisions to deny less appealing. Clearly, there is some overlap with this procedure and the decision-making model, although in some respects the fact that the suspect must make a decision to confess or deny means that decision making must be a component of any model seeking to explain confessions. The "Reid technique" forms the basis of one of the most popular police interrogation training manuals available, and espouses nine basic steps for an effective interrogation (e.g., Inbau et al., 1986).

According to Inbau et al. (1986), the nine steps for effective interrogation are: (i) direct positive confrontation (the interviewer directly and confidently accuses the suspect of being guilty, and advises them of the benefit of telling the truth and admitting their guilt); (ii) theme development (the interviewer demonstrates an understanding of the suspect's way of thinking, and appears to minimize, normalize, justify or rationalize their offending); (iii) handling denials (the interviewer does not allow the suspect to deny the offence, and instead interrupts their denials and tells them to listen to the evidence etc.); (iv) overcoming objections (the interviewer does not allow the suspect to argue or explain their "innocence"); (v) procurement and retention of the suspect's attention (if the suspect seems to be withdrawing from the process or not paying attention, the interviewer regains their attention by speaking to the suspect, touching them, or moving closer to them); (vi) handling the suspect's passive mood (the interviewer must show sympathy for the suspect and focus their mind on a particular theme of their guilt, e.g., the reason for their offence; they can also attempt to make the suspect feel more guilty about their offending); (vii) presenting an alternative question (the interviewer may present the suspect with two different scenarios for the offence, where one scenario is clearly worse than the other; this will encourage the suspect to choose the seemingly less serious scenario); (viii) having the suspect orally relate various details of the offence (the suspect is required to provide an oral confession regarding their actual offence, and their motives for committing the offence); (ix) and finally, converting an oral confession into a written confession (the suspect is required to sign a written confession which is developed from their oral confession).

Though this interrogation technique is popular, and is often widely regarded as the most successful police interrogation approach, some researchers consider this technique to be ethically questionable and controversial (e.g., Gudjonsson, 2003; Kassin & Gudjonsson, 2004). This is because the technique is considered to be highly coercive and because limited empirical data exists regarding its effectiveness in yielding a greater percentage of true confessions (as opposed to no confessions or false confessions) (Gudjonsson, 2003). According to Gudjonsson (2003), any confessions that result from this technique should be viewed with caution.

The Interaction Process, Cognitive Behavioural and Psychoanalytic Models

Moston, Stephenson and Williamson (1992) suggest an interaction process model of confession, where the background characteristics of the suspect and offence, contextual characteristics of the case (e.g., legal advice) and the interviewer's questioning technique interact to influence decisions to confess. Again, this is similar to the decision-making model, but with the addition of a consideration of the changing influence of the interviewer's questioning over time. Similarly, Gudjonsson (1989) suggests a cognitive-behavioural model of confession that is similar to that of Moston et al. (1992), but additionally emphasizes the fact that the suspect may "learn" to respond in ways encouraged by the interviewer. Finally, there is the psychoanalytic model (Reik, 1959) in which confessions are seen as arising from internal conflict and feelings of guilt (this is likely to be particularly relevant to sex offenders and their offences).

To date, what the different models presented above share, is a lack of systematic research aiming to test the models. While this is not particularly unusual in the field of forensic psychology (Ogloff, 1999; Small, 1993), refutable theoretical work is still vital if suspect interviewing is to become a science rather than an art (Popper, 1963). Clearly, this is an important area to be tackled if our understanding of suspect interviewing is to be improved.

THE IMPORTANCE OF EVIDENCE

We turn now to the important factor of evidence, and attempt to examine its impact on suspects' decisions to confess or deny. One way of shedding light on offenders' reasons for confessing generally is to ask them directly. Gudjonsson and Petursson (1991) used this approach with 74 Icelandic prisoners who had admitted to their crimes. Respondents were required to respond to questions using a Likert scale that was labelled "not at all" (1 or 2) to "very much so" (6 or 7). The majority (55%) of offenders gave scores of 6 or 7 to the question, "Did you think the police would eventually prove you did it?" and this was the most frequently rated reason for confessing. Gudjonsson and colleagues have replicated this finding (Gudjonsson & Sigurdsson, 1999, 2000), although it must be noted that what they label the "perception of proof" factor in these later papers involves a combination of questions including, "Did you think the police would eventually prove you did it?" as well as some which are not directly related, other than by factor analysis, to perceptions of proof such as "Were you under the influence of alcohol when you committed the offence?".

While this approach provides some apparently useful information, the data has to be treated with some caution. As with all self-report data, participants are likely to be motivated to portray themselves in a good light, and saying they confessed because of evidence may be more desirable for them to say than, for example, the police cleverly tricked them into confessing. Another drawback to this approach is that offenders are relying on their memories for what happened, in some instances, many years ago. Nevertheless, a field study conducted by Moston et al. (1992) in England provides additional support for the importance of evidence.

Moston et al. (1992) investigated confession rates for 1 067 suspects who had been interviewed by detectives. Again the majority of cases concerned nonsexual offences. The results showed that when the researchers rated the evidence against the suspect as weak, confessions occurred less than 10% of the time, and denials occurred 77% of the time. When the evidence was rated as strong by the researchers, confessions were frequent, occurring in 67% of cases, while denials were infrequent, occurring in 16% of cases. While this study provides more powerful evidence for the importance of evidence than those of Gudjonsson and colleagues, it is still possible that confounds exist. For example, if the interviewing officer was aware that there was a great deal of evidence against the suspect, he or she may have been more relaxed and less aggressive during the interview, and this may have been an influence on the suspect's decision to confess. We return to the issue of officer demeanour in a later section.

Kebbell, Hurren and Roberts (2006) addressed the issue of potential confounds by using an experimental design. Participants were asked to commit a mock crime that involved them stealing a wallet. Later, the mock offenders were interviewed and presented with evidence from a witness who was said to have seen the offence. Participants were randomly assigned to one of two conditions in which they were presented with a witness statement that either contained detailed information concerning their description and their actions, or not-detailed information. For half the participants in each condition the information was correct, while for the other half some of the information was incorrect. The results showed that participants were more likely to confess if the evidence against them was accurate, but the level of detail of the evidence made no difference. Interestingly, participants who had accurate evidence presented against them felt more guilty than those who had less accurate evidence against them, suggesting that expressions of guilt may be more related to the amount of evidence against an offender than genuine remorse (for another laboratory approach see Russano, Meissner, Narchet & Kassin, 2005, discussed in more detail later).

Finally, although it may seem to be tangential to the police interviewing literature, recent research into the polygraph also supports the assertion that presentation of convincing evidence has a crucial impact on suspects' decisions to confess. In one study, sex offenders were found to increase their reports of sexual deviancy, and were more likely to disclose adult and juvenile victims and offences against males and females, when they were in a polygraph group compared with a non-polygraph control (English, Jones, Patrick & Cooley-Towell, 2000). Similarly, others have found that polygraphed offenders admit to more victims, increased numbers of offences and an earlier onset of offending (Ahlymeyer, Heil, McKee & English, 2000; Wilcox, 2000). The reason for these admissions appears to be that the offenders believe the polygraph will provide evidence that they are lying if they do not tell the truth, and hence can be construed as a form of strong evidence. Taken as a whole, the triangulation of the self-report, field and experimental studies all point to the critical importance of presentation of evidence against a suspect.

The most frequent form of evidence against a suspect is an eyewitness account (Kebbell & Milne, 1998). Importantly, police interviewing can have a dramatic impact on the quantity, quality and accuracy of eyewitness accounts (see Chapter 1). A clear implication of the current review is that police officers should interview witnesses effectively, and in turn, present the obtained witness information effectively to the suspect. In particular, this means that police officers must not only interview effectively, but must also be sufficiently familiar with the evidence to present it effectively, something that requires preparation which is not always apparent (Baldwin, 1993). Interviewers are also required to remember what the evidence is, which is an area where they also seem to have problems (Kohnken, Thurer & Zoberbier, 1994).

The issue of presentation of evidence raises some intriguing empirical issues. For example, if the negative effects of inaccurate information are robust, should police officers only present information that they are absolutely certain about? Clearly, also of relevance here would be the substantial literature concerning eyewitness accuracy and perceived credibility. Mock-jury research suggests that witness confidence increases jurors' perceptions of the credibility of eyewitness evidence (Wells, Ferguson & Lindsay, 1981). For example, an officer could present a witness's evidence as follows, "Jane picked you out of the lineup". However, this may be perceived as weaker evidence than if it were presented as follows. "Jane picked you out of the lineup. She says she's absolutely certain it is you. This is likely to be very powerful evidence if it is presented to a jury". The way in which evidence is presented is an important issue which should be considered in future research.

POLICE INTERVIEWING TECHNIQUES

The way that a police officer conducts an interview may also have a great influence on the likelihood of a confession, regardless of the evidence they present, and so we turn to this issue now. The work of Leo (1996) is particularly relevant here. He conducted a systematic evaluation of 182 suspect interviews in the United States which resulted in the most detailed documentation of how police officers interview, and the impact this has on suspects' decisions to confess. The majority of the cases analysed were crimes against the person, for example, homicide, robbery and assault, including sexual assault.

The study showed that police officers used a number of tactics frequently. The tactic used most often was an appeal to the suspect's self-interest, which was used in 88% of cases, and confronting the suspect with existing evidence of guilt, which was used in 85% of cases. Other tactics were also used relatively often. These included undermining the suspect's confidence in their denial of guilt (43% of cases), identifying contradictions in the suspect's story (42% of cases), behavioural analysis questions such as behavioural indicators of guilt (40% of cases), an appeal to the importance of cooperation (37%), offering moral or psychological justifications (34%), confronting the suspect with false evidence of guilt (30%), the use of flattery or praise (30%), pointing out the detective's expertise or authority (29%), appealing to the suspect's conscience (23%) and minimizing the moral seriousness of the offence (22%).

Leo found that the length of interrogation and the number of tactics used were significantly related to the likelihood of a confession. Further, he found that a confession was significantly more likely when certain techniques were used. For example, when police officers appealed to suspects' consciences they confessed significantly more often (confessions in 97% of cases). Similarly, confessions were frequent if police officers identified inconsistencies in suspects' stories (confessions in 91% of cases), used praise or flattery (confessions in 91% of cases) and offered moral justification and moral excuses (confessions in 90% of cases). Interestingly, confronting a suspect with false evidence of guilt (confessions in 83% of cases) or confronting a suspect with existing evidence of guilt (confessions in 78% of cases) were not significantly associated with confessions.

Unfortunately there are confounds in these data, as is often the case with field data. For example, it is reasonable to expect that police interviewers who interview for a long period of time are going to use more tactics, so the number of tactics used and the length of the interview are confounded. Importantly, police officers may interview more confidently and competently where there is strong evidence because they feel less pressure to achieve a confession, and clearly evidence is relevant to many of the techniques (e.g., pointing out inconsistencies in the case). In turn, in these situations they might be more relaxed, and so less aggressive to the suspect, which could impact on suspects' decisions to confess. Nevertheless, the results of the previously mentioned study by Gudjonsson and Petursson (1991) indicate that 40% gave a "very much so" rating to the question: "Did you confess because you felt guilty about the offence?" (although 38% responded "not at all" to this question). This suggests that many suspects confess to get things "off their chest", supporting some of the assertions made by Leo (1996).

A survey of 83 men convicted of murder or sexual offenses by Holmberg and Christianson (2002) is also especially relevant here. They found aggression, hostility and insulting and condemning behaviour, which they labelled "dominance", reduced the likelihood of a confession. However, friendliness, the suspect feeling acknowledged and respected as a human being and a feeling of cooperation, which they labelled "humanity", were associated with increases in the numbers of confessions.

Perhaps the lack of effectiveness of dominance may be due to "psychological reactance" (Brehm, 1966). Brehm showed that when individuals perceive an unfair restriction on their actions, in this case their ability to deny an offence or give their own account of an event, an intense motivational state is produced that means the individual attempts to challenge the restriction, and obtain the denied item, choice or behaviour. In other words, we want what we can't have. In an interview situation characterized by dominance and pressure to confess, psychological reactance is likely to take the form of a decision to deny the alleged offence and terminating the discussion with the interviewing officer. Furthermore, Holmberg (2004) points out that an extensive literature on attitudes indicates that if an individual perceives themselves to be emotionally threatened, ego defence may occur (Katz, 1960). In these circumstances, once the suspect has become suspicious, then it may prove very difficult to change their mind, and they are likely to be far more critical of any further information that is generated by the police officer.

Conversely, the fact that the humanistic approach can be successful could be explicable in terms of offenders feeling more comfortable with the officer, and thus, more able to reduce their guilt and to get things of their chest, particularly compared to an officer who displays dominance. Again, however, there is a problem with the correlational nature of this study, which makes it impossible to determine a causal relationship between these variables and outcomes. For example, offenders could be more likely to confess because officers responded positively to them, or alternatively, officers could have responded more positively to the offenders *because* they were confessing, at this stage we do not know for sure. There may also be problems with this data, as it is self-report data.

There is further support for the idea that displaying positive attitudes to offenders may increase confessions, while displaying negative attitudes may decrease confessions. For example, Kebbell, Hurren and Mazzerole (in press) questioned 19 convicted sex offenders concerning their beliefs about how the police can increase or decrease the likelihood of a sex offender confessing. Participants suggested that interviewers were most likely to secure confessions if they were compassionate, neutral and fair, while aggressive and biased interviewers were reported as being less likely to be successful. Though this study is limited by the small sample size, and the fact that there may be differences between how sex offenders say they react to an interviewer and how they do react to an interviewer, the results suggest some form of cause and effect relationship. The implication of these findings is that police interviewers should be encouraged to have, or at least display, more positive attitudes to suspects, which may in turn increase the likelihood of obtaining a confession.

As mentioned previously, the correlational nature of most field studies reduces the inferences that can be drawn. To date, in contrast to the false-confession literature where experimental methods are having an increasingly important impact (for example see Horselenberg, Merckelbach & Josephs, 2003; Kassin & Kiechel, 1996), little laboratory-based research has been conducted on suspect interviews where the suspect is actually guilty. One exception is an innovative study by Russano et al. (2005). In this experiment, participants were asked by a confederate to help "cheat" in an experimental task. Most did so and were later accused of cheating by the experimenter.

Two conditions were used. In one, labelled the "minimization" condition, the interrogator was instructed to express sympathy and concern (e.g., "I'm sure you didn't realize what a big deal it was"). In the other condition, labelled the "deal" condition, the experimenter told participants that if they signed a confession then, "things would probably be settled pretty quickly", they would receive their research credit for the day but would have to return and do the experiment again, however, if they did not confess they were told the professor in charge of the experiment would come, and it was implied the consequences could be more severe. The results indicated that without any tactics 46% of the guilty participants confessed. However, these figures increased to 72% and 81% in the deal and minimization conditions, respectively. Importantly, when both a deal and minimization were combined, the confession rate was 87%.

While caution must clearly be used in extrapolating from this experimental study, the implications are that offering a deal and minimization, are potentially likely to be critical to suspects' decisions to confess.

It is important to note here, that while minimization does seem to have the potential to improve confession rates, the concept of "minimization" is still somewhat broad. For example, on the one hand minimization could include suggesting to the suspect that the victim encouraged the attack, which, if not true, could be considered unethical police interviewing behaviour (we will return to the issue of ethics later). On the other hand, a police officer could state that the attack was not the worst he had ever seen, which is a more ethical form of minimization if it is also true, and perhaps should be more accurately labelled normalization. The issue of minimization and normalization appears to be an important avenue of research in reducing the stigma associated with sex offending in particular (Bhaghwan, 2003; McGrath, 1990; Quinn, Forsyth & Mullen-Quinn, 2004). An example of one way of reducing stigma is given by Pearse and Gudjonsson (1999) where a female officer said the following:

> So were you playing with your penis? I'm married, I've got a husband, I know men and men do masturbate. It's not an unusual thing so don't, I know it's probably not easy for you to talk in front of me but I've heard all this before and there's nothing you're going to say that's going to shock me so don't, try not to feel embarrassed. I know it's not easy for you (p. 238).

Immediately after this, the suspect admitted he was playing with his penis.

Another form of minimization is demonstrating an understanding of cognitive distortions. Some offenders may have particularly distorted ways of thinking about their victims, which supports their offending (Swaffer, Hollin, Beech, Beckett & Fisher, 1999; Ward, Hudson, Johnston & Marshall, 1997). For example, many who offend against children agree with statements such as, "Having sex with a child is a good way for an adult to teach the child about sex", "A child who doesn't physically resist an adult's sexual advances, really wants to have sex with the adult", and "When a young child walks in front of me with no or only a few clothes on, she is trying to arouse me" (Abel, Gore, Holland, Camp, Becker & Rathner, 1989).

Police officers may have little insight and understanding of these cognitions (which are essentially a form of minimization for the offender). Perhaps an effective strategy would be for the interviewing officer to present an understanding of these cognitive distortions to the suspect (without actually condoning them). This may be effective in gaining confessions for two reasons. First, because it shows a level of understanding of the suspect's thinking. Secondly, if the officer talks about these distortions without becoming angry it suggests to the suspect that the officer is less likely to become aggressive if he confesses to the crime. For example, an officer may say, "I know some people think that when a young child walks in front of them with no or only a few clothes on, she is trying to arouse them. Perhaps that is how you felt?" Of course understanding the offender's thinking is not the same as condoning it. The above approach differs from the less ethical approach advocated by Inbau et al. (1986) who suggest officers say they have thought about committing the same crime.

Baldwin (1993) conducted a field study in the United Kingdom. He evaluated 600 video and audiotaped suspect interviews. While many of his findings concur with those of Leo (1996), Baldwin's study provides additional information. Importantly, he studied suspects' admissions and denials, as well as when they occurred. Full confessions, or confessions to some part of the allegation, occurred immediately in 51.9% of interviews, while 32.7% denied immediately and continued that denial throughout the interview. Baldwin (1993) found that 2.3% denied at first but subsequently admitted some part of the allegation, 4.2% denied but did shift their position during the interview, and 3.3% completely changed their account and confessed. This could be taken to suggest that police interviewing has little impact on suspects' decisions to confess or deny, and that the suspect has usually decided beforehand whether they will confess to or deny the allegation.

Alternatively, however, Kebbell et al. (in press) found that half of their sample of convicted sex offenders had not made a decision to confess or deny prior to their police interview. Potentially, this can be interpreted as indicating that suspects make up their mind to confess or deny early in the interview, and then subsequently rarely deviate from this decision. This seems plausible. An extensive social psychological literature shows a "commitment bias", whereby people remain committed to an initial position even when extensive evidence suggests they should change their position (e.g., Edwards & Smith, 1996). For criminal suspects in particular, changing an account is even more difficult than usual, as they must not only change their position but also admit that their previous account was false and that they lied to the police. One technique that the police could use is to ask the suspect not to comment immediately but rather advise them to listen to the evidence before speaking.

The Baldwin (1993) study is also relevant here, because of his assertions concerning the quality of police interviews. Baldwin identified a discrepancy between how the police *say* they interview and how they *actually* interview. Baldwin (1993) stated that the police officers

in their sample often spoke of high-level psychological conce
they applied in their interviewing, but in reality their intervie
more closely characterized by ineptitude and limited social s
fact that some offenders (particularly sex offenders) have personality
deficits (e.g., Fisher, Beech & Browne, 1999) may make interviewing
more difficult, because of the suspect's poor interpersonal skills. Of
course, if the interviewing officer also has poor interpersonal skills, it is
unlikely that the interview will be effective. Clearly, one implication of
this is that police officers with good interpersonal skills may be better
at interviewing.

ETHICAL ISSUES AND FALSE CONFESSIONS

As argued previously in this chapter, offenders are more likely to confess
if they perceive there is strong and accurate evidence that they committed the crime. The obvious implication of this is that police interviewers
should, prior to the suspect interview, establish strong evidence which
suggests the suspect's guilt, and then present that evidence effectively
to the suspect during the interview. Interestingly, some practitioners
have suggested that this may be achieved by fabricating evidence. For
example, in the third edition of their police interrogation training manual regarding the previously mentioned "Reid technique", Inbau et al.
(1986) suggest fabricating evidence, such as nonexistent eyewitnesses,
in order to make the suspect more likely to confess.

Importantly though, there is no available empirical evidence that
suggests that fabricating evidence is effective in increasing rates of
confession. Alternatively, findings from the previously outlined Kebbell
et al. (2006) study suggests that if the suspect is presented with fabricated evidence that the suspect believes to be incorrect, then their likelihood of confessing may be reduced. Further, such fabrications could
lead to an increase in the likelihood of an innocent individual making a
false confession. Research shows that false confessions can be a problem
(again the reader is referred to Chapter 7, for a discussion of this issue).
Clearly then, there are limits to the utility of this ethically dubious
method.

It is particularly important to remember that not all people who are
suspected of committing offences are actually guilty. For example, some
victims identify the wrong person as an offender (Connors, Lundregan,
Miller & McEwan, 1996), and although specific figures are difficult to
come by, it is also clear that some individuals, perhaps a small minority, make malicious allegations, for example in cases concerning sexual
offences (Oates, Jones, Denson, Sirotnak, Gary & Krugman, 2000). In
these cases suspects are likely to be particularly sensitive to the way in

which they are interviewed, and this must be borne in mind in devising effective and ethical police interviewing techniques.

SUMMARY AND CONCLUSION

In this chapter, the state of our knowledge concerning effectively and ethically interviewing suspected offenders and increasing rates of confession, has been summarized. As argued previously, there are three key benefits to an offender confessing, including an increased likelihood of a conviction, the decreased likelihood of a victim being required to testify and the reduction in costs associated with a lengthy trial and prosecution. We have presented an overview of theoretical models which can assist us in understanding why suspects decide to confess or deny an alleged crime, and have demonstrated how these models can be used to develop effective interviewing techniques.

We have reviewed the literature, and have presented important findings, which have a variety of implications. First, police officers should attempt to ensure they have sufficient strong and accurate evidence to present to a suspect during an interview. This requires preparation and familiarity with the evidence prior to beginning the interview. Secondly, aggression and dominance appear to be important attributes for police officers to avoid, while humanity, displaying positive attitudes, compassion, neutrality, fairness and strong interpersonal skills are highly desirable attributes for police interviewers. Thirdly, preventing the suspect from denying the offence early on in the interview, as well as using minimization and normalization where legally permissible, and demonstrating an understanding of the suspect's cognitive distortions, may help to increase the likelihood of a confession from a guilty suspect.

REFERENCES

Abel, G.G., Gore, D.K., Holland, C.L., Camp, N., Becker, J.V. & Rathner, J. (1989). The measurement of the cognitive distortions of child molesters. *Annals of Sex Research, 2*, 135–153.

Ahlymeyer, S., Heil, P., McKee, B. & English, K. (2000). The impact of polygraphy on admissions of victims and offenses in adult sex offenders. *Sexual Abuse: A Journal of Research and Treatment, 12*, 123–139.

Baldwin, J. (1993). Police interview techniques. *British Journal of Criminology, 33*, 325–352.

Bhaghwan, W.B., (2003). Pedophilia: Psychiatric insights. *Family Court Review, 41*, 497–532.

Brehm, J. (1966). *A theory of psychological reactance*. New York: Academic Press.

Bruton *v.* United States, 391 U.S. 123, 140 (1968)

Connors, E., Lundregan, T., Miller, N. & McEwan, T. (1996). *Convicted by juries, exonerated by science: Case studies in the use of DNA evidence to establish innocence after trial.* Alexandria, VA: National Institute of Justice.

Eastwood, C. & Patton, W. (2002). *The experiences of child complainants of sexual abuse in the criminal justice system.* Report for the Criminology Research Council. Australia: Queensland University of Technology.

Edwards, K. & Smith, E.E. (1996). A disconfirmation bias in the evaluation of arguments. *Journal of Personality and Social Psychology, 71,* 5–24.

English, K., Jones, L., Patrick, D. & Cooley-Towell, S. (2000). *The value of polygraph testing in sex offender management.* Research report submitted to the National Institute of Justice. Denver: Colorado Department of Public Safety.

Epstein, J.N., Saunders, B.E. & Kilpatrick, D.G. (1997). Predicting PTSD in women with a history of childhood rape. *Journal of Traumatic Stress, 10,* 573–588.

Fisher, D., Beech, A. & Browne, K. (1999). Comparison of sex offenders to nonoffenders on selected psychological measures. *International Journal of Offender Therapy and Comparative Criminology, 43*(4), 473–491.

Gudjonsson, G.H. (1989). The psychology of false confessions. *The Medico-Legal Journal, 57,* 93–110.

Gudjonsson, G.H. (2003). *The psychology of interrogations, confessions and testimony: A handbook.* Chichester: John Wiley & Sons, Ltd.

Gudjonsson, G.H. & Petursson, H. (1991). Custodial interrogation: Why do suspects confess and how does it relate to their crime, attitude and personality. *Personality and Individual Differences, 12,* 295–306.

Gudjonsson, G.H. & Sigurdsson, J.F. (1999). The Gudjonsson confession questionnaire-revised (GCQ-R): Factor structure and its relationship with personality. *Personality and Individual Differences, 27,* 953–968.

Gudjonsson, G.H. & Sigurdsson, J.F. (2000). Differences and similarities between violent offenders and sexual offenders. *Child Abuse and Neglect, 24,* 363–372.

Hilgendorf, E.L. & Irving, B. (1981). A decision-making model of confessions. In M.A. Lloyd-Bostock (Ed.), *Psychology in legal contexts: Applications and limitations* (pp. 67–84). London: Macmillan.

Holmberg, U. (2004). Police interviews with victims and suspects of violent and sexual crimes: Interviewees' experiences and outcomes. PhD thesis, Department of Psychology, Stockholm University, Sweden.

Holmberg, U. & Christianson, S. (2002). Murderers' and sexual offenders' experience of police interviews and their inclination to admit or deny crimes. *Behavioral Sciences and the Law, 20,* 31–45.

Horselenberg, R., Merckelbach, H. & Josephs, S. (2003). Individual differences and false confessions: A conceptual replication of Kassin and Keichel (1996). *Psychology, Crime and Law, 9,* 1–8.

Inbau, F.E., Reid, J.E. & Buckley, J.P. (1986). *Criminal interrogation and confessions,* 3rd edn. Baltimore, MD: Williams and Wilkins.

Kassin, S.M. & Gudjonsson, G.H. (2004). The psychology of confessions: A review of the literature and issues. *Psychological Science in the Public Interest, 5*(2), 33–67.

Kassin, S.M. & Kiechel, K.L. (1996). The social psychology of false confessions: Compliance, internalization, and confabulation. *Psychological Science, 7,* 125–128.

Kassin, S.M. & Neumann, K. (1997). On the power of confession evidence: An experimental test of the fundamental difference hypothesis. *Law and Human Behavior, 21,* 469–484.

Katz, D. (1960). The functional approach to the studies of attitudes. *Public Opinion Quarterly, 24*, 187–203.

Kebbell, M.R., Hurren, E.J. & Mazerolle, P. (in press). Sex offenders' perceptions of how they were interviewed by the police. *Canadian Journal of Police & Security Services*.

Kebbell, M.R., Hurren, E.J. & Roberts, S. (2006). Mock suspects' decisions to confess: Accuracy of eyewitness evidence is crucial. *Applied Cognitive Psychology, 20*, 477–486.

Kebbell, M.R. & Milne, R. (1998). Police officers' perception of eyewitness factors in forensic investigations: A survey. *Journal of Social Psychology, 138*, 323–330.

Kohnken, G., Thurer, C. & Zoberbier, D. (1994). The cognitive interview: Are the interviewers' memories enhanced, too? *Applied Cognitive Psychology, 8*, 13–24.

Larrick, R.P. (1993). Motivational factors in decision theories: The role of self-protection. *Psychological Bulletin, 113*, 440–450.

Leo, R.A. (1996). Inside the interrogation room. *Journal of Criminal Law and Criminology, 86*, 266–303.

Lipovsky, J.A. (1994). The impact of court on children: Research findings and practical recommendations. *Journal of Interpersonal Violence, 9*, 238–257.

Mackey, T., Sereika, S.M., Weissfeld, L.A., Hacker, S.S., Zender, J.F. & Heard, S.L. (1992). Factors associated with long-term depressive symptoms of sexual assault victims. *Archives of Psychiatric Nursing, 6*, 10–25.

McGrath, R.J. (1990). Assessment of sexual aggressors: Practical clinical interviewing strategies. *Journal of Interpersonal Violence, 5*(4), 507–519.

Moston, S., Stephenson, G.M. & Williamson, T.M. (1992). The effects of case characteristics on suspect behaviour during questioning. *British Journal of Criminology, 32*, 23–40.

Oates, R.K., Jones, D.P.H., Denson, D., Sirotnak, A., Gary, N. & Krugman, R.D. (2000). Erroneous concerns about child sexual abuse. *Child Abuse and Neglect, 24*, 149–157.

Ogloff, J.R.P. (1999). *Law and Human Behavior*: Looking back and reflecting forward. *Law and Human Behavior, 23*, 1–7.

Pearse, J. and Gudjonsson, G.H. (1999). Measuring influential police interviewing tactics: A factor analytic approach. *Legal and Criminological Psychology, 4*, 221–238.

Popper, K. (1963). *Conjectures and refutations: The growth of scientific knowledge*. Routledge, London.

Quinn, J.F., Forsyth, C.J. & Mullen-Quinn, C. (2004). Societal reaction to sex offenders: A review of the origins and results of the myths surrounding their crimes and treatment amenability. *Deviant Behavior, 25*, 215–232.

Reik, T. (1959). *The compulsion to confess: On the psychoanalysis of crime and punishment*. New York: Farrar, Straus and Cudahy.

Russano, M.B., Meissner, C.A., Narchet, F.M. & Kassin, S.M. (2005). Investigating true and false confessions within a novel experimental paradigm. *Psychological Science, 16*(6), 481–486.

Small, M.A. (1993). Legal psychology and therapeutic jurisprudence. *Saint Louis University Law Journal, 37*, 675–700.

Swaffer, T., Hollin, C., Beech, A., Beckett, R. & Fisher, D. (1999). An exploration of child sexual abusers cognitive distortions with special reference to the role of anger. *Journal of Sexual Aggression, 4*, 31–44.

Ward, T., Hudson, S.M., Johnson, L. & Marshall, W.L. (1997). Cognitive distortions in sex offenders: An integrative review. *Clinical Psychology Review, 17*, 479–507.

Wells, G.L., Ferguson, T.J. & Lindsay, R.C. (1981). The tractability of eyewitness confidence and its implications for triers of fact. *Journal of Applied Psychology, 66*, 688–696.

Wilcox, D. (2000). Application of the clinical polygraph examination to the assessment, treatment and monitoring of sex offenders. *Journal of Sexual Aggression, 5*, 134–152.

CHAPTER 7

Strategies for Preventing False Confessions and Their Consequences

DEBORAH DAVIS AND RICHARD LEO

Shortly after midnight on 18 October 1986, medical student Lori Roscetti was raped and murdered as she started home after a late night of studying. Having failed to solve the crime for some months, and faced with escalating public pressure, Chicago police hired noted Federal Bureau of Investigation (FBI) profiler Robert Ressler to profile the perpetrator. Ressler soon offered his opinion that there were multiple perpetrators, including 3–6 black males, ages 15–20, who had previously been incarcerated, and who lived near the location where Roscetti's body had been found. Based on Ressler's profile, police soon targeted three black teenagers with juvenile records who lived in the housing project near the location of the murder – Marcellus Bradford, Larry Ollins and Omar Saunders.

No specific evidence existed to tie the boys to Roscetti's rape or murder. Yet, police soon engaged in a virtual rampage of coercive questioning that led Bradford and Ollins to confess to their own involvement, led Bradford to implicate Larry Ollins as well as Larry's cousin Calvin Ollins (who later also confessed after being shown Larry's statement) and led several witnesses to provide false testimony against them. Even Chicago crime laboratory analyst Pamela Fish testified falsely that semen samples from the victim could have come from the defendants, though this was impossible since the perpetrators were "secretors" and

Practical Psychology for Forensic Investigations and Prosecutions.
Edited by Mark R. Kebbell and Graham M. Davies. © 2006 John Wiley & Sons, Ltd.

the defendants were all "nonsecretors". The "evidence" appeared over-whelming, and all four boys were convicted. Although Bradford received a reduced sentence for having implicated others, Saunders and Larry and Calvin Ollins received life sentences.

Nearly 15 years later, DNA testing proved that the perpetrator's DNA failed to match any of the four boys, leading prosecutors to agree to their release. Nevertheless, Chicago police insisted the boys were some-how guilty, offering explanations of why the DNA did not match – such as the use of condoms, failure to ejaculate or the existence of addi-tional unidentified but associated perpetrators. Their scepticism was soon proven unfounded when the true perpetrators were identified less than two months later. The real perpetrators confessed, and these con-fessions were confirmed by DNA and fingerprint evidence linked to the crime scene (see account of the Roscetti case in Drizin & Leo, 2004).

The multiple wrongful convictions in the Roscetti case represent only a few among the rising tide of documented wrongful convictions caused wholly or in part by coerced false confessions. Systematic stud-ies of wrongful convictions (e.g., Bedau & Radelet, 1987; Connors, Lun-dregan, Miller & McEwen, 1996; Drizin & Leo, 2004; Leo & Ofshe, 1998; Radelet, Bedau & Putnam, 1992; Scheck, Neufield & Dwyer, 2000; Warden, 2003; the Innocence Project case files (maintained at their website – http://www.innocenceproject.org/case/index.php)) have docu-mented over 300 cases involving false confessions, and have made clear that these false confessions prominently contribute to wrongful con-victions. These studies have shown that 14% to 25% of the wrongfully convicted had confessed to the crimes of which they were later proven innocent, and that among those who confessed and yet went to trial conviction rates have ranged from 73% to 81%. What caused so many innocents to generate false confessions that could have, and in many cases did, send them to jail – even to death row? How can such false confessions be prevented while still allowing police to obtain true con-fessions from the guilty? And, recognizing that false confessions can and do occur, what can be done to recognize them in time to prevent the ter-rible miscarriages of justice such as those that occurred in the Roscetti case, and the many others documented in published case histories and systematic studies of wrongful convictions?

This chapter reviews the primary causes of false confession and resultant miscarriages of justice *that are subject to the influence of law enforcement and the courts*. We first review the major identifiable causes of false confession, offering suggestions for ways to minimize or avoid them. We then turn to strategies for recognizing false confessions when they do occur, and thereby for minimizing their consequences. (See also Chapter 6 concerning ethical ways of interviewing suspected offenders.)

CAUSES AND PREVENTION OF FALSE CONFESSIONS

Probable Cause to Interrogate

The path to false confession begins, as it must, when police target an innocent suspect. Therefore, as many have pointed out, the best way to prevent false confession is to limit interrogation to suspects for whom there is sufficient probable cause supporting guilt (e.g., Davis & O'Donohue, 2004; Drizin & Leo, 2004; Kamisar, 1980; Ofshe & Leo, 1997a, 1997b). As we shortly discuss, modern interrogation techniques incorporate highly sophisticated powerful psychological weapons of influence that can persuade innocent and guilty alike to confess. This being the case, it is clear that the frequency of false confessions will depend upon the base rate of innocent suspects among those subjected to interrogation. Unfortunately, police commonly interrogate suspects who are targeted for unreliable reasons well before sufficient evidence – or, in some cases, any at all – is available to indicate guilt. These deficits in probable cause tend to elevate the base rate of innocents among those who are interrogated.

Identifying the Suspect

Accounts of wrongful convictions have often revealed that innocent persons are targeted for suspicion for reasons not actually probative of guilt. The suspect may simply be the most readily noticed person who fits a very general description given by an eyewitness or others. Although many may fit the description, the target may be chosen simply because he happens to be noticed by police, reported by someone who had seen a police sketch or falsely identified from a mugshot or lineup. Or, as in the Roscetti case, suspects who fit an official "profile" of the perpetrators may be targeted for no other reason.

A suspect may also be targeted based on widespread crime-related schemas including likely motives for the crime, as well as perpetrators likely to have such motives (e.g., Davis & Follette, 2002, 2003; Vanous & Davis, 2002). Family members, for example, have been led to confess falsely to murdering wives, children or parents, largely because police start with the assumption that most such murders are committed by family and proceed by ruling out family before looking for other suspects. Eighteen-year-old Peter Reilly, for example, was led to confess falsely to murdering his mother. Police targeted Peter immediately after he reported the murder, subjected him to a long and coercive interrogation, and elicited the confession before investigation of any other possibilities had begun (Connery, 1977). Family members may also be targeted because their reactions to a relative's death seem inappropriate. Michael Crowe was subjected to interrogation regarding the death of his sister because detectives believed he reacted with insufficient emotion to her brutal stabbing (Sauer, 2004).

Sometimes police target the innocent suspect for reasons idiosyncratic to the case. Timothy Hennis, for example, was identified as a suspect in the triple murder of a mother and two of her three children simply because he had bought a dog from the family during the week before the murders (Loftus & Ketcham, 1991). Sixteen-year-old Allen Chesnet was brought to the attention of police by reporters who noticed his bleeding hand while asking him directions to a murder victim's house (Drizin & Leo, 2004). Others, such as Michael Gayles, are targeted when police receive misleading tips of various sorts (Drizin & Leo, 2004).

The Presumption of Guilt

"For cops, the presumption of innocence is a rarity, not a right".
New York City Police Officer, Edward Conlon (2004), *Blue Blood*, pp. 182–183

Whatever the reasons, once specific suspects are targeted, police interviews and interrogations are thereafter guided by the presumption of guilt. This very presumption is perhaps the root cause of false confessions and their far-reaching consequences. It engages strong "confirmation biases" that lead police to misinterpret evidence and to employ powerful coercive influence techniques that cause the suspect to seemingly confirm the presumption of guilt through incriminating statements and behaviours; that prevent police from identifying and investigating even strong evidence of innocence; and that similarly bias forensic experts and laboratories that examine trace evidence, handwriting and other ostensibly objective "scientific" evidence (see Kassin & Gudjonsson, 2004; Meissner & Kassin, 2004; Nickerson, 1998; Risinger, Saks, Thompson & Rosenthal, 2002 for reviews).

The Pre-interrogation Interview

These biasing confirmatory processes can begin when investigators conduct pre-interrogation "interviews" in which they attempt to assess the suspect's deceptiveness and probable guilt. The popular interrogation manual by Inbau, Reid, Buckley & Jayne (2001), widely considered the most influential among American law enforcement, advises investigators to conduct a "behaviour analysis interview" for this purpose, which, it is claimed, will allow the investigator to determine truth or deception at a rate of 85% accuracy. In fact, this rate seems to be represented in John E. Reid and Associates training seminars as 100%. As per their website, their seminars have been attended by several hundred thousand law enforcement personnel at all levels (http://www.reid.com). Joseph Buckley, Reid and Associates president and co-author of the Inbau et al. manual, claimed at least as recently as 2004 that their interrogation methods do not ever induce false confessions "because we don't interrogate innocent people" (see Kassin & Gudjonsson, 2004, p. 36) – a claim that has been widely made among interrogators. Such a claim rests, of course, on the assumption that interrogators trained to conduct effective behaviour analysis interviews can then detect guilt and innocence faultlessly, such that they proceed to interrogate only those who are actually guilty. Clearly, if investigators use the behaviour analysis interview, then its outcome will determine whether the person subsequently goes home or is subjected to the full force of the ensuing interrogation.

These exaggerated claims of accuracy fly in the face of a vast empirical literature on the accuracy of human lie detection. First, most of the criteria Inbau et al. (2001) advise investigators to use to determine deception are actually not diagnostic of deception (Kassin & Fong, 1999), and investigators and laypersons trained to use these criteria have been shown to: (i) perform more poorly than untrained controls; (ii) exhibit a general bias towards judging targets as deceptive; and (iii) feel greater confidence in their judgements (see Kassin & Gudjonsson, 2004; Meissner & Kassin, 2004 for reviews).

Second, hundreds of studies on detection of deception have found that people, regardless of profession, perform no better than chance (see Chapter 5 for a detailed discussion concerning the detection of deception). Virtually none achieve the levels of 85%–100% claimed by Buckley and others. Indeed, O'Sullivan and Ekman (2004) reported that having tested over 13 000 people from all walks of life, they have identified only 15 who could achieve accuracy rates of 80% or more. Professionals such as police, judges, psychiatrists, polygraph examiners and those from other relevant professions exhibit accuracy rates between 45% and 60%, averaging 54% (Vrij, 2000). Many such studies have been criticized for use of relatively low-stakes lying. However, researchers have recently employed higher stakes situations, and several studies have examined police officers' ability to detect deception in high-stakes crime-related circumstances. Vrij and Mann (2001), for example, asked police officers to judge truthfulness in videotaped press conferences in which family pleaded for help finding missing relatives – some of whom had actually killed their "missing" kin. Even in this situation, accuracy rates were low. Hartwig, Granhag, Strömwall and Vrij (2004) asked law enforcement personnel to judge truthfulness among students alleged to have committed a mock crime. Whether they personally interrogated these students or watched interrogations conducted by others, the investigators did not exceed chance performance in their attempts to distinguish between students who actually had, and those who had not, committed the mock crimes. These and many other studies have clearly shown that even in crime-relevant contexts investigators fail to exceed chance performance (see Kassin & Gudjonsson, 2004; Meissner & Kassin, 2004; Vrij, 2004, Chapter 5, this volume, for reviews).

Although investigators in practice usually do not conduct a pre-interrogation behaviour analysis interview, there have been prominent cases of interrogation-induced false confessions in which the suspect was subjected to interrogation based upon the investigators' use of faulty indices of deception recommended by Inbau et al. (2001). Tom Sawyer, for example, was accused of sexual assault and murder, and interrogated for 16 hours – based on the fact that his face flushed and he appeared embarrassed during an initial interview. These reactions were interpreted as deceptive by detectives who were unaware that Sawyer was a recovering alcoholic suffering from a disorder that caused profuse sweating and blushing in evaluative social situations (Leo & Ofshe, 1998).

Available Evidence

In the absence of any specific evidence against the suspect, police judgements of deceptiveness clearly do not constitute adequate probable cause to interrogate. Police are predisposed to see deception whether or not it exists (see Kassin & Gudjonsson, 2004), and achieve no better than chance accuracy in their determinations of deceptiveness. Likewise, targeting persons as suspects for unreliable reasons, such as fit to professional or intuitive profiles of perpetrators, or others such as reviewed earlier, does not constitute probable cause to subject a suspect to interrogation. Without specific evidence linking the specific suspect to the crime, the base rate of innocent persons among those who are interrogated will be enhanced, thereby increasing the potential for false confession.

The Interrogation

Ideally, interrogation tactics would effectively induce the guilty, but not the innocent, to confess. Unfortunately, some of the most prominent tactics are implicated as causes of false confession in documented cases of wrongful conviction and/or in laboratory studies of interrogation-induced compliance. Space does not permit a full review of all tactics and how and why they may induce false confessions (for detailed reviews see Davis & O'Donohue, 2004; Gudjonsson, 2003; Ofshe & Leo,

1997a, 1997b). Here, we focus on three: (i) the length and aversiveness of the interrogation; (ii) the use of false evidence; and (iii) false characterization of the consequences of confession versus denial.

Length, Aversiveness and Stress-Induced Confessions

Both by their very nature, and by deliberate design, interrogations are stressful and aversive. Interrogative stresses derive from a number of essential features of the process: confinement, social isolation, physical discomfort, the sense of helplessness and lack of control, the aversiveness of the interrogation tactics and the fear and anxiety surrounding the immediate situation and its anticipated consequences (Davis & O'Donohue, 2004). These stresses can be exacerbated when those who enter the process are already distressed by grief, other reactions to the crime itself, physically exhausted, intoxicated or otherwise mentally or physically distressed for any of a variety of reasons. As well, some individuals are dispositionally psychologically or physically vulnerable and therefore unable to tolerate even low or moderate levels of stress.

As with any form of aversive stimulus, the longer it persists, the stronger the motivation to escape becomes. And, given a long and aversive interrogation, some individuals become willing to do almost anything to escape, including to confess falsely, even to the most heinous crimes. Whereas most interrogations on average last under two hours (Leo, 1996a), the interrogations leading to false confessions tend to last much longer. In a recent analysis of 125 proven false confessions for example, Drizin and Leo (2004) found the average interrogation to be 16.3 hours. Hence, excessively lengthy interrogations – particularly when accompanied by physical discomfort, aversive interactions or deprivations of sleep, food, water or other physiological necessities and promises or threats – may lead the innocent to confess simply in order to escape. This tendency can be exacerbated, particularly among the innocent, when police imply or state that confessing will carry minimum, if any, consequences (see below).

Interrogative stresses also contribute to the tendency to confess falsely through their impact on the self-regulation abilities of the target (see Davis & O'Donohue, 2004 for review re interrogation and Baumeister & Vohs, 2004 for reviews of self-regulation, behavioural self-control and intellectual functioning). That is, stress impairs the ability to think clearly and make reasonable judgements, and the ability to control behavioural impulses and act in one's own long-term best interest. Specifically, stress impairs the ability to accurately understand and analyse incoming information, to retrieve relevant information from long-term memory, to avoid distractions and focus on relevant information, to hold all relevant information in working memory while attempting to assess it and form judgements and to form reasonable conclusions based upon all available information. Impairment of these capacities facilitates the interrogator's goal of making the decision to confess seem like the rational and optimal choice under the circumstances. Further, even if one can reasonably see the undesirable consequences of confessing, stress can yet facilitate confession by undermining the ability to exert one's will to resist or one's ability to control short-term impulses in favour of long-term outcomes (Davis, 2004; Davis & O'Donohue, 2004).

Investigations of the reasons for confessing, true or false, have shown that many do confess simply to escape (see reviews by Drizin & Leo, 2004; Gudjonsson, 2003; Kassin & Gudjonsson, 2004; Ofshe & Leo 1997a, 1997b). Indeed, some documented cases of wrongful conviction have illustrated the role of impaired thinking in promoting the belief that confession will result in escape. Consider, for example, 16-year-old Allen Chesnet's comment (ABC news 20/20, 2002): "They kept telling me I know you did it so why are you lying to me. They had me so upset I wasn't thinking right... [I]f I said, yeah, I did it, I could go home. If I said I didn't do it, I could go to jail so I said I did it and I want to see my parents and everything". Suspects may also be prone to waive their *Miranda* rights in order to be released. A suspect in one of the first author's recent cases, having been read his rights and asked if he was still willing to talk to the investigators, responded "How I'm gonna get outta here if I don't talk to ya'll".

Given the importance of stress-induced impairments in thinking and self-control, and ultimately in promoting false confessions, investigators should exert greater care to exert limits on the length of uninterrupted interrogation and associated deprivations of basic needs. Further, given the enhanced vulnerability of some groups (for example, juveniles) or individuals, investigators should become more aware of those who may be more likely to confess falsely simply to escape, and those who may do so in response to less stress than the less vulnerable.

The "Borg Maneuver" and the Role of False Evidence

"You believe everything a cop tells you, you're a damn fool!"

Lieutenant Colombo

Interrogation may be thought of as an extended "anti-*Miranda*" warning, in which the suspect is led to believe that *failure to tell* his version of the events in question can and will be held against him in a court of law, and that, conversely, everything he *does tell* the investigators can and will work to his benefit. This message is conveyed in two parts. First, the suspect is convinced that the investigators have overwhelming proof of guilt, and therefore he cannot hope to establish his innocence because no one will believe him. Second, given the futility of denial, the suspect is led to believe that he will achieve the best outcomes, legal and otherwise, by complying with the interrogator's wishes and making or agreeing to an incriminating statement, admission or full confession (Ofshe & Leo, 1997a, 1997b).

The popular Reid nine-step method of interrogation (Inbau et al., 2001) begins with "positive confrontation", in which the investigator accuses the suspect of the crime, expresses complete confidence in his guilt, and offers supporting "evidence" in the form of real or falsified trace, eyewitness or other evidence. The purpose of this is to instill a sense of futility and hopelessness, and to convince the suspect that he will be unable to establish his innocence. Davis and O'Donohue (2004) dubbed this the "Borg maneuver" after television's *Star Trek* nemesis race, the Borg, whose signature saying was "Resistance is futile! You will comply!" Subsequent steps of the Reid method are designed to reinforce this sense of futility through continued presentation of "evidence" and arguments supporting guilt, refusal to acknowledge the suspect's protestations or arguments for innocence and continued displays of absolute confidence in guilt (Ofshe & Leo, 1997a, 1997b).

This strategy is very effective in inducing confession. Surveys of prisoners and others who have been interrogated by police have shown that the most powerful reason for confession is the perception of strong evidence against them (see review in Gudjonsson, 2003; Kassin & Gudjonsson, 2004; see also Moston, Stephenson & Williamson, 1992). A series of laboratory studies has likewise shown that presentation of false evidence substantially increases the rate of false confession to various undesirable, but non-criminal, behaviors (Forrest, Wadkins & Miller, 2002; Horselenberg, Merckelbach & Josephs, 2003; Kassin & Kiechel, 1996; Redlich & Goodman, 2003).

Given the effectiveness of the presentation of evidence for inducing true confessions, we do not suggest that this should be avoided. However, the presentation of *false* evidence should be minimized, particularly when there is no supporting actual evidence. American law does not prohibit lying and fabrication of evidence, even in the extreme circumstances where no true evidence exists (unless these lies about evidence communicate threats or promises), and such strategies are commonplace and varied. Among the most common false evidence is falsified polygraph or other lie-detection tests such as so-called computer voice-stress analyser or others (Lykken, 1998). Falsified polygraph results have been prominently implicated among strategies employed in documented cases of false confessions (see Connery, 1977; Drizin & Leo, 2004; Leo & Ofshe, 1998). Other prominent strategies included claims of non-existent fingerprints, DNA and other trace evidence; alleged eyewitness identifications; alleged confessions and incriminating statements by co-perpetrators; and claims involving completely fabricated forms of evidence, such as "penis prints" left in the vagina of rape victims (Davis & O'Donahue, 2004; Ofshe & Leo, 1997a, 1997b). Many variations of such false evidence ploys are commonly implicated in documented cases of false confession. Several notorious cases in which multiple confessions have been obtained have involved false claims of confessions and incriminating statements of alleged co-perpetrators – including the Roscetti case described in the opening of this chapter, and the well-known case of the "New York Jogger" in which false confessions were obtained from five teenagers, partly through use of this co-perpetrator ploy (which is among those recommended by Inbau et al., 2001 and other manuals) (Kassin, 2002).

The Benefits of Confession

Given that the suspect has been led to believe he cannot hope to establish innocence, he is next led to believe that confession will best serve his long-term interests by reducing his culpability, or that perhaps it may result in immediate release and possibly no consequences at all (Ofshe & Leo, 1997a, 1997b). Interrogators use "themes" (i.e., scenarios that provide moral, psychological or legal excuses or justifications for committing the alleged act) and suggest inducements to *motivate* the suspect to perceive that it is in his self-interest to comply with the interrogator's wishes and confess. Interrogators try to persuade suspects of this by implying that the crime may be understandable or excusable and thus that a full admission will cause the case to be treated more leniently by the legal system.

The Sympathetic Detective with the "Time-Limited Offer"

'I've heard the sum of these techniques referred to as "jerkology" '
New York City Police Officer Edward Conlon (2004), *Blue Blood,* p. 185

Resistance to influence is minimized when the source is well liked or viewed as lacking self-serving motives (see Davis & O'Donohue, 2004 for review). Playing upon this principle, investigators are trained to establish rapport with and flatter the suspect, and to portray themselves as sympathetic to the suspect and motivated by the desire to help him, a tactic which may be more effective than hostile dominating tactics (Holmberg & Christianson, 2002). For example, Davis and her colleagues (2006) have shown that the addition of sympathy/flattery (and a time-limited offer of help, see below) to an interrogation including other typical strategies such as confrontation with evidence against the suspect, and a minimizing scenario for the nature of the crime (see below), successfully altered perceptions of both the detective's motives and the likely outcomes of confession. Those in the sympathy/flattery condition were more likely to believe that the detective liked the suspect and wanted to help him achieve the best legal outcomes, and more likely to expect that the detective would actively try to minimize the charges filed against him, and that a suspect who confessed would actually face less serious legal charges.

Such sympathetic offers of help are portrayed as "time limited", however, and unavailable once the suspect leaves the interrogation. Unfortunately, the only way the suspect can obtain this "help" is by agreeing to or providing a full incriminating account of the crime of which he is accused. If the suspect does not comply with the interrogator's demands to "tell your side of the story before it's too late" the suspect will suffer worse outcomes. For example, interrogators may suggest any one of the following types of scenarios: that the co-perpetrators may implicate the suspect as having a primary role in the crime – such as the shooter rather than getaway driver; that the eyewitness accounts will have to be believed because the suspect hasn't contradicted them; that there will be no other explanation for why his fingerprints were found at the scene or of what he might have been lying about during the polygraph exam; that the district attorney and judge will not be willing to listen to him; that jurors will be offended that he would not take responsibility for what he has done – and on and on.

Techniques in which interrogators implicitly or explicitly threaten suspects with harsher treatment or punishment if they do not confess are sometimes referred to as "maximization" (Kassin & McNall, 1991; Ofshe & Leo, 1997a, 1997b). Maximization strategies communicate, implicitly or explicitly, that the suspect will be charged with more crimes, will be more likely to be convicted and will receive a longer sentence and/or differential punishment if he fails to comply with the detectives' wish or demand that he agree to or make a full confession. For example, detectives may repeatedly tell a murder suspect that if he fails to acknowledge his role in the killing of the victim, the prosecutor, judge and jury will all assume that it was premeditated and will treat him as a cold-blooded murderer – implying that he will receive the harshest possible charge and punishment if he does not comply with the detectives' demands for confession (Kassin & McNall, 1991; Ofshe & Leo, 1997a, 1997b).

Minimization and the Misunderstood Consequences of Confession

The trained interrogator may also misportray the other side of the coin – that is, the very real harm done to the suspect who makes incriminating statements of various sorts. These are not limited to full confession. As New York City detective Conlon states, "the detective... is looking for any kind of useful admission – if a robbery suspects says, 'I was there, but I didn't do anything,' he might have effectively owned up to the crime" (2004, p. 185). Similarly, Inbau et al. (2001) recommend eliciting any and all admissions, no matter how apparently benign, as a "stepping-stone" approach to eliciting a full confession.

A central strategy for eliciting such admissions is to "minimize" (Kassin & McNall, 1991) the seriousness of the offence in question. This is often done through the process of "theme" development (Inbau et al., 2001), whereby the investigator suggests various scenarios that would tend to minimize criminal intent or redefine the nature of the act so that it is no longer criminal and thus imply less serious consequences – for example, that a murder occurred by accident or was committed in self-defence, that the crime was provoked, committed while intoxicated, well intentioned or otherwise justifiable. The Inbau et al. (2001) manual suggests a number of specific themes tailored to the type of suspect and type of crime (see also Senese, 2005 for a catalogue of such themes). Although Inbau et al. deny that the use of such themes are coercive, research has clearly shown that they communicate and are perceived to imply leniency and reduced punishment in exchange for admissions (e.g., Gudjonsson, 2003; Kassin & McNall, 1991; Ofshe & Leo, 1997a, 1997b). Further, the use of such minimizing themes and explicit promises of leniency increases the rate of both true and false confessions at equivalent rates, and the use of each increases the ratio of false to true confessions, making the confession less diagnostic of guilt (Ofshe & Leo, 1997a, 1997b; Russano, Meissner, Narchet & Kassin, 2005).

As noted earlier, such tactics may be particularly effective with innocent persons. They are prone to waive their *Miranda* rights largely because they feel they have nothing to hide and nothing to lose by talking with investigators (Kassin & Norwick, 2004; Leo & White, 1999). Similarly, innocents may believe that their innocence will be proven when police investigate further or scientific evidence is tested (Kassin, 2005). When these expectations combine with minimization tactics portraying the suspect's role as accidental, self-defence or other characterizations implying that there may be no crime at all or the suspect bears no culpability for it, innocent suspects may be particularly likely to misperceive the consequences of confession as minimal to none.

Indeed this is true of many suspects, guilty and innocent. Interrogators often lead suspects to believe that confession may result in their release (see Gudjonsson, 2003 for review). For example, the first author watched a suspect who had just confessed to the attempted rape of a nine year old burst into tears with disbelief when he was told he was to be arrested, crying "I'm going to jail? I thought you wanted to help me!" This may seem counterintuitive to those who have not seen effective theme development and minimization tactics in practice, but in fact, it attests to how minimizing themes pragmatically communicate leniency, freedom and/or immunity in exchange for confession (Kassin & McNall, 1991; Ofshe & Leo, 1997a, 1997b).

Vulnerable Suspects

Interrogation tactics are most likely to induce false confessions when practised on vulnerable suspects. Some types of individuals – the mentally handicapped, the mentally ill and juveniles in particular – are especially susceptible to the psychological pressures of accusatorial interrogation. As a result, they tend to be more easily coerced or led into giving involuntary and/or unreliable statements (Gudjonsson, 2003; Kassin & Gudjonsson, 2004) and are thus disproportionately represented in the documented false confession cases (Drizin & Leo, 2004). There are good psychological reasons for why these types of individuals tend to be less able to withstand accusatorial police questioning, and to be more compliant and suggestible and thus at increased risk for interrogation-induced false confession (Gudjonsson, 2003; Kassin & Gudjonsson, 2004). Such vulnerabilities may be heightened, such as when the suspect is intoxicated, physically ill or exhausted, or suffering acute distress. As noted earlier, physical or emotional distress or impairments can compromise self-regulation resources, and the ability to make reasonable judgements and decisions or to resist immediate behavioural impulses in favour of long-term outcomes (see Davis & O'Donohue, 2004 for review). These self-regulatory functions can also be compromised by youth, lower IQ or mental illness.

The outward characteristics displayed by the mentally handicapped and mentally ill are not always obvious to the untrained eye. As a result, police should receive additional training on how to recognize such persons as well as how to most effectively elicit information from them. There are a number of practices and policies that law enforcement can enact to increase their knowledge about vulnerable individuals and decrease the risks of eliciting unreliable statements from them.

The Broward County, Florida Sheriff's Office – whose investigators had elicited notable false confessions from developmentally disabled suspects in several high-profile cases (Drizin & Leo, 2004) – has adopted policies for interrogating mentally vulnerable suspects that suggest a model for how police can more effectively elicit information from them while decreasing the risk of false confessions. Pursuant to this new policy, Broward County detectives must annually receive specialized training to assist them in recognizing the characteristics of a developmentally disabled suspect and on how to properly question them to avoid or minimize the risk of false confessions. Before questioning a developmentally disabled suspect, Broward County detectives are instructed to immediately notify their supervisors and to make a reasonable effort to notify and afford an appropriate adult the opportunity to be present during all questioning. Interrogators are also instructed to take special care in advising developmentally disabled suspects of their constitutional rights, requiring them to "speak slowly and clearly and ask subjects to explain their response rather than simply answer yes or no". Because the developmentally disabled are "easily persuaded" and "eager to please authority figures", detectives are trained to avoid leading or suggestive questions and questions that "tell the suspect the answer the detectives expect".

As a final check against false confessions, before a developmentally disabled suspect can be charged with a crime, each confession taken from a developmentally disabled suspect must undergo a thorough "post-confession analysis" by a unit supervisor, or, if there is no evidence corroborating the confession, by a team consisting of a psychologist, an assistant state's attorney and a criminal investigation commander. This evaluation involves weighing numerous factors, including whether the suspect was able to provide an accurate description of the major and minor details of the crime and crime scene, whether the suspect was able to identify unusual or unique elements of the crime or its scene which were not publicly known, and whether the suspect provided information to the police that led to the discovery of other previously unknown evidence.

Because they share many of the same characteristics as the developmentally disabled – such as an eagerness to comply with adult authority figures, impulsivity, immature judgement and inability to recognize and weigh risks in decision making – juvenile suspects should be afforded the same protections (Drizin & Colgan, 2004). Police detectives should receive specialized training on the vulnerabilities and psychological traits of juveniles that predispose them to comply more readily with interrogation demands that they confess. Prior to any questioning, police detectives should notify a supervisor so that the interrogation can be monitored. When interrogating juveniles, police detectives should use simple language; speak slowly and clearly; avoid leading, suggestive and forced choice questions; and take regular breaks. Once detectives have elicited a statement or admission from a juvenile suspect, they should subject it to the same post-confession analysis described above in order to more fully analyse its reliability and protect against the possibility of false confession. In addition, juveniles should also be provided with an appropriate adult during questioning, such as a lawyer or other person (independent of police) who is specially trained to fill this role.

MINIMIZING CONSEQUENCES OF FALSE CONFESSIONS

Those who confess tend to be thereafter presumed guilty and treated more harshly at every remaining stage of the case (see Davis & O'Donohue, 2004; Gudjonsson, 2003; Leo & Ofshe, 1998). Because police assume the confession to be true, they are unlikely to pursue exculpatory evidence or follow leads to other suspects and tend to consider the case solved (e.g., Leo, 1996a; Leo & Ofshe, 1998). Instead, police may so strongly pursue evidence of the defendant's guilt that other evidence may become tainted in the process – for example, through inadvertent but powerful biasing of eyewitness identifications or accounts, and even through alteration or deliberate falsification of evidence (see Drizin & Leo, 2004 for multiple case examples).

Judges tend to view a defendant who has confessed as guilty and refuse to grant bail, and on the strength of the confession, prosecutors tend to charge a defendant with more serious offences and to be less inclined to plea bargain. Even defence attorneys, anticipating the impact of the confession, often pressure the client to plead guilty (Davis & O'Donohue, 2004; Leo & Ofshe, 1998).

False confessions are typically retracted once the suspect is free of the coercive influences of the interrogation, or when he obtains an attorney and is apprised of the likely consequences of the confession (Ofshe & Leo, 1997a). Police tend to be unresponsive to such claims, however, and remain unlikely to further investigate the case or pursue evidence of innocence. Likewise, judges confronted with motions to exclude such confessions from trial as involuntary are generally unreceptive. Most suspects waive their *Miranda* rights (Leo, 1996a, 1996b; White, 2001a), and innocent suspects are particularly likely to do so (Kassin, 2005). If the suspect is *Mirandized* but confesses anyway, the courts often automatically find the confession to be voluntary (White, 2001b, p. 1220), despite evidence that suspects commonly fail to understand their rights even when apprised of them (e.g., Grisso, 1998a, 1998b). In theory, a confession will be excluded if elicited via actual physical violence, threats of harm, promises of leniency or without proper *Miranda* warnings (Kamisar, Lafave, Israel & King, 2005). However, in the absence of such egregious violations, it is often ruled voluntary and admissible despite the use of implied threats and promises, falsified evidence, lengthy and stress-filled interrogations and other tactics known to induce false confessions (Kassin, 1997; Ofshe & Leo, 1997a, 1997b). Such practices are only a factor in the "totality of the circumstances" test of voluntariness (Kamisar et al., 2005).

If a confession is admitted into evidence (as are the overwhelming majority) and the defendant is convicted (as, again, are the overwhelming majority), the defendant may appeal, arguing that the confession was actually coerced and inappropriately admitted (see Gudjonnson, 2003 for a discussion of case law regarding challenges of confessions). Prior to 1991, if the confession was deemed coerced on appeal, the conviction was routinely reversed. However, in the *Arizona* v. *Fulminante* (1991) decision, the US Supreme Court ruled that in certain circumstances the admission of a coerced confession may be "harmless error". The appellate court is required to consider the confession in the context of all of the evidence to determine whether it exerted significant prejudicial effect upon the outcome. If not, the conviction will stand.

As reviewed in detail by Davis and O'Donohue (2003), the various tasks of judges and juries require, at a minimum: (i) accuracy in understanding interrogation practices that are actually coercive, and their abilities to elicit both true and false confessions; (ii) the ability to ignore a confession deemed involuntary and to eliminate both direct and indirect influences it may have on their judgements; and (iii) the ability to ignore the trial jury verdict in evaluating the strength of evidence without the confession (for appellate judges). Substantial research suggests, however, that neither judges nor juries can meet these requirements (see Davis & O'Donohue, 2004; Kassin & Gudjonsson, 2004 for reviews), and instead, the overwhelming majority of those who confess are found guilty at trial, only to have the verdict upheld upon appeal.

Given the pervasive use of psychologically manipulative, deceptive and/or coercive tactics such as those reviewed in the preceding sections, we can expect that police will continue to obtain false confessions for the foreseeable future. False confessions can and do occur with troubling regularity (Drizin & Leo, 2004), and continue to be a leading source of wrongful prosecution and erroneous conviction in America (Scheck et al., 2000). Nevertheless, the consequences of such false confessions can be minimized if law enforcement, judges and juries develop greater understanding of the potential for police interrogation procedures to elicit false statements and of the conditions under which they are most likely to do so. In the absence of such understandings, defendants who falsely confess will continue to be disadvantaged in every respect as their case proceeds through the justice system.

As the preceding section implies, the consequences of false confession can be minimized when law enforcement, attorneys, judges and juries remain open to disconfirmation. This requires both an attitude of openness to disproof and active investigation of all evidence and leads (including those inconsistent with the confession), as well as documentation of the interviews and interrogations leading to the confession.

Remaining Open to Disproof

Intuitions of police, prosecutors, judges and jurors alike deem the notion that an innocent person would confess falsely to be inherently lacking in credibility (Davis & O'Donohue, 2004; Kassin & Gudjonsson, 2004; Ofshe & Leo, 1997a, 1997b). This cascade of disbelief begins, of course, with the detectives who identify and interrogate the suspect.

Unfortunately, criminal investigators are neither trained to believe that false confessions can be elicited from innocents nor to understand the processes by which this may occur. Nor are they trained to avoid tactics that have been shown to elicit false confession or to recognize them when they do occur. Instead, the most popular criminal investigation manuals specifically instruct the reader that false confessions cannot be extracted from innocent persons via the techniques they recommend. For example, two prominent interrogation proponents (Jayne & Buckley, 1992), argued in defence of common interrogation tactics that "none of these techniques, in and of themselves, is unique to interrogations, and none of them would cause an innocent suspect to confess to a crime" (p. 69). In the latest edition of the Inbau et al. police interrogation training manual (2001), the authors repeat earlier claims that: "It must be remembered that none of the steps is apt to make an innocent person confess and that all the steps are legally as well as morally justifiable" (p. 212).

In part, this belief is founded on investigators' unjustified confidence in their ability to conclusively determine guilt prior to the interrogation, as discussed earlier. As indicated by Reid Associates' president Joseph Buckley's statement that they don't interrogate innocent people (referenced earlier), investigators may simply discount the potential for those they interrogate to confess falsely on this basis.

In contrast to such presumptions, investigators should not simply assume that a confession is true merely because the suspect has acknowledged guilt, agreed to a scenario that incriminates him or even provided "details". Absent external corroboration, confessions should always be treated as potentially, if not inherently, unreliable.

Distinguishing True From False Confessions

Even if open to the possibility that a confession may be false, investigators and fact finders must have the necessary evidence to distinguish the reliable from the unreliable. This requires a three-pronged analysis of: (i) police interviews and interrogations of the suspect; (ii) the incriminating statements and admissions themselves; and (iii) all relevant case evidence.

It should be noted that one should *not* attempt to distinguish true from false confessions through subjective determinations of truthfulness. As reviewed earlier, human lie-detection abilities are no better than chance, and the ability to distinguish true from false confessions is no better. Hence, one must rely on more systematic analyses of the evidence and the circumstances under which the confession was elicited.

Analysis of the Interviews/Interrogations

What occurred during an interrogation may be crucial to assessing whether a confession is likely to be true. Two issues are important: (a) whether the interrogation involved coercive tactics such as those discussed in previous sections that could have induced the suspect to confess falsely; and (b) where the suspect could have learned the details included in his statements and admissions (see section on post-admission narrative analysis below).

A Requirement to Record All Interviews/Interrogations

In many cases – especially high-profile cases – there may be little to no evidence other than a suspect's statements. For example, in the case of Gary Gauger, who was wrongly convicted and sentenced to death for the murder of his parents, the only evidence against Gauger was his statements to police interrogators after nearly 20 hours of overnight interrogation (Leo & Ofshe, 1998). Although it is important to evaluate all suspected false confessions, particularly when there is little relevant evidence of other kinds, the details of police interactions with the suspect may be crucial.

Unfortunately, memory for conversation (including interviews) is unreliable, particularly memory for such issues as who first introduced crime-relevant facts, how many times particular behaviours (such as offers of sympathy or help) occurred, how long the interaction lasted, what one did to elicit particular responses from the other, and other behaviours crucial to determine *why* the suspect made various statements and admissions. Of particular importance, neither interrogator nor suspect is likely to be able to recall features of the interrogation in terms different from how they were originally encoded. Hence, features not noticed or thought of in a particular way at the time will not be available for retrieval later (see reviews of foibles of memory for conversation by Davis & Friedman, in press; Davis, Kemmelmeier & Follette, 2005; Davis & Loftus, in press). Evidence of the capacity of the stresses of interrogation to impair memory was also recently obtained by Morgan and colleagues (2004), who found that high (relative to lower) stress interrogations led targets to offer fewer true, and more false, positive identifications of their interrogators from either photo spreads, sequential photo lineups or live lineups.

The only way to reliably evaluate the potentially coercive force of an interrogation is through careful examination of objective records, in the form of electronic recordings of the entire set of police interactions with the suspect, from the initial interview through the full-documented confession – a practice endorsed by a virtual chorus of confession scholars (see reviews by Davis & O'Donohue, 2004; Drizin & Reich, 2004; Kassin & Gudjonsson, 2004; Lassiter & Greers, 2004a, 2004b; Leo, 1996b). Unfortunately, only a few states – Alaska, Minnesota, Illinois, Maine, New Mexico, Wisconsin and Washington DC – currently require electronic recording of some or all interrogations, although many other jurisdictions do so voluntarily (see Drizin & Reich, 2004 for an historical review), and many of their personnel favour the practice and find it useful (Geller, 1993). Sullivan (2004) interviewed detectives from 38 states in jurisdictions that have practised such voluntary recording. Many viewed recording as useful, citing such advantages for police as less need to focus on note taking, ability to gain information through review of tapes, increased accountability and less need to defend the interrogations in court.

Unfortunately, in many cases the only recorded phase of the interrogation is the final confession in which the person is asked to narrate the details of his commission of the crime. This is, of course, the worst basis for determination of whether the confession is true or false. Fact finders see a very incriminating and detailed account of the crime that seems compelling, with no access to *how* the narrative was developed or potentially fed to the suspect during the interrogation phase.

Even if interrogations are fully recorded, *how* they are recorded may be important. Lassiter and his colleagues (see Lassiter, Greers, Munhall, Handley & Beers, 2001; Lassiter & Greers, 2004a, 2004b) have done a series of studies demonstrating that to fairly evaluate the coercive properties of an interrogation it must be taped from a "neutral focus" perspective focusing upon the detective and suspect equally. Most videotapes, however, focus on the suspect, showing only the back of the detective's head, if anything. As shown by Lassiter's research, such practices lead observers to underestimate the amount of pressure exerted by detectives, and tend to enhance observer perceptions of the suspect's guilt.

Post-Admission Narrative Analysis

A second tool for distinguishing between reliable and unreliable statements is the post-admission narrative analysis, comparing a suspect's post-admission narrative – that is, the account he gives of how and why he committed the crime – against the objectively knowable facts of the crime as well as the presence or absence of physical, medical or other credible evidence (Leo & Ofshe, 1998, 2001). When a guilty suspect gives a true confession, he will know both mundane and dramatic crime scene details and case facts that are not publicly known, cannot be easily guessed by chance and are capable of verification. The true confessor's post-admission narrative will therefore fit the crime scene facts. The true confessor should be able to explain aspects of the crime that may not be already known or readily observable. In addition, if the perpetrator left physical evidence at the crime scene, it should match to the confessor. The confessor may also be able to lead police to new, missing or derivative case evidence (Leo & Ofshe, 1998, 2001). Absent contamination from external sources, all of this should corroborate the suspect's underlying admission.

By contrast, an innocent person who falsely confesses will provide a post-admission narrative that does not fit the crime scene details or case facts – unless, of course, the innocent suspect has been fed the correct answers by police interrogators or he has learned crime details from the media or street gossip. Absent this kind of contamination, the innocent false confessor should not be able to provide police with accurate crime scene details and case facts, whether mundane or dramatic, unless they can be guessed by chance. Absent contamination, then, the innocent false confessor's post-admission narrative will likely be replete with factual errors. The innocent false confessor should not be able to explain unknown aspects of the crime or lead police to new, missing or derivative case evidence.

Clearly, the issue of contamination is crucial for an accurate and informative post-admission narrative analysis. But the most likely source of contamination for most cases – the interrogation itself – cannot be accurately assessed in the absence of objective recordings. Memory for who first introduced information into conversation has been shown to be poor (see Davis & Friedman, in press for review), and therefore interrogators cannot be expected to reliably report whether crucial information first came from the suspect.

To aid with the post-admission narrative analysis, the investigator should obtain as complete and detailed a post-admission narrative as possible, and should not ask any leading or suggestive questions in this post-admission portion of the interrogation (Ofshe & Leo, 1997b).

Collection and Analysis of All Relevant Evidence

Part and parcel of the post-admission narrative analysis is comparison to all known evidence, both immediately and as the investigation progresses. Case facts and evidence left behind at the crime scene will not match to the innocent false confessor. To distinguish between reliable and unreliable confessions, the interrogator needs first to keep an open mind about the possibility of eliciting a false confession, always seeking corroboration for any statements he elicits. In this sense, the properly trained interrogator is like a scientist seeking to test his hypotheses against the existing evidence. Like a scientist, the interrogator must not prejudge the evidence or seek to fit the evidence to a pre-existing belief. As one police interrogation training manual states, an uncorroborated confession is not worth the paper that it is written on (Oakland Police Department, 1998).

The problem here is, of course, confirmation biases that can prevent detectives from recognizing the possibility of having elicited a false confession because they are precommitted to the belief that a suspect is guilty even before he confesses. The confession may only fuel this belief further, causing a detective to seek out only evidence or circumstantial facts that appear to confirm the confession while selectively ignoring evidence that fails to corroborate the confession or evidence that strongly suggests the confession is, in fact, false. Erroneous prejudgements of guilt lead to what Meissner and Kassin (2002) have called the *investigator response bias* (i.e., the tendency to presume a suspect's guilt with near or complete certainty). The police detective who fails to keep an open mind about the possibility of a confession being false will be far less likely to investigate new or existing leads, evidence and/or theories of the case that point to other possible suspects. These confirmation biases can trickle down to police labs, sometimes up to and including deliberate falsification of lab results to support unreliable confessions, eyewitness identifications or other unreliable evidence (Scheck et al., 2000). This failure to keep an open mind among those at all levels perpetuates the injustice of the false confession in the first place and sometimes contributes to a wrongful prosecution and/or conviction (which may be a double tragedy if the true perpetrator remains at large).

There are a number of examples from false confession cases that illustrate how interrogators' failure to keep an open mind prevented them from seeing that they had in fact elicited a false confession and were contributing to an injustice (see many such accounts in Drizin & Leo, 2004; Kassin & Gudjonsson, 2004; Scheck et al., 2000). For example, Escondido, CA police detectives (after approximately 10–22 hours of psychologically coercive interrogation) elicited false confessions from teenagers Michael Crowe and Joshua Treadway in 1998 to the murder of Michael's younger sister Stephanie Crowe, who had been stabbed nine times. There was physical evidence (blood, DNA, fingerprints) left behind at the crime scene, yet none of it matched to Michael Crowe or Joshua Treadway. Moreover, both Crowe's and Treadway's post-admission narratives were full of errors and inconsistent with other case evidence. Yet the detectives refused to keep an open mind about the possibility that they had elicited false confessions. Both boys, charged and incarcerated for seven months, were released from custody only when, on the verge of trial, their defence attorneys had discovered DNA from the victim (Michael Crowe's sister) on the clothing of a Richard Tuite, a drug-addicted mentally ill drifter with a violent history who had been reported knocking on doors and menacing neighbours in the Crowe's neighborhood on the night of Stephanie Crowe's murder. Even with the DNA exoneration of Crowe and Treadway, however, the Escondido detectives continued to proclaim their belief in the boys' guilt and alleged reliability of the confessions, even self-publishing a book declaring Crowe and Treadway's guilt (Tracey, 2003). Notwithstanding such protestations, however, state prosecutors eventually filed charges against Tuite and he was convicted of the murder of Stephanie Crowe.

The Role of the Expert Witness

Unfortunately, investigators and prosecuting attorneys currently remain largely unreceptive to the notion that interrogation-elicited confessions can be false, leaving the testimony of experts on coercive influence as the last defence of false confessors. Experts from the fields of psychology, criminology and/or sociology are sometimes called to testify primarily at two points in the trial process. First, they may be called at motions *in limine* or suppression hearings, where judges must decide whether the confession was coerced and is therefore to be deemed "involuntary" (and hence inadmissible) or "voluntary" (and therefore to be admitted during trial). Second, the expert may testify at trial, where the jury must ultimately determine what weight to put on the confession for their determination of guilt. The expert's role at these trial phases is to educate judges or juries about the social science research on the psychology of police interrogation and the phenomenon, causes, characteristics and indicia of police-induced false confessions. This includes, for example, educating the jury about such counterintuitive issues as: (i) the very fact that police sometimes elicit false confessions from the innocent by using commonly taught and practised interrogation methods; (ii) how and why police interrogations methods and strategies sometimes lead the innocent to falsely confess; and (iii) the personal and situational risk factors that increase the likelihood that a false confession will be elicited. In some cases the expert may also discuss the generally accepted principles of post-admission narrative analysis and external corroboration to assist the jury in its evaluation of the reliability of confession evidence.

Jurors are ill-equipped to understand these issues or to distinguish true from false confessions in the absence of expert testimony. Based upon their commonsense, jurors and others are simply unwilling to believe that people will confess to crimes they did not commit – especially heinous crimes with devastating consequences. Generally, we tend to judge others in comparison to ourselves, and therefore tend to judge others based upon how we think we would act in a given situation. Unfortunately, predictions of how one would behave in unfamiliar or powerful situations tend to be highly inaccurate, and hence observers are unlikely to believe they could personally be led to confess falsely, and therefore disbelieve others' claims. In addition, research on the fundamental attribution error has shown that observers generally fail to recognize the importance of situational factors in explaining others' behaviour, and to make internal attributions for their behaviour (Ross, 1977). Hence the powerful force of the interrogation is not recognized as the primary cause of the decision to confess. Also, since neither judges nor jurors can reliably distinguish truth from falsehood, they are unable to reliably distinguish true and false accounts. Finally, the corrupting influences discussed earlier can cause suspects to appear guilty – both through their own coerced statements and through flawed evidence – making denials ineffective in the absence of external support from exonerating evidence or expert testimony (see Davis & O'Donohue, 2004; Kassin & Gudjonsson, 2004 for reviews of research support for these processes).

In the last two decades, the use of expert witness testimony has become increasingly common in cases involving disputed interrogations and/or confessions. For the most part, trial courts have accepted this testimony (see, for example, *California* v. *Page*, 1991; *United States* v. *Hall*, 1996, 1997), though a few courts have published written opinions rejecting it (see, for example, *New Jersey* v. *Patrick Free*, 2002). Despite these few written opinions, academic interrogation and confession experts have testified in hundreds of criminal and civil cases across the country in the last two decades, most of which have not generated published opinions (Kassin & Gudjonsson, 2004). The trend towards greater acceptance of this testimony is clear, for the basis of the testimony rests on generally accepted social science research dating back almost a century (Leo, 2001). As Kassin and Gudjonsson (2004, p. 59) point out, "In this new era of DNA exonerations, however, it is now clear that such testimony is amply supported not only by anecdotes and case studies of wrongful convictions, but also by a long history of basic psychology and an extensive forensic science literature".

In sum, expert witness testimony may reduce the number of police-induced false confessions that lead to wrongful convictions in three ways: by its direct effect on the decision making of the judge at pretrial suppression hearings (at which time the judge decides which evidence to allow at trial and which to exclude); its direct effect on the decision making of jurors at trial; and perhaps less obviously, its indirect effect on the behaviour of police and prosecutors. When interrogation experts testify, police and prosecutors take notice – especially in high-profile cases that rest entirely on disputed confession evidence (like the Central Park Jogger case, for example). Police do not like to have their poor training, technical flaws or courtroom lies exposed; to be criticized for using inappropriate or coercive methods or to be shown to have elicited demonstrably false confessions. Prosecutors do not like to be criticized for indicting defendants based solely on coerced or false confessions, to be forced to dismiss charges after a judge suppresses the defendant's confession or to have defendants acquitted. By exposing flaws in a detective's interrogation methods or in the prosecution's case against a defendant, social science expert witness testimony in disputed confession cases may deter police misbehaviour in the long run and improve police and prosecutorial screening practices. It should lead to a decline in the use of psychologically coercive interrogation methods, the number of false confessions that police elicit and prosecutors introduce into evidence at trial, and thus the number of innocent men and women who are wrongfully convicted every year due to false confessions.

CONCLUSIONS

As this chapter has shown, social scientists, legal scholars and independent researchers have amply documented that contemporary methods of psychological interrogation can, and sometimes do, lead innocent individuals to confess falsely to serious crimes. The consequences of these false confessions can be disastrous for innocent individuals who are wrongfully convicted and incarcerated. The consequences of false confession may be disastrous even for those who are not convicted at trial. Some experience rape or other violence, loss of reputation or damage to family or careers as a result of their pretrial incarceration (Drizin & Leo, 2004; Leo & Ofshe, 1998). Two recent studies have documented that when false confessors refuse to plead guilty and go to trial, conviction rates range from 73% (Leo & Ofshe, 1998) to 81% (Drizin & Leo, 2004). Although some have been proven innocent and freed, many spend considerable time in prison for acts they didn't commit. And when that happens, the true perpetrators remain free to commit more crimes.

We have offered four primary strategies for prevention of false confessions: (i) interrogation only of those for whom there is sufficient probable cause to support guilt; (ii) educating law enforcement concerning the potential for and causes of false confessions (including confirmatory biases at all phases of investigation); (iii) avoiding practices known to promote false confession; and (iv) greater training and sensitivity to the psychological vulnerabilities that render some suspects unusually susceptible to influence, and adjustment of the police interrogation policies and practices based on these vulnerabilities. We do not expect that these remedies will prevent all false confessions. Contemporary American police interrogation techniques remain psychologically powerful, and some suspects are vulnerable even to lesser forms of influence and milder interrogation processes. However, we do expect that our proposed suggestions would reduce the number of false confessions and the rate at which they occur.

Such reforms are likely to occur slowly in the United States. Great Britain has adopted a number of reforms, based on growing documentation and awareness of the problem of false confessions (see Bull & Milne, 2004; Gudjonsson, 2003). But American law enforcement remains steeped in the traditions of interrogation via the Reid technique and similar procedures, including near absolute denial that these techniques can and do induce false confessions (see Davis & O'Donahue, 2004; Gudjonsson, 2003; Kassin & Gudjonsson, 2004; Ofshe & Leo, 1997a, 1997b). Until this misconception is fully dispelled by the steadily increasing tide of empirical documentation of false confessions and the interrogative influences that promote them, police interrogations will continue to elicit false confessions. In turn, many will remain undiscovered by detectives and others in the legal system who fail to maintain an attitude of open investigation and receptiveness to disproof.

REFERENCES

Arizona v. Fulminante, 499 US 279 (1991).

Baumeister, R.F. & Vohs, K.D. (2004). *Handbook of self-regulation: Research, theory, and applications*. New York: Guilford Press.

Bedau, H.A. & Radelet, M.L. (1987). Miscarriages of justice in potentially capital cases. *Stanford Law Review, 40*.

Bull, R. & Milne, B. (2004). Attempts to improve the police interviewing of suspects. In G.D. Lassiter (Ed.), *Interrogations, confessions, and entrapment* (pp. 182–196). New York: Kluwer Academic.

California v. Bradley Page, 2 Cal. App. 4th 161 (1991).

Conlon, E. (2004). *Blue blood*. New York: Riverhead Books.

Connery, D.S. (1977). *Guilty until proven innocent*. New York: Putnam's Sons.

Connors, E., Lundregan, T., Miller, N. & McEwen, T. (1996). *Convicted by juries, exonerated by science: Case studies in the use of DNA evidence to establish innocence after trial*. Washington, DC: Department of Justice.

Davis, D. (2004, February). *The road to perdition*. Paper presented at the California Attorneys for Criminal Justice, Monterey, CA.

Davis, D. & Follette, W.C. (2002). Rethinking probative value of evidence: Base rates, intuitive profiling and the postdiction of behavior. *Law and Human Behavior, 26*, 133–158.

Davis, D. & Follette, W.C. (2003). Toward an empirical approach to evidentiary ruling. *Law and Human Behavior, 27*, 661–684.

Davis, D. & Friedman, R.D. (in press). Memory for conversation: The orphan child of eyewitness researchers. In M.P. Toglia, J.D. Read, D.R. Ross and R.C.L. Lindsay (Eds), *Handbook of eyewitness memory (Vol. 1): Memory for events*. Mahwah, NJ: Erlbaum.

Davis, D., Kemmelmeier, M. & Follette, W.C. (2005). Conversational memory on trial. In Y.I. Noy and W. Karwowski (Eds), *Handbook of human factors in litigation* (pp. 12–29). New York: CRC Press.

Davis, D., Leo, R., Knaack, D. & Bailey, D. (2006). Sympathetic detectives with time limited offers: Effects on perceived consequences of confession. *Association for Psychological Science*, New York, NY.

Davis, D. & Loftus, E.F. (in press). Internal and external sources of distortion in adult witness memory. In M.P. Toglia, J.D. Read, D.R. Ross and R.C.L. Lindsay (Eds), *Handbook of eyewitness memory (Vol. 1): Memory for events*. Mahwah, NJ: Erlbaum.

Davis, D. & O'Donahue, W. (2004). The road to perdition: Extreme influence tactics in the interrogation room. In W. O' Donahue (Ed.), *Handbook of forensic psychology* (pp. 897–996). San Diego: Academic Press.

Drizin, S. & Colgan, B. (2004). Tales from the juvenile front: A guide to how standard police interrogation tactics can produce coerced and false confessions from juvenile suspects. In G.D. Lassiter (Ed.), *Interrogations, confessions, and entrapment* (pp. 127–162). New York: Kluwer Academic.

Drizin, S.A. & Leo, R.A. (2004). The problem of false confessions in the post-DNA world. *North Carolina Law Review*, 82, 891–1007.

Drizin, S.A. & Reich, M.J. (2004). Heeding the lessons of history: The need for mandatory recording of police interrogations to accurately assess the reliability and voluntariness of confessions. *Drake Law Review, 52*, 619–646.

Forrest, K.D., Wadkins, T.A. & Miller, R.L. (2002). The role of preexisting stress on false confessions: An empirical study. *Journal of Credibility Assessment and Witness Psychology. 3*, 23–45.

Geller, W.A. (1993). *Videotaping interrogations and confessions. National Institute of Justice: Research in Brief*. Washington, DC: US Department of Justice.

Grisso, T. (1998a). *Forensic evaluation of juveniles*. Sarasota, FL: Professional Resources.

Grisso, T. (1998b). *Instruments for assessing understanding and appreciation of Miranda rights*. Sarasota, FL: Professional Resources.

Gudjonsson, G.H. (2003). *The psychology of interrogations and confessions*. New York: John Wiley & Sons, Inc.

Hartwig, M., Granhag, P.A., Strömwall, L.A. & Vrij, A. (2004). Police officers' lie detection accuracy: Interrogating freely vs observing video. *Police Quarterly*, 7, 429–456.

Holmberg, U. & Christianson, S.A. (2002). Murderers' and sexual offenders' experiences of police interviews and their inclination to admit and deny crimes. *Behavioral Sciences and the Law, 20*, 31–45.

Horselenberg, R., Merckelbach, H. & Josephs, S. (2003). Individual differences and false confessions: A conceptual replication of Kassin and Keichel (1996). *Psychology, Crime and Law, 9*, 1–8.

Inbau, F.E., Reid, J.E., Buckley, J.P. & Jayne, B. (2001). *Criminal interrogation and confessions* (4th ed.). Maryland: Aspen Publishers.

Jayne, B.C. & Buckley, J.P. (1992). Criminal interrogation techniques on trial. *Security Management, 36*, 64–67.

Kamisar, Y. (1980). *Police interrogation and confessions: Essays in law and policy.* Ann Arbor: University of Michigan Press.

Kamisar, Y., LaFave, W., Israel, J. & King, N.J. (2005). *Modern criminal procedure: Cases, comments and questions* (11th ed.). St Paul, MN: West.

Kassin, S.M. (1997). The psychology of confession evidence. *American Psychologist, 52*(3), 221–233.

Kassin, S.M. (2002, November 1). False confessions and the jogger case. *The New York Times.*

Kassin, S. (2005). On the psychology of confessions: Does innocence put innocents at risk? *American Psychologist, 60*, 215–228.

Kassin, S.M. & Fong, C.T. (1999). "I'm innocent!": Effects of training on judgments of truth and deception in the interrogation room. *Law and Human Behavior, 23*, 499–516.

Kassin, S.M. & Gudjonsson, G.H. (2004). The psychology of confessions: A review of the literature and issues. *Psychological Science in the Public Interest, 5*, 33–67.

Kassin, S.M. & Kiechel, K.L. (1996). The social psychology of false confessions: Compliance, internalization & confabulation. *Psychological Science, 7*, 125–128.

Kassin, S.M. & McNall, K. (1991). Police interrogations and confessions: Communicating promises and threats by pragmatic implication. *Law and Human Behavior, 15*, 233–251.

Kassin, S.M. & Norwick, R.J. (2004). Why people waive their Miranda rights: The power of innocence. *Law and Human Behavior, 28*, 211–221.

Lassiter, G.D. & Greers, A.L. (2004a). Bias and accuracy in the evaluation of confession evidence. In G.D. Lassiter (Ed.), *Interrogations, confessions, and entrapment.* New York: Kluwer Academic.

Lassiter, G.D. & Greers, A.L. (2004b). Evaluation of confession evidence: Effects of presentation format. In G.D. Lassiter (Ed.), *Interrogations, confessions, and entrapment.* New York: Kluwer Academic.

Lassiter, G.D., Greers, A.L., Munhall, P.J., Handley, I.M. & Beers, M.J. (2001). Videotaped confessions: Is guilt in the eye of the camera? In M.P. Zanna (Ed.), *Advances in experimental social psychology* (Vol. 33, pp. 189–254). San Diego: Academic Press.

Leo, R.A. (1996a). Inside the interrogation room. *Journal of Criminal Law and Criminology, 86*, 266–303.

Leo, R.A. (1996b). The impact of Miranda revisited. *Journal of Criminal Law and Criminology, 86*, 621–692.

Leo, R.A. (2001). False confessions: Causes, consequences and solutions. In S.D. Westervelt (Ed.), *Wrongly convicted: Perspectives on failed justice* (pp. 36–54). Newark, NJ: Rutgers University Press.

Leo, R.A. & Ofshe, R.J. (1998). The consequences of false confessions: Deprivations of liberty and miscarriages of justice in the age of psychological interrogation. *Journal of Criminal Law and Criminology, 88*, 429–496.

Leo, R.A. & Ofshe, R.J. (2001). The truth about false confessions and advocacy scholarship. *Criminal Law Bulletin, 37*, 293–370.

Leo, R.A. & White, W.S. (1999). Adapting to Miranda: Modern interrogators' strategies for dealing with the obstacles posed by Miranda. *Minnesota Law Review, 84*, 397–472.

Loftus, E. and Ketcham (1991). *Witness for the defense*. New York: St. Martin's Press.

Lykken, D.T. (1998). *Tremor in the blood: Uses and abuses of the lie detector*. New York: Plenum.

Meissner, C.A. & Kassin, S.M. (2002). "He's guilty!": Investigator bias in judgments of truth and deception. *Law and Human Behavior, 26*, 469–480.

Meissner, C.A. & Kassin, S.M. (2004). "You're guilty, so just confess!" Cognitive and behavioral confirmation biases in the interrogation room. In G.D. Lassiter (Ed.), *Interrogations, confessions, and entrapment* (pp. 85–106). New York: Kluwer Academic.

Morgan, C.A., III, Hazlett, G., Doran, A., Garrett, S., Hoyt, G., Thomas, P., et al. (2004). Accuracy of eyewitness memory for persons encountered during exposure to highly intense stress. *International Journal of Law and Psychiatry, 27*, 265–279.

Moston, S., Stephenson, G.M. & Williamson, T.M. (1992). The effects of case characteristics on suspect behavior during questioning. *British Journal of Criminology, 32*, 23–40.

Nickerson, R.S. (1998). Confirmation bias: A ubiquitous phenomenon in many guises. *Review of General Psychology, 2*, 175–220.

Oakland Police Department (1998).

Ofshe, R.J. & Leo, R.A. (1997a). The social psychology of police interrogation: The theory and classification of true and false confessions. *Studies in Law, Politics and Society, 16*, 189–251.

Ofshe, R.J. & Leo, R.A. (1997b). The decision to confess falsely: Rational choice and irrational action. *Denver University Law Review, 74*, 979–1122.

O'Sullivan, M. & Ekman, P. (2004). The wizards of deception detection. In P.A. Granhag & L.A. Strömwall (Eds), *Deception detection in forensic contexts* (pp. 269–286). Cambridge: Cambridge University Press.

Radelet, M.L., Bedau, H.A. & Putnam, C.E. (1992). *In spite of innocence: Erroneous convictions in capital cases*. Boston: Northeastern University Press.

Redlich, A.D. & Goodman, G.S. (2003). Taking responsibility for an act not committed: The influence of age and suggestibility. *Law and Human Behavior, 27*(2), 141–156.

Risinger, D.M., Saks, M.J., Thompson, W.C. & Rosenthal, R. (2002). The Daubert/Kumho implications of observer effects in forensic science: Hidden problems of expectation and suggestion. *California Law Review, 90*, 1–56.

Ross, L.D. (1977). The intuitive psychologist and his shortcomings: Distortions in the attribution process. In L. Berkowitz (Ed.), *Advances in experimental social psychology* (Vol. 10, pp. 173–220). New York: Academic Press.

Russano, M.B., Meissner, C.A., Narchet, F.M. & Kassin, S.M. (2005). Investigating true and false confessions within a novel experimental paradigm. *Psychological Science, 16*(6), 481–486.

Sauer, M. (2004). Former detective won't say Tuite was overlooked. *Union-Tribune*, p. B1.

Scheck, B., Neufield, P. & Dwyer, J. (2000). *Actual innocence*. Garden City, NY: Doubleday.

Senese, L.C. (2005). *Anatomy of interrogation themes: The Reid technique of interviewing and interrogation*. Chicago: John Reid Assoc.

State of New Jersey *v.* Patrick Free, 798 A.2d 83 (NJ 2002).

Sullivan, T.P. (2004). *Police experiences with recording custodial interrogations*. Chicago: Center on Wrongful Convictions, Northwestern University School of Law.

Tracey, P. (2003). *Who killed Stephanie Crowe?* Dallas: Brown.

United States *v.* Hall, 93 F.3d 1337 (7th Cir. 1996).

United States *v.* Hall, 974 F. Supp. 1198 (1997).

Vanous, S. & Davis, D. (2002). *Murder scripts: Perceived motives and means for spouse murder.* Salt Lake City: Rocky Mountain Psychological Association.

Vrij, A. (2000). *Detecting lies and deceit: The psychology of lying and the implications for professional practice.* Chichester: John Wiley & Sons, Ltd.

Vrij, A. (2004). Why professionals fail to catch liars and how they can improve. *Legal and Criminological Psychology, 9,* 159–181.

Vrij, A. & Mann, S. (2001). Who killed my relative? Police officers' ability to detect real-life high stakes lies. *Psychology, Crime and Law, 7,* 119–132.

Warden, R. (2003). *The role of false confessions in Illinois: Wrongful murder convictions since 1970.* Chicago: Center on Wrongful Convictions, Northwestern University School of Law.

White, W.S. (2001a). *Miranda's waning protections.* Ann Arbor: Michigan University Press.

White, W.S. (2001b). Miranda's failure to restrain pernicious interrogation practices. *Michigan Law Review, 99,* 1211–1247.

CHAPTER 8

Offender Profiling: Limits and Potential

LAURENCE ALISON AND MARK R. KEBBELL

Typically, the aim of an offender profile has been to determine an offender's likely characteristics by analysing the way in which he or she committed a particular crime, thus helping the police to identify the perpetrator (Blau, 1994). For example, Douglas, Ressler, Burgess and Hartman (1986) describe offender profiling as "a technique for identifying the major personality and behavioral characteristics of an individual based upon an analysis of the crimes he or she has committed" (p. 405). Further, according to Pinizzotto and Finkel (1990), an offender profile "... focuses attention on individuals with personality traits that parallel traits of others who have committed similar offences" (p. 216). The aim of this chapter is to outline how offender profiles have, until very recently, been constructed, and to illustrate the theoretical underpinnings that these views have traditionally relied upon. This chapter will also evaluate the effectiveness of typical approaches to offender profiling, and identify the ways in which more recent developments have sought to improve the scientific status of profiles and their effectiveness.

THE CONSTRUCTION OF OFFENDER PROFILES

Many statements concerning offender profiling tend to attribute behaviours to underlying, relatively context-free dispositional traits of the offender. As is the case with traditional trait theories (Mischel, 1968),

Practical Psychology for Forensic Investigations and Prosecutions.
Edited by Mark R. Kebbell and Graham M. Davies. © 2006 John Wiley & Sons, Ltd.

most forms of offender profiling make general predictions about offenders from their crime scene behaviours, assume that most offenders' behaviours are affected in predictable ways and suggest that offenders' behaviours remain stable in the face of different environmental influences (Alison, Bennell, Mokros & Ormerod, 2002).

The assumption regarding primary dispositional traits is that they are stable and general, in that they determine a person's inclination to act consistently in a particular and stable way across a variety of situations. In the case of profiling, these traits are inferred from crime scene actions. For example, if a crime is particularly violent, it may be concluded that the offender is particularly aggressive. Similarly, aggressive offenders would be expected to commit any given crime in a particularly violent way. Thus, traits are both inferred from and explained by behaviour.

Perhaps the most frequently cited theory of offence behaviour, which is consistent with this simple model, is exemplified in the Federal Bureau of Investigation's (FBI) suggestion of differences between "organized" and "disorganized" offenders (Douglas et al., 1986). This model suggests, for example, that offenders will vary according to the degree of "organizational control" over a victim, and this will also reflect a stable trait emergent in other features of the offender's life. Therefore, the "traditional" profilers will argue that factors such as social maturity, intelligence and previous convictions can all be "profiled" on the basis of the level of organization observed at the crime scene (Alison et al., 2002).

The propositions described in these last two examples, that clusters of specific characteristics about the offender can be derived from examining crime scene actions, are not unique. Indeed, many of the most widely recognized and frequently employed experts in the UK, the US and several other European countries have made similar claims (Åsgard, 1998; Boon, 1997; Douglas, Burgess, Burgess & Ressler, 1992; Douglas et al., 1986). They reflect the widely held belief that the same behavioural dispositions that determine the style of crime scene behaviour of the offender are reflected in more general, non-offence behaviour patterns in the individual's general life. In fact, some profiling advice claims that these dispositions are linked directly with certain demographic features. This process is illustrated in a quotation from Douglas et al. (1992) where they state that "...[t]he crime scene is presumed to reflect the murderer's behavior and personality in much the same way as furnishings reveal the homeowner's character" (p. 21).

In their comparative study of profilers, groups of homicide detectives, psychologists and students, Pinizzotto and Finkel (1990) described five steps that lead to profiling inferences. They state that professional profilers: (i) assess the type of criminal act with reference to individuals who have committed similar acts previously; (ii) thoroughly analyse the crime scene; (iii) scrutinize the background of the victim as well as any possible suspects; and (iv) establish the likely motivations of all parties involved. Finally, a description of the perpetrator is generated as the fifth step, from the characteristics supposedly connected with such an individual's "psychological make-up" (p. 216).

It is argued that the inferential process accomplished in the five steps described above can be represented in the question series "What to Why to Who" (Pinizzotto & Finkel, 1990). Based on the crime scene material (What), a particular motivation for the offence behaviour is attributed to the perpetrator (Why). This, in turn, leads to the description of the perpetrator's likely characteristics (Who). This simple "What to Why to Who" inference assumes that the supposed specific motivations that drive the initiation of the offence, are consistently associated with specific types of background characteristics of the offender (e.g., "... if motivation X then characteristics A, B, C and D"). This particular approach to profiling is limited and problematic because it is not clear how a profiler moves from one point to the next (i.e., what rules of thumb connect each inferential leap) (Pinizzotto & Finkel, 1990). Moreover, profilers commonly do not specify which (if any) behavioral, correlational or psychological principles they rely on. Therefore labels such as "organized" and "disorganized" (Ressler, Burgess, Douglas, Hartman & D'Agostino, 1986) may simply be the result of a readiness to attribute a latent trait to a set of crime scene behaviours, despite the lack of clear evidence for the existence of such traits or factors. Finally, some profilers appear to engage in little more than what one would expect from detective work, i.e., generating logical, deductive inferences from what is known about the crime scene (McNamara, 2005). Thus, while such inferential processes are, in themselves, interesting aspects of decision making and situational awareness, they are not scientific contributions.

ASSUMPTIONS UNDERLYING OFFENDER PROFILING

There are two key assumptions that underpin the profiling methods outlined so far. The first is that the actions of any given offender are consistent across offences. That is to say, the behavioural variation across offences for a particular offender is smaller than the behavioural variation between different offenders. This has been called the "consistency assumption" (Mokros & Alison, 2002). Clearly, if the behaviour of the same offender varied more than between offenders it would not be logical to look for behavioural indicators of the same person committing multiple crimes. The second assumption is that similar offence styles have to be associated with similar offender background characteristics.

To use the previous example, aggressive individuals are expected to be aggressive both in the way they commit offences and in the way they live their day-to-day life. This is called the "homology assumption" (Mokros & Alison, 2002).

Offenders' behavioural consistency can be defined as the repetition of particular aspects of behaviour when the same offender engages in the same type of offence (Canter, 1995). Numerous studies have provided some support for the notion of offender consistency. For example, 1 study examined the consistency of behaviours displayed by different burglars of residential properties (Green, Booth & Biderman, 1976). Based on 14 aspects of the crimes, such as "location of entry", "method of entry" and "value of property taken", Green and his colleagues were able to use cluster analysis to assign accurately 14 out of 15 cases of burglary to the 3 actual perpetrators. Mokros and Alison (2002) investigated the behavioural consistency of 100 British male stranger rapists of which 39 were serial rapists. The offenders' offence behaviour was coded including, for example, their style of attack, their use of violence and the sexual acts they performed. The results indicated that there were lower levels of variance within a series of offences than between random sets of offences, which supports the idea of behavioural consistency.

The homology assumption has been demonstrated by Davies, Wittebrood and Jackson (1998) and House (1997) who observed the relationship between previous convictions and certain crime scene actions of rapists. Davies et al. (1998) used odds ratios and base rates (i.e., probabilities derived from percentages), and House (1997) reported percentages, to describe the relationship between pairs of crime scene actions and previous convictions. Davies et al. (1998) noted that offenders who display awareness of forensic procedures by destroying or removing semen, have a likelihood of a previous conviction for a sexual offence which is almost four times higher than those offenders who do not take such precautions.

These simple relationships between a given action and a given characteristic are very different from the far more ambitious accounts that are often referred to by practitioners and researchers in the profiling field (e.g., see Blau, 1994; Douglas et al., 1986; Pinizzotto & Finkel, 1990). In these latter ambitious cases, attempts are made to profile clusters of background features from crime scene actions to develop a psychological profile of the offender. They are concerned with multiple forms of prediction, in which particular configurations or sets of actions are linked to particular sets of characteristics. When tested, however, the results of this ambitious approach to profiling are not very promising.

For example, in the study by Davies et al. (1998) the integration of a range of crime scene actions as predictors within logistic regression models, failed to show a substantial improvement over the information obtained through simple base rates in the majority of instances. Similarly, in the study by House (1997), the 50 rapists in his sample appeared relatively homogeneous with respect to their criminal histories, regardless of whether they acted in a primarily aggressive, pseudo-intimate, instrumental/criminal or sadistic manner during the sexual assault. Similarly, the previously mentioned study by Mokros and Alison (2002) also showed no relationship between specific rape behaviours and subsets of offender background characteristics.

The readiness to invoke dispositions rather than to explain behaviour in terms of situational influences, may explain this disparity between intuitive offender profiling and empirical findings, or in other words, the disparity between an intuitive belief within most people that behaviour is cross-situationally consistent versus much empirical evidence that suggests it is not (Bem & Allen, 1974). Bem and Allen (1974) have called this disparity "the personality paradox", and according to their observations, individuals are prone to infer stable dispositions from behaviour even though evidence has consistently demonstrated that global trait constructs fail to accurately predict behaviour over time and across specific situations. Further, as Alison et al. (2002) point out,

> Most varieties of offence behavior for which profiling may be of relevance involve intense, relatively short-lived and potentially traumatic interactions that are generally characterized by the diametrically opposed interests of the offender and victim. Therefore, the influence of situational factors and the role of the victim should not be neglected, and a theoretical framework that emphasizes the importance of person _ situation interactions in generating behavior may provide a more productive model for offender profiling (p. 123).

From this perspective, the fact that situational factors are so important means that making accurate attributions concerning an offender will be difficult. Thus, it is to be expected that offender profiles are likely to not be particularly accurate when evaluated.

THE UTILITY OF OFFENDER PROFILES

Typically, evaluations of offender profiling have focused on post hoc assessments of accuracy, based on the degree to which police officers claimed they were satisfied with the advice that they received. For example, a number of reviews of profiling have been carried out based primarily on the opinions of detectives about its utility (Britton, 1992; Copson, 1995; Douglas, 1981; Goldblatt, 1992; Jackson, Van Koppen & Herbrink, 1993). Broadly, all of these reviews have concluded that investigators approved of the advice given, and in various ways found it useful. However, none of these reviews are definitive and all were somewhat limited in the extent to which they were able to obtain a representative sample of profiles. They were also limited by the fact that they relied almost entirely on the subjective opinions of the investigators subsequent to the conclusion of the case.

In contrast, Alison, Smith, Eastman and Rainbow (2003) used Toulmin's (1958) philosophy of argument to assess the appropriateness of 21 offender profiles primarily from the US and the UK but also including 3 other European countries. Toulmin suggested that strong arguments should contain 6 interrelated components: (i) the claim; (ii) the strength of the claim; (iii) the grounds supporting the claim; (iv) the warrant; (v) the backing; and (vi) the rebuttal. For example, if it is suggested in an offender profile that, "the murderer is under 30 years of age" this represents the claim. In order to substantiate this claim certain components must be present. The first involves the strength of the claim, for example, whether this claim is "possible", "probable" or "definite". The grounds are the support for the claim argument, in this example it could be that "the majority of offenders who murder women under 25 years of age are under 30 years of age themselves". The warrant authorizes the grounds, for example, citing specific research. Finally, the rebuttal allows the consideration of conditions in which the claim ceases to be likely. Thus, if further evidence becomes known the claim may have to be adjusted accordingly, for example, if the victim's partner is over 30 and has a history of spousal abuse against the victim, then the victim's partner should also be considered to be a strong potential suspect.

While not definitive, the profiles included in Alison et al.'s (2003) study included many prominent profiling figures' work. The profiles yielded 3 090 statements that were examined as units of text for coding. The mean average number of statements per profile was 147. Of these, 25% were statements about the characteristics of the offender, while the remaining 75% included repetition of the details of what occurred in the offence (factual statements already known by the police), references to the profiler's competence (affiliation and background), or caveats about using the material in the investigation. Of the 780 statements that were claims made about the characteristics of the offender, 92% were unsubstantiated and lacked backing. That is, in terms of Toulmin's system, they involved simply a claim with no form of justification at all. Just under 5% (38 statements) included some grounds for the claim, 1.4% (11) involved illogical grounds for the claim and just under 1.5% (12 statements) also incorporated a warrant with backing as well as the grounds.

These results demonstrate that the overwhelming majority of profilers' statements made about the offender were not discussed in terms of any grounds, warrants or backing to support the claim. In other words, over 80% were unsubstantiated. Moreover, only 12 statements in the entire set (just over 1%) included the full gamut of the Toulminian framework. Significantly, these same statements were also all falsifiable and nine of these statements were from one profile. Just over 15% included some substantiation, although 13 of the 21 profilers' reports contained fewer than five substantiated statements. Over 50% of the statements were unverifiable (e.g., he will fantasize about coercive sex) while just under 45% were verifiable (e.g., he will live with his mother).

Thus, the majority of these profiles can be defined as not actually having anything to do with outlining the characteristics of the offender and a majority of claims were made (either intentionally or unintentionally) without any justification. Of course it could be the case that the authors of the profiles simply did not include the support for their assertions, although given the available literature, another possibility is that there exists no justification for their claims – they are simply opinions based on supposition. If so, they are at best, as useful as any detective opinion or, at worst, potentially dangerous because they carry the presumed weight of an expert opinion but are not formulated with recourse to either (a) any body of research or (b) a credible level of relevant experience.

However, if this were the case, this raises the question, "If offender profiles were not useful, why would police officers who have used them rate them as useful?" (Britton, 1992; Copson, 1995; Douglas, 1981; Goldblatt, 1992; Jackson et al., 1993). Here the " Barnum effect" is relevant in relation to the statement by the circus entrepreneur that his circus included "a little something for everyone". Studies have shown that participants tend to view generalized summaries as accurate summaries of their own personalities. For example, in several experiments participants were required to complete a personality inventory and a few days later they were given a personality report in an envelope. Unknown to them, all participants received the same report (e.g., including information such as "at times you are extraverted, affable, sociable, while at other times you are introverted, wary, reserved"). Most said the description fitted them fairly well (Forer, 1949). It is possible then that a contributory factor in the perception of usefulness of profiles can be explained by a willingness to selectively fit ambiguous, unverifiable information from the profile to the offender. Therefore, after a suspect has been apprehended, or if the investigating officer has a type of offender in mind, it is possible that the inquiry team engage in an inferential process that validates the profile.

To test this hypothesis Alison, Smith and Morgan (2003) conducted a study to investigate the hypothesis that the Barnum effect might account for favourable assessments of offender profiles. Their first study used bogus profiles of an offender who had killed a young boy, with two distinctly different offender profiles given to each of two groups of police officers. Over half of both groups classified their profile as accurate, and despite distinct differences between the two offender profiles, there were no differences in accuracy ratings of either profile. This study lends preliminary support to the hypothesis that individuals tend to construct their own meaning around ambiguous statements about a third party within the context of profiling.

IMPROVING THE UTILITY OF OFFENDER PROFILES

So far, the research presented gives a somewhat negative picture of profiling, and it certainly seems to be the case that our current scientific knowledge concerning inferring characteristics of offenders from their actions in committing a crime is limited and in particular, offender profiles have the potential to mislead an enquiry. Nevertheless, there are a number of ways in which offender profiling can (and has) provide(d) useful information, and importantly, improve the future utility of offender profiles. We use a case example to illustrate this and set out a template for a useful offender profile. The case example involves the abduction, sexual assault and murder of a 12-year-old girl, a missing 14-year-old girl who may have been abducted and murdered, and an unknown young girl whose naked body had been found near to where the 12-year-old's body was found and the 14-year-old went missing. This case is described in detail by Alison, Goodwill and Alison (2005) and the reader is referred to this source for more detail (for a different case example using a similar systematic approach, see Alison, West & Goodwill, 2004). The following information presents only an overview of the above-mentioned case example.

First of all, the profile includes basic information such as the names and addresses of the authors and the instructions that were given to the authors for providing the report. A caveat is then provided. This states that the profile is not intended to point towards the guilt or innocence of an individual, rather it is intended to be an investigative tool to be used at the investigating team's discretion. Further, an acknowledgement of the limitations of the methodologies used is included because as Alison, West and Goodwill (2004) point out,

> Psychologists cannot assume that police officers seeking their advice know what the profiling process consists of, or of the methodology of that profiler, or on which scientific principles it purports to be based. It is essential that its limitations are understood and accepted both by the police and profilers involved in any investigation, otherwise advice could seriously mislead an inquiry, wasting valuable time and resources, as well as jeopardizing a suspect's liberty (p. 78).

Next, the profile includes information concerning the author's competence. Often the inquiry team may be embarrassed about asking this directly so it should be included as a matter of course, again to allow a critical approach to be taken to the credibility of the profile and the author. After outlining the instructions, caveats and competence, the authors consider the case at hand, moving on to the material upon which claims are made. We will use a couple of examples next but for space reasons we are not able to include most details. Importantly, the sources of data described below were included in the profile to show the reason for the assertions and where the data had come from.

For the confirmed sexual murder, it is possible to suggest that it is unlikely that the murderer is a family member, and there is a much greater chance that the offender is a stranger or acquaintance of the victim. Sexual assault is highly unlikely to precede the murder of a child by a parent. The data to back up this assertion comes from the Bureau of Justice in the US that reports that when a person under 12 is murdered a family member is the most likely suspect (Greenfield, 1997). However, when family members killed their children the rate of sexual assault occurring prior to death was 1%. Due to the lack of forensic evidence found at the site where the body was disposed of for both the 12-year-old girl and the unidentified body, it is likely that the victims were assaulted at another location from where they were discovered. This suggests that the attack location is likely to be indoors (including in a vehicle). In the UK the CATCHEM database of sexual murders of female children aged between 6 to 21, and where the body was transported, suggest in 53% of cases the offence was committed by a killer who is a stranger to the victim, in 39% of cases the offence was committed by a friend or acquaintance, and in 9% of cases the offence involved the family.

The vast majority of the offenders in the CATCHEM study lived within 5 miles of the point of contact with the victim, 95% had their residence there, 3% had work, previous residence, or relatives within a 5-mile radius of the point of encounter suggesting the offender is likely to live nearby. A review of the CATCHEM database of sexually motivated murders in the UK shows that 44% of offenders who murder female victims under the age of 18 and transport the victim's body are married at the time of the offence. Thus, married men should not be ruled out as significantly less likely than single males or males with partners.

The offender is likely to have a previous criminal history, including sexual offences and more general criminality such as convictions for theft and dishonesty. Thus the investigation of sexually motivated homicides of abducted children, especially pubescent children, should not be limited to or even automatically focused on individuals with a history of sex offences against children. For example, Canter and Kirby

(1995) examined the prior convictions of 416 detected child sex offenders and report that contrary to popular belief, child molesters did not have an exclusive offence history relating to assaults on children; 44% had previous criminal convictions of which 86% were for dishonesty. Goetting (1990) examined the case details of 93 incidents of child homicide in Detroit, USA, and found the majority had an established criminal history. The implication of this is that the offender is already likely to be known to the police and likely to be in police records.

Prentky et al. (1991) found that child abductors motivated by a drive for sexual gratification had committed an average of four previous sexual offences. Greenfield (1997) further identified this recidivist feature of sexually motivated child abduction, finding that offenders convicted for the forcible rape or sexual assault of a child were more than twice as likely to have other victims than sexual offenders of adults. Thus, in cases of child abduction it is not uncommon for the offender to commit several offences.

The implications of this profile are reasonably clear. The offender is likely to be a stranger or an acquaintance of the murdered child, and is likely to live within five miles of where they first made contact with the child. The offender is likely to be single, but married men should not be ruled out either, as there is also a good chance that he is married. There is a strong likelihood the offender has a criminal record although this is not inevitable. Further, there is a reasonable possibility the offences are linked.

While only a somewhat cursory outline has been given of this case example, several points should be immediately clear. First, a much more critical approach by an inquiry team to an offender profile is encouraged. The caveat and outline of competence encourage this, but perhaps more importantly, the fact that the data on which the profile is based is outlined, means the reader is able to determine *why* comments have been made and on what bases they rest. The fact that statements are backed up by data means if the profile is not supported by data, or indeed, unsupportable by data, this becomes painfully obvious with this approach. In this respect this style of profile is much more able to withstand scrutiny from Toulmin's philosophy of argument and in turn this sheds light on the abilities of the author.

Furthermore, the presentation of data in this way means that alternative hypotheses are not ruled out. For example, although it is likely that the offender is a stranger or an acquaintance of the murdered child, the data presented does indicate that it is far from unheard of for the offender to be a family member, although this is unusual. This approach is also verifiable. Popper (1963) argues that for a science to progress, the theories underpinning that science must be refutable. As Alison et al. (2003) point out, much of what offender profiles have typically included has been unverifiable (e.g., the offender will be angry or socially immature). Contrast this with the information in the example profile, which includes factors such as marital status, offending history, place of residence, all of which can be verified. Furthermore the reasons for assertions are mapped out. Thus, if the profile is not accurate, reasons for this can be explored, for example, maybe European child abductors behave differently from US child abductors and so results from the US cannot be generalized to Europe and vice versa.

CONCLUSIONS

Offender profiling has considerable potential to help in the identification of offenders and in the linking of offences. Unfortunately, due to the fact that the way an offence is committed is so dependent on situational factors, particularly the response of the victim, any attempt at extrapolating precise details concerning the offender from the way the offence was committed, is always likely to be an inexact science. Fortunately, the utility of offender profiles can be improved in future, simply by applying an appropriate caveat and using data to inform a profile. Once these changes have been taken into consideration, offender profiling has the potential to take one of the tools at the disposal of an inquiry team.

REFERENCES

Alison, L.J., Bennell, C., Mokros, A. & Ormerod, D. (2002). The personality paradox in offender profiling: A theoretical review of the processes involved in deriving background characteristics from crime scene actions. *Psychology, Public Policy, and Law, 8*, 115–135.

Alison, L.J., Goodwill, A. & Alison, E. (2005). Guidelines for profilers. In L.J. Alison (Ed.), *The forensic psychologist's casebook* (pp. 235–277). Culmcott: Willan.

Alison, L.J., Smith, M.D., Eastman, O. & Rainbow, L. (2003). Toulmin's philosophy of argument and its relevance to Offender Profiling. *Journal of Psychology, Crime and Law, 9*(2), 173–181.

Alison, L.J., Smith, M.D. & Morgan, K. (2003). Interpreting the accuracy of offender profiles. *Psychology, Crime and Law, 9*, 185–195.

Alison, L.J., West, A. & Goodwill, A. (2004). The academic and the practitioner: Pragmatists' views of offender profiling. *Psychology, Public Policy, and Law, 10*, 71–101.

Åsgard, U. (1998). Swedish experiences in offender profiling and evaluation of some aspects of a case of murder and abduction in Germany. In Case Analysis Unit (BKA) (Eds), *Method of case analysis: An international symposium* (pp. 125–130). Weisbaden: Bundeskriminalamt Kriminalistisches Institut.

Bem, D.J. & Allen, A. (1974). On predicting some of the people some of the time: The search for cross-situational consistencies in behavior. *Psychological Review, 81*, 506–520.

Blau, T.H. (1994). Psychological profiling. In T.H. Blau (Ed.), *Psychological services for law enforcement* (pp. 261–274). New York: John Wiley and Sons, Inc.

Boon, J. (1997). Contribution of personality theories to psychological profiling. In J.L. Jackson & D.A. Bekarian (Eds), *Offender profiling: Theory, research and practice* (pp. 43–59). Chichester: John Wiley & Sons, Ltd.

Britton, P. (1992). *Review of offender profiling*. London: Home Office.

Canter, D.V. (1995). Psychology of offender profiling. In R. Bull and D. Carson (Eds), *Handbook of psychology in legal contexts* (pp. 343–355). Chichester: John Wiley and Sons, Ltd.

Canter, D. and Kirby, S. (1995). Prior convictions of child molesters. *Science and Justice, 35*, 73–78.

Copson, G. (1995). *Coals to Newcastle (Part 1): A study of offender profiling*. London: Home Office (Police Research Group).

Davies, A., Wittebrood, K. & Jackson, J.L. (1998). *Predicting the criminal record of a stranger rapist*. London: Home Office, Policing and Reducing Crime Unit.

Douglas, J.E. (1981). *Evaluation of the (FBI) psychological profiling program*. Unpublished manuscript.

Douglas, J.E., Burgess, A.W., Burgess, A.G. & Ressler, R.K. (1992). *Crime classification manual: A standard system for investigating and classifying violent crime*. New York: Simon and Schuster.

Douglas, J.E., Ressler, R.K., Burgess, A.W. & Hartman, C.R. (1986). Criminal profiling from crime scene analysis. *Behavioral Sciences and the Law, 4*, 401–421.

Forer, B.R. (1949). The fallacy of personal validation: A classroom demonstration of gullibility. *Journal of Abnormal and Social Psychology, 44*, 118–123.

Goetting, A. (1990). Child victims of homicide: A portrait of their killers and their circumstances of their deaths. *Violence and Victims, 5*, 287–296.

Goldblatt, P. (1992). *Psychological offender profiles: How psychologists can help the police with their enquiries*. Unpublished manuscript.

Green, E.J., Booth, C.E. & Biderman, M.D. (1976). Cluster analysis of burglary MOs. *Journal of Police Science and Administration, 4*, 382–388.

Greenfield, L. (1997). *Sex offences and offenders: An analysis of data on rape and sexual assault*. US Department of Justice, Office of Justice Programs, Bureau of Justice Statistics.

House, J.C. (1997). Towards a practical application of offender profiling: The RNC's criminal suspect prioritization system. In J.L. Jackson & D.A. Bekerian (Eds), *Offender profiling: Theory, research and practice* (pp. 177–190). Chichester: John Wiley and Sons, Ltd.

Jackson, J.L., Van Koppen, P.J. & Herbrink, C.M. (1993). *Does the service meet the needs: An evaluation of consumer satisfaction with specific profile analysis and investigative advice as offered by the Scientific Research Advisory Unit of the National Criminal Intelligence Division (CRI), The Netherlands*. Unpublished manuscript.

McNamara, J., (2005). *Case study example of the use of FBI approaches to profiling*. AGIS Conferences (6–8 September). Dublin, Ireland.

Mischel, W. (1968). *Personality and assessment*. New York: John Wiley and Sons, Inc.

Mokros, A. & Alison, L. (2002). Is offender profiling possible? Testing the predicted homology of crime scene actions and background characteristics in a sample of rapists. *Journal of Legal and Criminological Psychology*, 7, 25–43.

Pinizzotto, A.J. & Finkel, N.J. (1990). Criminal personality profiling: An outcome and process study. *Law and Human Behavior*, 14, 215–233.

Popper, K. (1963). *Conjectures and Refutations: The Growth of Scientific Knowledge*. London: Routledge.

Prentky, R.A., Knight, R.A., Burgess, A.W., Ressler, R., Campbell, J. & Lanning, K.V. (1991). Child molesters who abduct. *Violence and Victims*, 6, 213–224.

Ressler, R.K., Burgess, A.W., Douglas, J.E., Hartman, C.R. & D'Agostino, R.B. (1986). Sexual killers and their victims: Identifying patterns through crime scene analysis . *Journal of Interpersonal Violence, 1*, 288–308.

Toulmin, S. (1958). *The Uses of Argument*. Cambridge: Cambridge University Press.

CHAPTER 9

Deciding to Prosecute

ELIZABETH GILCHRIST

This chapter outlines key factors affecting the decisions to prosecute offences, with particular reference to two prosecutorial systems in the UK. Considerations as to broader issues relating to evaluating the workings of a prosecution process are discussed. The stages of the processes are outlined and the influence of philosophy, structure, the working practices of the various professionals involved, factors relating to the victim, the defendant and other sources are considered. Systematic biases in the prosecution of offences, the implications for differential progress of categories of different types of cases, and differential treatment of categories of offenders and victims are considered.

To an extent, this chapter identifies many aspects of this stage of the criminal justice system which have yet to be fully addressed by forensic psychology but which are ripe for investigation by our discipline.

THE DECISION TO PROSECUTE

The decision to prosecute is likely not to be the first decision affecting the interaction between the criminal justice system and either the victim or the suspects. It is highly likely that there has been a previous decision to report an offence, a previous arrest decision, or some form of previous encounter which has an influence on what follows. The decision to prosecute is, however, a very important one as it has a critical effect on the likely outcome of the encounter with a formal criminal justice system and it has a great influence on perceptions of

Practical Psychology for Forensic Investigations and Prosecutions.
Edited by Mark R. Kebbell and Graham M. Davies. © 2006 John Wiley & Sons, Ltd.

fairness, justice and the utility of the system, by suspects and victims alike.

Over the past 20 years there have been significant changes in the structure of the decision to prosecute in England and Wales (Sanders, 1985b), which received attention within the criminal justice research literature and to a lesser extent within the criminological literature (Hall Williams, 1988). This work identified some key aspects and general issues surrounding the decision to prosecute in any system, worthy of further study. In the late 1980s, the National Audit Office (NAO) conducted research into both the workings of the English and Welsh and the Scottish prosecution systems and suggested that in terms of outcome, both systems were working appropriately. The NAO used conviction rates, acquittals at court, and in particular, directed acquittals, to assess the systems. The NAO identified, at that point, in England and Wales, only around 17% of contested trials resulted in an acquittal and less than 4% of those were directed acquittals, and in Scotland over half of contested trials resulted in a conviction and suggested that, on this basis, the prosecution systems were functioning correctly in terms of selecting and preparing cases for court (NAO, 1989a, 1989b). However the NAO also identified that there was considerable variation across both systems in terms of the percentages of cases which proceeded. In Scotland it was suggested that the rate varied from 2.5% no proceedings rate in some areas to a 25% rate in others (NAO, 1989b).

In England the Crown Prosecution Service (CPS) was also criticized on similar grounds, a wide variation in discontinuances across areas having been identified, but more than this, the CPS was also criticized for the fact that two-thirds of the cases were not discontinued until the first court hearing (NAO, 1989a). There were also suggestions that lack of information from the police and lack of consultation and feedback between the police and the prosecutor might also be considered problematic. At points, the prosecutors in England and Wales and in Scotland have been criticized for failing to discontinue cases (Gilchrist, 1995) and also for discontinuing too many cases (Crisp, Whittaker & Harris, 1994). The rate of nonprosecution has certainly varied. Work by the Scottish Consortium on Criminal Justice identified that the rate had varied between 7% in 1982 and 39% nonprosecution decisions in 1999 (Scottish Consortium on Criminal Justice, 2000).

The lack of consistency across areas and the difficulties in using convictions to assess prosecutorial practice (there are many reasons why a case which is properly pursued may not result in a conviction, and equally as many reasons why a case which should have been discontinued early in the process might result in a conviction of some sort), suggest that perhaps there are more appropriate measures for the evaluation of prosecution decisions.

It is of note that little forensic psychological research has focused around this area. Forensic psychology and indeed criminology has tended to focus more on the earlier interactions between police and suspects, exploring stop and search decisions and arrest decisions (McConville, Sanders & Leng, 1991; Reiner, 2000; Smith & Gray, 1983). Further work has considered factors influencing jury and judicial decision making, including the effect of factors such as expert evidence and risk assessments on juries (Guy & Edens, 2003; Schuller, 1992), and the impact of specific defence information, such as the insanity defence on juror decision making where jurors understanding of this defence was identified as limited (Ogloff, 1991), and the order of presentation of evidence on judicial decision making (Kerstholt & Jackson, 1999), but little has been directly applied to the decision to prosecute. Much of the previous work has included discussion of fairness, justice, openness and systematic bias and possible prejudice within the system (Corsianos, 2001). Indeed many so-called "extra-legal" factors have been identified which have been found to influence all of these stages and decisions, ranging from ethnicity of both victim and suspect, age of suspect, perceptions of socioeconomic status of both, (Geller & Toch, 1996; Tonry, 1995) to "worthiness" of the victim in terms of whether they could be seen as a deserving victim or not (Chambers & Miller, 1987; Greene & Dodge, 1995). Again little of this knowledge has been applied to the decision to prosecute by forensic psychologists.

It may be that the very specific issues raised by the decision to prosecute, the key role played by lawyers, and the importance of the legal roles and legal definitions, may heighten the importance of the consideration of broader contextual issues linking to jurisprudence and legal philosophies, which are of relevance in all legal contexts but thrown into sharper focus here. It may also be that the presentation of the decision as a purely legal one has greatly influenced the disciplines who have sought to explore this key decision point, notably legal and sociolegal scholars. However, it is highly likely that many of the factors seen to influence earlier and later parts of the system equally apply in this context and are worthy of further exploration by forensic psychologists and criminologists alike.

DUE PROCESS OR CRIME CONTROL

One of the first issues to identify in a critique of a process, particularly one within the criminal justice system, is what the key focus ought to be. Is there a notion of "fairness" or "justice" which ought to be employed as a measure against which the process can be measured, or should the question be focused around how effective the process is in terms of an outcome, for example crime prevention, or in terms of identifying and responding to perpetrators. One of the key distinctions within socio-legal approaches is the distinction between a "due process model" of criminal justice and a "crime control model" (Packer, 1968). While this may sound as if it is a philosophical question rather than a practical one, it is crucial for us to have an understanding of these issues for us to unpick some of the conflicts affecting the decision to prosecute, and for us to set appropriate standards against which such decisions could be evaluated.

With a "crime control" approach, the rules of the system and the "fair" functioning of the process would be subsumed by the needs for a practical and effective system of dealing with alleged offenders, which would result in an outcome-focused evaluation and be less concerned with bias and justice in the process. With a "due process" model the key issues relate to the appropriateness of all stages of the system, and the strength of any system is based in the clarity, fairness and inherent justice of all steps within the process. This would lead to the outcome of the process being less important than the system itself but could fail to meet the practical needs of criminal justice while serving the higher order desire for fairness.

This balancing between due process and crime control can be translated into a conflict between "expediency" and "legality", which is interesting to consider in terms of the smaller decision points involved in the prosecution process. This area can also be researched in terms of factors influencing these, and what this might mean in terms of "justice". Consideration can also be given to what requires challenge and change, and how this might be achieved.

Moran and Cooper (1983) have identified that there is a tension which can be seen as deriving from the fact that the prosecutor is "foremost an administrator" (and so pressure to deal with caseloads efficiently is high, resulting in pressure towards solutions such as the acceptance of negotiated pleas), but also has a duty to the public and to justice. This would suggest that prosecutorial practice may be more driven by a "crime control" model rather than a "due process" one, but what does it mean in terms of consistency, or fairness? And what might it mean in terms of bias and prejudice?

The use of shortcuts to deal with workload cannot be seen as surprising for psychologists; perhaps the more interesting issues to address would focus more around whether any of these shortcuts has a differential effect on any particular group, and some of the broader issues raised in relation to justice and fairness, such as "whose interests are served by the ways in which the rules are subverted to save time and to deal with the work?" Moran and Cooper (1983) identify that while most prosecutors will identify that they are making decisions in the public interest, as they put it, all too often their personal or individual interests frequently coincide with alleged societal interest. Balancing the scales of justice can come down to personal needs and wishes against the demands of a private organization.

Malcolm Feeley (1973) identified two competing approaches which might be applied to the study of organizations within the criminal justice system: the "rational goal approach" and the "functional-systems approach". Feeley (1973) suggests that a "functional-systems" approach may be more beneficial in explaining the behaviour of the actors involved, as it sees the formal rules of the system as being only one of the many influences shaping and controlling individuals' decisions, and suggests that the most interesting rules to study and those which are likely to be most influential are the "rules of the game" or "folkways" of the organization. It is within the "folkways" of prosecutorial practice across all jurisdictions that the integrity, fairness, biases and prejudices of the system will be found. It is those rules that forensic psychology needs to identify and to study, and where knowledge and methodology from within forensic psychology should be applied.

FOLKWAYS IN PROSECUTORIAL PROCESS

In comparing prosecutorial systems where the relative roles of the police and the prosecutors differ, the influence of working practice and "folkways" can be distinguished from the influence of a particular legal system or a "legal approach" to decision making, and likely sources of bias, reasons for lack of consistency and implications of these, can be more fully explored.

PROFESSIONALS INVOLVED, ROLES AND INDEPENDENCE

Within adversarial systems there are at least two major professional bodies involved in the decision to prosecute: the police and the prosecution authority. The relationship between these two bodies and their roles has been the subject of comment, research, criticism and to some extent controversy over the years (Ashworth, 1984; McConville et al., 1991; Sanders, 1986). One of the key tenets of prosecution authorities is that of independence. It was in independence that fairness from previous bias, protection for innocent suspects and appropriate responses to victims were to be found.

Traditionally the criminal justice systems of England and Wales and that of Scotland have varied quite considerably. Although both systems are fundamentally adversarial in nature, the English system has followed this philosophy more closely than its Scottish counterpart. The relatively recent introduction of an independent prosecution authority in England and Wales reflects this. The different roles of the police and the prosecutor within the two systems results in slightly different approaches to the prosecution of offences, and the comparisons highlight how underlying philosophies and organizational cultures affect these decisions.

When the CPS in England and Wales was being introduced, the relative authority of the two bodies, and the roles they would perform, were the focus of some attention. For some geographic areas the introduction of a specialist legal authority heralded the loss of an area of control and influence for the police, who until then had been responsible for the investigation and prosecution of cases taken forward by the police. In other areas, where there had previously been police prosecution services, the new Crown Prosecution Service meant a change in the relationship between the police and "their" lawyers, as the Crown Prosecutors were set up to be independent of the police, and to follow their own policies and procedures rather than to provide legal advice for the police prosecution. The current situation is that the police are the public body responsible for the investigation of the majority of alleged offences and the initial decision to prosecute, and the CPS then makes the decision as to whether to continue or discontinue these cases and is then responsible for the legal conduct of these cases (Sanders, 1985b).

In Scotland, the Procurator Fiscal and the Crown Office had developed alongside the police forces, and their relationship and relative authority had been established historically so that the investigation and prosecution of offences was officially the remit of the Fiscal, and the role of the police was either "the enforcement of the criminal law ... " or the "prevention of crime and the suppression of vagrancy" for urban and rural police, respectively (Gordon, 1980).

The role of the Crown Prosecutor is to review the evidence and the circumstances surrounding the offence and then decide whether there is sufficient evidence and whether it is in the public interest to continue or discontinue with this prosecution. In Scotland, in general, the very early decisions as to investigation of potential offences and the arrest decisions tend to be implemented by the police, although they can be instigated by the prosecution authorities, but one of the key differences is that following a decision that a potential offence has been committed there is no discretion as to whether or not to report this to the police and there is no requirement to consider the strengths or weaknesses of the case. All cases recorded as potential offences, whether by the police or other agencies, in Scotland are reported to the Procurator Fiscal who then makes the decision to prosecute or not, or to offer an alternative disposal. The relative authority and the defined roles of those involved in the decision to prosecute has a great influence on the "folkways" likely to influence such decisions.

Previous work (Ashworth, 1984; Sanders & Young, 2002) has identified that "cop culture" and police "working rules" greatly influence early police decisions to arrest suspects and to initiate a prosecution in England and Wales. The "working rules" were greatly influenced by such factors as social dimensions such as ethnicity, class, age and gender (Sanders & Young, 2002). Previous involvement with criminal justice was also influential. Research into the decision to prosecute juveniles suggested that when juveniles had had previous involvement with the criminal justice system, "legal" factors such as previous referral to court and previous court appearance, did predict prosecution outcome, however, when there had been no previous involvement, legal factors, such as type and seriousness of the offence, did not predict outcome (Landau, 1978). An interesting study with police recruits in Scotland identified that the factors involved in the decision to prosecute changed following a socialization period, implicating professional culture (the "folkways"?) as being a strong influence (Tuohy, Wrennall, McQueen & Stradling, 1993).

MARKING VS REVIEW AND THE ROLE OF DECISION REVERSER

In addition to the organizational and cultural, it is suggested that structural factors also have an effect on the decision to prosecute. In England the process that is undertaken by the lawyers involved in the prosecution decision is "review", the Crown Prosecutor is in the position of decision reverser. In Scotland the process is described as "marking". Even from the terms used, it is clear that there is a difference in approach; the English prosecutors are expected to review a previous police decision and review the evidence in order to make a decision as to whether to continue with the prosecution or discontinue. In Scotland the prosecutor has to mark a case for prosecution or for nonprosecution (Gilchrist, 1995). In recent work, the role of the Crown Prosecutor was described as being one where "poor police decisions can be corrected by the CPS" (Sanders & Young, 2002, p. 1057) but the structural arrangements may not facilitate this.

In England, the prosecuting solicitors department identified that the prosecuting solicitors simply implemented decisions already taken by the police, did not give policy advice and restricted their advice to specific legal issues (Weatheritt, 1981). Weatheritt (1981) suggested that any decision not to proceed with a case tended to be made in conjunction with the police, and the prosecuting solicitors only achieved independence when the police were willing to allow them this independence.

Despite structural changes with the implementation of the CPS, Sanders (1988a) suggested that with the police retaining the initial decision as to whether or not to prosecute, the prosecutor cannot be seen as independent, and that the freedom to make an independent decision is severely curtailed. There is a possibility of pro-prosecution momentum, and early biases within the process may be replicated and maintained throughout the process, rather than being challenged.

Interestingly, although the Scottish Procurator Fiscal is not structurally constrained in the same way, as they are officially making the decision to prosecute or not, research by Moody and Tombs (1982) suggested that the Fiscals tended to "rubber stamp" for prosecution all cases reported to them by the police. Further research in Scotland also suggests that when a Procurator Fiscal is put in the position of being a decision reverser, for example, when the decision has been made to hold a suspect in custody, hence signalling a serious intention to proceed with a case, then it is more likely that the Fiscal will decide to continue a prosecution (Gilchrist, 1995). Work exploring the use of diversionary procedures in cases involving mentally disordered offenders suggests that the police play a key role in the diversionary process, and the prosecutors tend to respond "neutrally" to cues presented by the police. The conclusion of this work was that any systematic bias within the system was "not caused by prosecutorial decision making but [was] imported at an earlier stage in the process" (Duff, 1997, p. 15), again highlighting the importance of earlier police decisions.

It appears that the desire to "let things run" (perhaps with the understanding that at some later stage in the process the case will be fully reviewed, whether this be in preparation for a trial, in response to evidence refuting the case being presented by the defence solicitor or at trial), is strong enough to influence even those who officially have the role of making the first decision. In fact this decision avoidance has been identified as a positive feature, for example, prosecutors have suggested that they should not usurp the position of the court by prematurely making decisions which ought to be decided in open court (Gilchrist, 1995). It is clear that there are further debates to be had surrounding the "justice" or otherwise of early prosecutorial decisions, generally made in private as opposed to later decisions based within the public arena of the court.

An interesting point to note here is that the structures in the two different systems differ in terms of the level of authority required to discontinue cases, which in turn affects the likelihood of discontinuance. In the CPS a higher level of authority is required to discontinue a case, and there is more justification required, while in the Scottish Fiscal service, despite justification being needed for making a "no pro" decision, all Depute Fiscals have the authority to drop cases (Gilchrist, 1995). This indicates a disparity between the rhetoric of independent rigorous review of evidence and prosecution only in evidentially sufficient cases which are in the public interest, and the norm to suggest the normal working practices as being pro-prosecution.

STAGES OF THE DECISION

In terms of making a specific decision to prosecute, there are different approaches within different systems; however, within an adversarial system, there is a requirement to assess evidence and to balance the benefits of prosecution against any costs of that prosecution, including practical considerations such as the likely success of proceedings.

In England and Wales, the decision is described as being a two-stage process: the first stage to assess evidence and the second stage to decide whether a prosecution is "in the public interest". The public interest and the considerations that have to be balanced are provided in internal guidance documents within the CPS, and are also specified within the publicly available *Code for Crown Prosecutors* (CPS, 2004).

In Scotland, the decision is described as a process involving a number of considerations, both evidential and legal, but is not specified as a two-stage process. The considerations include whether there is corroborated evidence of a criminal offence having been committed, of the accused having committed the offence and public interest factors such as nature and gravity of the offence, the impact of the offence on the victim, the age, background and personal circumstances of the accused, the age and circumstances of the victim and so on (Crown Office, 2001). Guidance for these decisions is also reinforced by circulars which are sent out from the Crown Office, the central office.

Research in the socio-legal arena suggests that many of the public interest criteria conflict (Ashworth, 1984). How, for example, does one balance the victim's wishes against the needs of a mentally disordered offender? Additionally, within the higher level structure of the CPS there is a conflict between a call for efficiency and also a call for adherence to public policy (Bennion, 1986).

Observational research suggests that the distinction between legal and public interest factors tends to be less clear in practice. Decisions tend to be made in a far more holistic manner, with issues as to media interest, mental health of the defendant, parental wishes in a case of underage sexual activity, being considered alongside issues as to credibility of witnesses and corroboration (Gilchrist, 1995). This parallels judges' decisions regarding bail, where it was identified that a simple heuristic model of decision making was more predictive of decisions than an alternative decision-making strategy (Dhami, 2003). Indeed this work identified that the judges' decisions were greatly influenced by one cue which incorporated previous decisions by the police, the previous bench and the prosecutor, and suggested that there was a tendency to "pass the buck" (Dhami, 2003).

Research in Scotland suggests that factors such as the background and social characteristics of the defendant, the wishes of the victim and the characteristics of the victim were inconsistently applied so that very similar factors could be both a reason for prosecution and a reason for discontinuance (Gilchrist, 1995). This work also identified previous police decisions as being highly influential.

Similar findings led McConville et al. (1991) to suggest that the CPS were neither decision makers, nor decision reversers, but decision avoiders. McConville et al. (1991) identified that the CPS rarely dropped cases, even when evidentially weak, and when this did occur, this was generally instigated by another agency (for example the police), and often this was only after the suspect had made a number of court appearances. They identified three main reasons for the lack of discontinuance, which included adherence to shared police–prosecutor working rules which drive toward prosecution, the possibility of a freak conviction and the possibility of a guilty plea (McConville et al., 1991). More recent work found that while there was a move towards more discontinuances on evidential grounds, many discontinuances on "public interest" grounds were of trivial cases, and the decisions appear to be driven by consideration of cost rather than criminal justice policy (Sanders & Young, 2002). Research in the USA on prosecution of minor cases also identified that previous decisions in the process were highly influential. This work suggested that while race and gender are significant predictors of decisions to prosecute in minor cases, legal factors also play a role and were most predictive of outcome. These "legal" factors were number of offences and prior arrest record (Adams & Cutshall, 1987). An interesting note from this work was that the use of social characteristics within legal decision making was interpreted as perhaps being indicative of perceptions of which groups pose the greatest threat to society, rather than merely bias.

Interestingly, recent research has shown that not all classes of case will continue to court. Mhlanga (2000) identified that ethnic minority suspects were more likely to have their cases discontinued by the CPS (Mhlanga, 2000). This has been interpreted as indicating that the CPS are, to some extent, counteracting earlier race biases in the system, which is seen as positive. However, taking into account the research indicating that it is "trivial" cases which tend to be discontinued, and recognizing the factors involved in the public interest aspect of decision making, it may be that the injuries to the victims in cases involving ethnic minority defendants are seen as less serious, and so the drive towards prosecution is less. Work in the USA has certainly identified that ethnicity has a complex influence on pre-sentence decisions and that it, in addition to covarying factors and wider influences, is not only the ethnicity of the accused but also that of the victim, the prosecutor and others that must be considered (Free, 2002). It is suggested that systematic research into issues like this might greatly aid our understanding of these complex issues.

FACTUAL BASIS FOR DECISIONS: QUALITY OF INFORMATION

A further issue affecting the decision to prosecute is that of the quality of the information on which the decision is based. Early research into prosecution in Scotland suggested that "if one accepts the premise the quality of decision making in most social contexts is directly related to the amount of relevant information available to the decision makers, it follows that the role of the police as reporters is a crucial one" (Moody & Tombs, 1982, p. 30). More recent work in England and Wales also identified that the quality of police evidence and the particular construction and presentation of cases as prosecutable (where evidence supportive of prosecution was selected and facts that do not support prosecution are ignored, hidden or undermined) (Sanders & Young, 2002, p. 1058), had a great influence on prosecution decisions. Duff (1997) and Gelsthorpe and Giller (1990) also identified that the police only tended to present the information that seemed relevant to them as prosecutors and supportive of prosecution, rather than presenting all information. Work by Crisp, Whitaker and Harris (1994) supported this assertion by showing that cases which had been conducted under an experimental "Public Interest Case Assessment" scheme (where more attention was focused on the public interest information), were more likely to be discontinued. Gilchrist (1995) also identified that the information included by police was influential, particularly identifying this as an issue where the police considered a "no pro" decision to be appropriate.

Innovative work in England suggested that technological solutions could be applied to the CPS decisions to increase consistency and to ensure that all factual information was included in the first element of the decision process, to establish that the "realistic prospect of conviction test" might be satisfied prior to consideration of the public interest test. However, barriers in the form of quality of information to input, and the acceptability of this approach to criminal justice decisions, means that this work is at the early stages of development (Greenfield, 1998).

It is clear that the outcome suggested by previous decisions influences prosecutors not only through the rules governing the structure of the system but also through the indirect influence of file construction.

FACTORS TO INCLUDE OR EXCLUDE

In addition to prosecution decisions being influenced by structural factors and pro-prosecution police working practices and philosophies, even individual decisions to prosecute might not be entirely based on unbiased criteria, and strategies should be implemented which addressed this. Ashworth (1987) explored this issue and suggested that to ensure fairness in decision making, there should be a list of criteria which should be excluded from the decision to prosecute. He suggested that factors such as race, politics, social standing, employment status, marital status and so on, could be stated as excluded factors. This approach has been implemented within other jurisdictions, for example in Tasmania, where, in addition to the provision of guidance as to factors that should be taken into account, it is clearly stated that "a decision whether or not to prosecute must clearly not be influenced by the race, religion, national origin or political associations, activities or beliefs or the alleged offender or any other person involved; personal feelings concerning the offender or victim; possible political advantage or disadvantage to the Government or any political group or party; or the possible effect of the decision on the personal or professional circumstances of those responsible for the prosecution decisions" (Director of Public Prosecutions, Tasmania, 2005). However, the need to serve both justice and administrative goals, the influence of "folkways" and working practices, and the lack of systematic interpretation and application of the current codes, might suggest that the introduction of further rules and lists might have less effect on fairness than might be desired.

Again this is an area where systematic study of factors involved in prosecutorial decision making, comparison of decisions including and excluding factors and cross-cultural work and application of psychological theory in this area would be hugely beneficial.

WHOSE INTERESTS DOES THE "PUBLIC INTEREST" SERVE?

A key issue to address is whether the discretionary application of specific, competing factors, allowed by the "public interest" element in the prosecutorial decision process, leads to more general bias. Whose interests does the public interest serve? There is general research that suggests bias does exist.

Sanders (1985a) has suggested that there is class bias in prosecution decisions in England and Wales. Sanders (1985a) suggests that bias is a byproduct of differential prosecution policies and due to the police involvement with mainly "working-class crime", and it is the involvement of alternative prosecution authorities, such as the Factory Inspectorate, in "middle-class" crimes. Interestingly while the Fiscal in Scotland is involved across all offences, qualitative research suggests that class-related factors appear to influence decisions in Scotland too (Gilchrist, 1995).

However, it is in the prosecution of specific types of offence which indicates the biases of the processes more clearly.

OFFENCES AGAINST WOMEN AND CHILDREN – STEREOTYPES AND BIASES

For historical and cultural reasons, definitions of, and responses to, many offences conducted in "private" space and involving women and children as victims, have created greater debate than those routinely involving men as victims and conducted in public. Consequently, the prosecution of these controversial sexual offences and "domestic" offences are areas where the beliefs of those involved are clearly exposed, and the limitations of discretionary public interest interpretations highlighted.

Research had suggested that sexual cases were inappropriately discontinued due to factors related to the victims' prior sexual experience, or credibility (Gilchrist, 1995). However, from research on sexual assault cases in the USA, victim characteristics and evidence of a prior relationship were not found to be influential in predicting prosecution decisions (Kingsnorth, MacIntosh & Wentworth, 1999), and, in a separate study, child sexual abusers were found to be treated similarly to nonsexual offenders, although it was noted that the child abuse offenders were more likely to be older, employed and have a previous sexual or violent record (Cullen, Hull Smith, Funk & Haaf, 2000). Work with care professionals identified that, in a sample of men with disabilities, convicted offenders were more likely to have targeted children, have males as victims and have perpetrated more serious offences (Green, Gray & Willner, 2002). Further work on sexual abuse cases identified general factors such as backround characteristics of the perpetrator and victim (e.g. victim age), severity of abuse (e.g. presence of oral-genital abuse), use of threat of force, duration of abuse and evidence (e.g. presence of physical or eyewitness evidence) were all related to acceptance of cases for prosecution (Cross, De Vos & Whitcomb, 1994). Research from Australia, however, identifies factors such as the requirement for corroboration of a child witnesses' testimony, reliance on admission to guarantee evidential sufficiency and the influence of the wishes of the victim or the parent of the victim as influencing prosecution decisions, and suggests that, despite a higher prosecution rate than might be perceived by the public, there continue to be obstacles to prosecution in this type of case (Brereton & Cole, 2000). These studies suggest that a range of factors linked with evidence, risk and public interest in different measure, are all mixed in the decisions to prosecute this type of offence, and also highlight the idiosyncratic nature of the application of discretion.

In cases of domestic violence similar criticisms had been levelled at the prosecution authorities, suggesting that decisions were being made on the basis of individual beliefs as to whether domestic violence was considered to be a serious crime, and overly influenced by beliefs about the protection of (male) privacy and notions of relationship (Gilchrist, 1995; Sanders, 1988b). Recent work has identified that often prosecutors will not proceed with a prosecution when the victim does not support this (Cretney & Davies, 1996) which is justifiable under the guidance, however, it can also be interpreted as continuing to view this type of behaviour through "the lens of "the couple" or "the family" (Cretney & Davies, 1996, p. 146), rather than as an offence. Recent research exploring the impact of children in domestic violence cases suggests that while the current CPS policy is to pursue prosecution even when a complainant withdraws their complaint, this rarely happened in practice, with the complainant's wishes being very influential. This work also highlighted the fact that a blanket policy of this type may not help either women or children victims (Burton, 2000). Across studies greater training, support and encouragement were identified as necessary to support victims in what could be "an arduous and possibly dangerous enterprise" (Cretney & Davies, 1996, p. 146). Clearly the unfettered use of discretion in classes of case where prosecutors' beliefs may be unhelpful and potentially dangerous is problematic. Again this highlights the importance of greater understanding of the factors and pathways leading to decisions to prosecute and the need for further research, particularly in atypical cases.

SUMMARY AND CONCLUSIONS

It is clear that the rhetoric of independent decision making, rigorous review of evidence and prosecution only when the public interest demands is not borne out in practice. Despite rhetoric to the contrary, Gandy (1988) claimed that by this stage in England and Wales "already ... a more robust approach by prosecuting lawyers has led to a number of cases being discontinued", and Robb (1988) suggested, as a rule the Procurator Fiscal Service would only prosecute "if the public interest leaves no suitable alternative". However, research indicates that there is a tendency to avoid making decisions. Structural features such as roles and relative powers, control over information and construction of cases, and philosophical issues such as the difficulties in balancing the competing public interest factors and the competing demands of efficiency and legality, mean that the decision to prosecute is complex, difficult to evaluate and the potential for differential treatment of types of cases or suspects is high. Systematic research by forensic psychology into many aspects of this process is long overdue.

A crucial message for those working and researching in this area is that the protection for the suspect provided through the requirement that a prosecution only proceeds in cases which have been rigorously scrutinized by legal professionals, where there is evidence, and where prosecution is deemed to be in the public interest, and the protection for victims from appropriate prosecution of all types of offences, seems to be more rhetoric than reality. As Sanders and Young (2002) suggest, it is possible that "prosecutors could become adequate reviewers of either evidence or public interest [but] only if placed in an entirely different structural relationship with the police ... and [this] might well then be unsuccessful" (Sanders & Young, 2002, p. 1058). The development of a successful prosecutorial process is possible, but further work is required to identify the key issues and to facilitate this. Forensic psychology has provided great insight into other aspects of criminal justice and perhaps now has a duty to become involved in this area too.

REFERENCES

Adams, K. & Cutshall, C. (1987). Refusing to prosecute minor offenses: The relative influence of legal and extra legal factors. *Justice Quarterly, 4*(4), 595–609.

Ashworth, A. (1984). Prosecution and the police and a guide to good gatekeeping. *Howard Journal of Criminal Justice, 23*(2), 312–325.

Ashworth, A. (1987). The public interest element in prosecution. *Criminal Law Review,* 596.

Brereton, D. & Cole, G. (2000). Obstacles to prosecution in child sexual assault cases: A preliminary report of some Victorian data. *Children as Witnesses*, 153–168.

Burton, M. (2000). Prosecution in cases of domestic violence involving children. *Journal of Social Welfare and Family Law, 22*(2), 175–191.

Bennion, F. (1986). The Crown Prosecution Service: The new prosecution arrangements. *Criminal Law Review*, 57–64.

Chambers, G. & Miller, A. (1987). Proving sexual assault: Prosecuting the offender or persecuting the victims? In P. Carlen & A. Worrall (Eds), *Gender, crime and justice*. Oxford: Oxford University Press.

Corsianos, M. (2001). Conceptualizing "justice" in detectives' decision making. *International Journal of the Sociology of Law, 29*, 113–125.

CPS, (2004). *The Code for Crown Prosecutors*. London: CPS.

Cretney, A. & Davies, G. (1996). Prosecuting domestic assault: Victims failing courts or courts failing victims. *Howard Journal of Criminal Justice, 36*(2), 146–157.

Crown Office, (2001). *The prosecution code*. Edinburgh: Crown Office.

Crisp, D., Whittaker, C. & Harris, J. (1994). Public interest case assessment schemes. *Home Office Research Study No 138*. London: HMSO.

Cross, T.P., De Vos, E. & Whitcomb, D. (1994). Prosecution of child sexual abuse: Which cases are accepted? *Child Abuse Neglect, 18*(8), 663–677.

Cullen, B., Hull Smith, P., Funk, J. & Haaf, R. (2000). A matched cohort comparison of a criminal justice system's response to child sexual abuse: A profile of perpetrators. *Child Abuse and Neglect, 24*(4), 569–577.

Dhami, M. (2003). Psychological models of professional decision making. *Psychological Science, 14*(2), 175–180.

Director of Public Prosecutions, (2005). *Prosecution guidelines for the Department of Justice, Tasmania*, at www.tas.gov.au.

Duff, (1997). Diversion from prosecution into psychiatric care. *British Journal of Criminology, 37*, 15–34.

Feeley, M. (1973). Two models of criminal justice: An organizational perspective. *Law and Society Review*, 407–425.

Free, M. (2002). Race and presentencing decisions in the United States: A summary and critique of the research. *Criminal Justice Review, 27*(2), 203–232.

Gandy, D. (1988). The Crown Prosecution System: Its organization and philosophy. In Eryl Hall Williams (Ed.), *The role of the prosecutor*. Aldershot: Avebury.

Geller, W. & Toch, H. (1996). *Police violence*. New Haven: Yale University Press.

Gelsthorpe, L. & Giller, H. (1990). More justice for juveniles: Does more mean better? *Criminal Law Review*, 153–164.

Gilchrist, E. (1995). Fairness in prosecutorial decision-making. *Scottish Journal of Criminal Justice Studies, 1*, 61–70.

Gordon, P. (1980). *Policing Scotland*. Edinburgh: Edinburgh University Press.

Green, G., Gray, N. & Willner, P. (2002). Factors associated with criminal convictions for sexually inappropriate behaviour in men with learning disabilities. *Journal of Forensic Psychiatry, 13*(3), 578–607.

Greene, E. & Dodge, M. (1995). The influence of prior record evidence on juror decision making. *Law and Human Behavior, 19*(1), 67–78.

Greenfield, J. (1998). Decision support within the criminal justice system. *International Review of Law Computers and Technology, 12*, 269–278.

Guy, L.S. & Edens, J.F. (2003). Juror decision-making in a mock sexually predator trial: Gender difference in the impact of divergent types of expert testimony. *Behavioural Sciences and the Law, 21*(2), 215–237.

Hall Williams, J.E. (Ed.) (1988). *The role of the prosecutor.* Aldershot: Avebury.

Kerstholt, J. & Jackson, J. (1999). Judicial decision-making: Order of evidence presentation and availability of background information. *Applied Cognitive Psychology, 12*(5), 445–454.

Kingsnorth, R., MacIntosh, R. & Wentworth, J. (1999). Sexual assault: The role of prior relationship and victim characteristics in case processing. *Justice Quarterly, 16*(2), 275–302.

Landau, S. (1978). Do legal variables predict police decisions regarding the prosecution of juvenile offenders? *Law and Human Behavior, 2*(2), 95–105.

Moran, T.K. & Cooper, J.L. (1983). *Discretion and the criminal justice process.* New York: Association Faculty Press.

McConville, M., Sanders, A. & Leng, R. (1991). *The case for the prosecution.* London: Routledge.

Mhlanga (2000). *Race and the CPS.* London: Stationery Office.

Moody, S. & Tombs, J. (1982). *Prosecution in the public interest.* Edinburgh: Edinburgh University Press.

National Audit Office (1989a). *Review of the Crown Prosecution Service.* London: HMSO.

National Audit Office (1989b). *Prosecution of Crime in Scotland: Review of the Procurator Fiscal Service.* London: HMSO.

Ogloff, J. (1991). A comparison of insanity defense standards on juror decision-making. *Law and Human Behavior, 15*(5), 509–531.

Packer, H.A.L. (1968). *The limits of the criminal sanction.* Stanford: Stanford University Press.

Robb, L. (1988). A Scottish contribution. In Eryl Hall Williams (Ed.), *The role of the prosecutor.* Aldershot: Avebury.

Reiner, R. (2000). *The politics of the police, third edition.* Oxford: Oxford University Press.

Sanders, A. (1985a). Class bias in prosecutions. *Howard Journal of Criminal Justice, 24*(3), 176–199.

Sanders, A. (1985b). Prosecution decisions and the Attorney-General's guidelines. *Criminal Law Review,* 4–19.

Sanders, A. (1986). An independent Crown Prosecution Service? The new prosecution arrangements. *Criminal Law Review,* 76–85.

Sanders, A. (1988a). The limits to diversion from prosecution. *British Journal of Criminology, 28,* 513–532.

Sanders, A. (1988b). Personal violence and public order: The prosecution of domestic violence in England and Wales. *International Journal of the Sociology of Law, 16,* 359–382.

Sanders, A. & Young, R. (2002). From suspect to trial. In M. Maguire, R. Morgan & R. Reiner (Eds), *The Oxford handbook of criminology, third edition.* Oxford: Oxford University Press.

Schuller, R. (1992). The impact of battered woman syndrome evidence on jury decision processes. *Law and Human Behavior, 16*(6), 597–620.

Scottish Consortium on Criminal Justice, (2000). *Rethinking criminal justice in Scotland.* Report of the Scottish Consortium on Crime and Criminal Justice, Edinburgh: SCCJ.

Smith, D. & Gray, J. (1983). *Police and people in London.* Aldershot: Gower.

Tonry, M. (1995). *Malign neglect: Race and punishment in America*. New York: Oxford University Press.

Tuohy, A., Wrennall , McQueen, R. & Stradling, S. (1993). Effect of socialization factors on decisions to prosecute: The organizational adaptation of Scottish police recruits. *Law and Human Behavior, 17*(2),167–181.

Weatheritt, M. (1981). The prosecution system: Survey of prosecuting solicitors' departments: Organizational implications of change. *Royal Commission on Criminal Procedure (1977–81) Research Studies No 11–12*. London: HMSO.

CHAPTER 10

Preventing Withdrawal of Complaints and Psychological Support for Victims

GRAHAM M. DAVIES AND HELEN WESTCOTT

INTRODUCTION

In many criminal cases, apparently well-founded allegations against named individuals are withdrawn, due to the reluctance of victims to speak out and sustain their allegations. Such incidents are particularly common among complainants of sexual or physical assaults, where the victims are often among the most vulnerable in society: children, the elderly or those with learning disabilities or psychiatric disorders. Given the interpersonal nature of such crimes, the principal or only evidence against the accused may be the testimony of the alleged victim. In the absence of such testimony, the case cannot go ahead, leaving the victim's personal distress unresolved and the perpetrator free to commit further offences.

What can be done to prevent the premature withdrawal of complaints and to provide the necessary psychological support for victims of such crimes? In this chapter we begin by examining the size of the problem of attrition in complaints, reviewing research on the pressure points within the investigative and legal process that lead to cases involving vulnerable victims not proceeding. We then go on to describe the different forms of support available, both procedural and social, and consider the effectiveness of these measures as attested by recent research.

Practical Psychology for Forensic Investigations and Prosecutions.
Edited by Mark R. Kebbell and Graham M. Davies. © 2006 John Wiley & Sons, Ltd.

Finally, we examine the lessons for the police, legal and other professionals on how to best sustain and support witnesses and ensure that justice is available for all groups within society.

PREVENTING THE WITHDRAWAL OF COMPLAINTS

Understanding Sources of Attrition

When searching for the causes of attrition in cases involving vulnerable and intimidated witnesses, the confrontation between the accused and the witness in the unfamiliar arena of the courtroom forms an obvious focus. However, as Sanders, Creaton, Bird and Weber (1997) have emphasized in their analysis of the difficulties facing complainants with learning disabilities, withdrawal of complaints does not arise solely from courtroom factors. Figure 10.1 is adopted from their report and illustrates the many points at which cases can be withdrawn in the investigative and prosecutorial process.

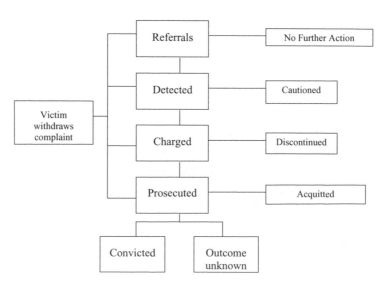

Figure 10.1 Summary of investigation and prosecution process, showing attrition points (developed from Sanders et al., 1997)

The causes of such attrition are not solely due to the victim withdrawing a complaint: they can also arise from a defendant fleeing before trial, or more often from legal decisions, such as the police or prosecutor involved terminating the enquiry or discontinuing the case. Sometimes the police will discontinue enquiries because they decide that no crime has been committed, but use of the "no-crime" procedure can be controversial. Harris and Grace (1999) in their study of attrition in rape cases in England and Wales showed that in around one-third of cases that were "no-crimed", the victims withdrew their complaint, and in a further 15% it was decided that there was insufficient evidence. They argue that these cases should not have been included in the "no-crime" category, which should be reserved for retractions and fabrications.

Kelly, Lovett and Regan (2005) identify four main pressure points in the investigative and prosecution process where attrition is likely to occur:

- the decision to report a crime;
- the investigative stage;
- the prosecution stage;
- at trial.

Kelly et al. (2005) argue that the decision of a victim to report a crime or to engage in the investigative process is easily overlooked as a cause of attrition, but may represent one of the most important causes, especially with vulnerable victims and witnesses. For example, a learning disabled victim may not know how to make a report (Sanders et al., 1997). Kelly et al. (2005) in their study of rape cases in England and Wales highlight the withdrawal of complaints at this early stage as a major cause of attrition: 14% of their total sample declined to complete the initial process, another 14% withdrew at the investigative stage and a further 2% withdrew at the decision to prosecute and trial stages: these represented 17% of cases remaining at the decision to prosecute stage, and 5% of all cases that reached trial.

Rates of Attrition in Cases Involving Vulnerable Victims and Witnesses

Controversy surrounds the definition of attrition. Kelly et al. (2005) define it as the process by which cases drop out of the system without a conviction and they lament the "justice gap" represented by high attrition rates. However, Sanders et al. (1997) argue that "a successful case is one in which the evidence of the victim is heard by a jury. Success should not necessarily be judged by convictions, for convictions are difficult to secure in these cases and results are unpredictable (as indeed they are in any sample of cases)" (p. 82). Even judged by this more liberal definition, attrition statistics in England and Wales depict a rather bleak picture for vulnerable victims and witnesses.

Regarding crimes against *adult and child victims who are learning disabled*, Sanders et al. (1997) used a case-study approach to examine 74 such cases. Of these 74,[1] they reported:

- 53% were subject to no further action (NFA);
- 47% were detected (of which 2% were cautioned);
- 45% were charged (of which 1% was discontinued);
- 18% resulted in a conviction;
- 23% resulted in an acquittal (two cases of unknown outcome).

Of the 15 cases relating specifically to children, only 1 resulted in a guilty plea, the remainder led to acquittals or a decision to take no further action. Overall, however, these are the most positive statistics included in this review, which is probably a reflection of the way cases were selected and obtained (the authors approached agencies for learning disabled people and searched newspapers for relevant reports).

The figures from Harris and Grace's (1999) study of *rape allegations* are more sobering. Of the 483 cases examined:

- 31% were subject to NFA;
- 64% were detected (of which 1% was cautioned);
- 31% were charged (of which 8% were discontinued);
- 6% resulted in a conviction of rape, and a further 7% in a conviction other than rape;
- 7% resulted in an acquittal.

Cases involving children less than 13 years old were least likely to be "no-crimed", and were most likely to proceed. These authors highlight plea-bargaining as a factor in attrition, with three-quarters of defendants pleading guilty to lesser charges in return for the withdrawal of more serious charges.

Kelly et al. (2005) found an overall conviction rate for all reported cases of rape of just 8%. Of the 2 284 cases in their study:

- 80% did not proceed beyond the police stage;
- a further 6% did not proceed beyond the prosecution stage; and
- just 14% proceeded to trial.

Fear of the criminal justice system (especially court), fear of disbelief and discouragement from the police featured strongly in reasons why victims withdrew complaints.

Finally, regarding *allegations of child abuse*, Davis, Hoyano, Keenan, Maitland and Morgan (1999) assessed the admissibility and sufficiency of evidence in prosecutions involving 124 children (most allegations concerned sexual assault). In all, 53 defendants were charged: 11 with physical assault, 31 with offences related to sexual abuse and 11 with rape. Twenty-five defendants pleaded guilty, but typically to lesser charges. Of the 28 defendants who entered a not-guilty plea and were tried, 8 were convicted on at least 1 count, or on a lesser charge. These authors highlighted the tensions in investigating and prosecuting cases of alleged abuse: for example, balancing concerns for the child's welfare against responsibilities as criminal investigators. They felt many unique features of these cases impacted upon the process, including the relationship between the child and the defendant, lack of corroboration and delay in the child's allegation.

Another study of 1 491 child abuse complaints in Northern England reported by Gallagher and Pease (2000) found that only 17% proceeded to prosecution, resulting in a 12% conviction rate over the total sample. Of the remainder:

- 76% were subject to NFA;
- 5% were cautioned;
- 2% resulted in an acquittal.

The authors found a drop in attrition rates once a case reached the prosecution stage: 85% of defendants were convicted of at least one of the indictments in the cases examined. Gallagher and Pease also noted differences in attrition and conviction rates depending on the nature of the alleged abuse, with sexual abuse allegations having the lowest attrition rate (63%), highest prosecution rate (26%) and second highest conviction rate (84% of the cases remaining at the prosecution stage). "Insufficiency of evidence" was the largest single reason given by police for taking no further action, with lack of corroboration also cited frequently, as well as concern about the "quality of the evidence" – specifically the credibility of the witness and the existence of conflict between the witness and the suspect. Gallagher and Pease estimated that approximately 10% of cases were not pursued because the child did not want to proceed, and a further 6% were not pursued on the basis of parental wishes. Fear of taking part in a criminal trial was cited as one of the major concerns for such decisions.

This section has revealed the high rates of attrition of various vulnerable witness groups and highlighted some of the reasons why cases involving vulnerable witnesses and victims do not proceed to trial, as suggested by researchers, practitioners and the victims themselves. These reasons include the long-term welfare of the victim or witness, fears of going to court and concerns about the courtroom experience. There are also concerns about insufficiency of evidence and the quality of evidence, especially in the context of close relationships between victim and defendant, lack of corroboration and lack of medical evidence that are typical features of such cases.

Concerns that Lead to Victims and Witnesses Withdrawing Complaints

This section examines in detail some of the fears and reasons cited by complainants as reasons for withdrawing allegations or not making them in the first place. It is important to acknowledge here, however, the disappointment and distress of victims and witnesses who do make a complaint, but whose cases are dropped, or who are told by the police that nothing more can be done (e.g. Keep, 1996; Sharland, Seal, Croucher, Aldgate & Jones, 1996).

The London Family Court Clinic, in Ontario, Canada has carried out a number of investigations relating to the discovery and prosecution of child sexual abuse among its clients (Sas, Cunningham, Hurley, Dick & Farnsworth, 1995; Sas, Hurley, Austin & Wolfe, 1991). On the basis of interviews with child victims, Sas and her colleagues proposed four hurdles to be overcome by children in order to disclose their abuse:

- recognising abuse as wrong;
- overcoming inhibitions to tell;
- deciding when to tell; and
- deciding who to tell.

A number of fears elicited from children contributed to inhibitions to the second hurdle, telling and pursuing complaints. These included:

- fear of harm by the abuser;
- fear of rejection by the family;
- fear of disbelief;
- fear of others' (typically parents') reactions;
- fear of family break-up, including being removed from the family;
- fear of embarrassment.

In addition a number of other feelings contributed to inhibitions, such as guilt, shame, feelings of responsibility, risk of loss of relationship with the abuser and fear of threats (e.g. if the child "told the secret"). Victims and witnesses in other studies, both adults and children, have reported many of these fears and feelings, even when such fears did not subsequently materialise (e.g. Gallagher and Pease, 2000; Kelly et al., 2005; Sanders et al., 1997; Westcott and Davies, 1996). Sas et al. (1991) noted that disclosure brought about a host of pressures on the child, and signalled a loss of control over the process that could be very disempowering. Some of these pressures, particularly family conflict, could lead to a retraction of a complaint.

In their later study, Sas et al. (1995) proposed a theoretical model to predict disclosure or non-reporting of abuse. Facilitators of reporting included that the abuser was a stranger, that force was used to obtain compliance, that the child was older at onset of abuse and that the child had a stable and supportive family. Inhibitors of reporting included a close relationship with the abuser, the abuser being a family member, "grooming" by the abuser, young age of child at abuse onset and a "dysfunctional" or neglectful family. This model therefore addresses cases that might not even engage with the investigation and prosecution process in the first place, as well as indicating which cases might lead to a more positive outcome. Although based on work with children, Sas's model is useful for considering the dynamics influencing other vulnerable groups as well, such as witnesses with learning difficulties or rape victims.

Victim and witness intimidation can also lead to withdrawal of complaints. Sas et al. (1991) noted pressures from some family members on children to retract allegations, and various surveys have documented intimidation from other sources, such as defendants and their supporters. A study by the Home Office Police Research Group (1993, cited in Home Office, 1998) found that 13% of crimes reported by victims and 9% of crimes reported by other witnesses, were followed by attempts at intimidation. Further, crimes were not reported to police because of intimidation in 6% of crimes experienced by victims, and 22% of crimes reported by other witnesses. The problem seems particularly acute for vulnerable witnesses: a recent survey (Hamlyn, Phelps, Turtle & Sattar, 2004) reported that 53% of vulnerable witnesses experienced some form of intimidation in the period leading up to the trial. Intimidation came mainly from the defendant (36%) or the defendant's family (21%).

Finally, what concerns motivate victims and witnesses to go ahead and make a report, despite fears and pressures to do otherwise? Research (e.g. Kelly et al., 2005; Sas et al., 1991) suggests that the following considerations are important:

- a desire to stop further assaults;
- a need to protect others;
- wanting the truth to come out;
- achieving accountability and sanctions against the offender; and
- fear of the perpetrator.

PSYCHOLOGICAL SUPPORT FOR VICTIMS

Given that a vulnerable and/or intimidated witness is prepared to press charges, what support can be provided for them in the run-up to the trial and in giving evidence at court? Psychologists have worked in tandem with legal professionals to develop and evaluate a range of innovations designed to facilitate the gathering and hearing of such evidence. These innovations have included both procedural and social support.

Procedural Support for the Witness: Videotechnology

Traditionally, evidence is delivered in person on the day of the trial. This emphasis upon oral evidence reflects a common belief that information bearing on the reliability and validity of the testimony can be gathered from the bearing and demeanor of the witness (Davies, 1999). In fact, the ability of observers to make accurate judgements from nonverbal information has been seriously challenged by experimental research (Landstrom, Granhag, & Hartwig, 2005; Orcutt, Goodman, Tobey, Batterman-Faunce & Thomas, 2001; Westcott, Davies, & Clifford, 1991). Moreover, vulnerable witnesses may find the experience of giving evidence in open court intimidating to the extent that they give fragmentary or incoherent accounts which depart from their previous written evidence: in lawyers' terminology, they "fail to come up to proof". Research suggests that such witnesses find giving evidence in front of the accused and in the often alien surroundings of the courtroom particularly stressful (Flin, Stevenson & Davies, 1989; Goodman et al., 1992). For these reasons, many countries have moved to exploit videotechnology to enable children and other vulnerable witnesses either to give their evidence via closed-circuit television (CCTV) from outside the courtroom or to permit prerecorded videotaped interviews with witnesses to be played at court to compliment, or as a substitute for, examination-in-chief on the day of the trial.

The use of CCTV to enable children to testify out of view of the accused was pioneered in the United States, but is rarely employed today because of concerns that such an arrangement violates a defendant's constitutional rights (Montoya, 1995). No such inhibitions exist in the United Kingdom and other Commonwealth countries and CCTV is now widely employed to assist witnesses in giving their evidence (Cashmore, 2002). In England and Wales, this arrangement was introduced for children as part of the *Criminal Justice Act, 1988* and further extended to all vulnerable witnesses under the *Youth Justice and Criminal Evidence Act, 1999*. The arrangement in use in Britain and other Commonwealth countries involves the witness, accompanied by an usher or other supporter, testifying from a small, specially equipped room, normally elsewhere in the court complex. Witnesses sit in front of a workstation which projects their image into the courtroom; the court always sees the witness while the witness only sees whomsoever is talking to them from the court. Other arrangements are in use in the United States, some of which involve the presence of the accused in the room, which defeats the purpose of the innovation (Cashmore, 2002). While the use of CCTV (known as the "live link") is now mandatory in England and Wales for children testifying in sexual abuse cases, its use in other cases and for other classes of witness is at the discretion of the presiding judge or magistrate.

An early evaluation of the English system suggested that the system had significant advantages for the reception of children's evidence. Lawyers and judges perceived children giving evidence via the live link to be less unhappy, to be more likely to "come up to proof" and to be more consistent in their answers compared to those questioned in open court. These views were supported by an analysis of ratings gathered in England in cases involving the live link, compared to similar ratings gathered in Scotland in cases where children gave their evidence in the conventional way (Davies & Noon, 1991).

Such overwhelmingly positive findings have not always emerged from evaluations in other countries, such as Scotland (Murray, 1995) and Western Australia (O'Grady, 1996). However, in both these legislatures, use of the live link is at the discretion of the court and the children permitted its use were significantly younger and involved in more serious allegations than the children testifying in open court (Westcott, Davies, & Spencer, 1999). The presumption of use that exists in England and Wales for complainants in sexual abuse cases robs older children of their right to confront the accused in open court if they so wish (Cashmore & de Haas, 1992) but avoids defence complaints that a discretionary decision is prejudicial in that it implies a special fear of the witness for the accused (Montoya, 1995). There is a general consensus that children and indeed, vulnerable witnesses in general (Hamlyn et al., 2004) find the live link helpful and generally preferable to open court testimony (Goodman et al., 1998).

Despite the apparent advantages, there remains considerable resistance, particularly among lawyers, to the widespread use of CCTV. Complaints include the difficulty in establishing rapport via the television link, and concerns that televised testimony will have less impact upon a jury than statements made in open court (Davies & Noon, 1991). Issues around rapport can be ameliorated by the increasingly accepted practice of advocates being prepared to meet witnesses prior to the formal examination. Issues around impact are more complex. Experimental studies in which the mode of giving statements has been manipulated suggest that jurors generally perceive "live" witnesses more positively than those on camera (Davies, 1999; Landstrom et al., 2005). However, the effects appear to be transient and have no measurable impact upon trial outcome (Goodman et al., 1998; Swim, Borgida & McCoy, 1993). This emphasis upon trial outcome also ignores the impact on the well-being of the witness and their reduced likelihood of "coming up to proof" when examined in open court (Davies, 1994; Swim, Borgida & McCoy, 1993). An alternative shielding arrangement to CCTV, which offers greater control to the advocate, is the use of screens in court to block the witness from sight of the accused. Little research has been conducted on their impact, though by bringing witnesses back into court, they rob them of one major advantage of the use of a televised link.

A second use of videotechnology is the pre-recorded video interview that can be played to judge and jury. The advantages of pre-recorded interviews were set out in the *Pigot Report* (1989), which urged their introduction into courts in England and Wales. Pigot argued that videotaping would enable evidence to be gathered soon after a complaint and so ensuring that the court could view as near a contemporaneous account as possible. Further, by gathering evidence at this point, vulnerable witnesses/victims could receive therapy with fewer concerns over the potential for evidence contamination. The use of pre-recorded video interviews as a substitute for the child's examination-in-chief in court became legal for children in England and Wales in the *Criminal Justice Act, 1991* and this facility was extended to all vulnerable witnesses in the *Youth Justice and Criminal Evidence Act, 1999*. Similar legislation has been enacted in other Commonwealth countries and the admission of pre-recorded evidence is also legal in many parts of the United States (Cashmore, 2002; Davies, 1999).

Videotaped interviews will normally be conducted by a non-uniformed police officer or a social worker. In England and Wales, the interview will take place in a specially equipped interview suite situated on "neutral ground" – a hospital or house, rather than a police station – and will be videotaped in its entirety, with the aid of a number of fixed cameras. The use of informal dress and a domestic setting reflects an implicit belief that witnesses will provide more complete and accurate testimony in informal situations, an assumption supported by research (Hill & Hill, 1987; Saywitz & Nathanson, 1993).

Such interviews require interviewers to probe for often sensitive issues while at the same time adhering to the rules of evidence in the framing of questions: interviews must be both simultaneously investigative and evidential (see the chapter by Milne and Bull in this book for a discussion of appropriate interviewing). In England and Wales, the conduct of such interviewing techniques is regulated by a series of guidelines. The original *Memorandum of Good Practice* (Home Office, 1992), written by a psychologist and a lawyer, drew widely on existing psychological research and best practice in the interviewing of children (Bull, 1996). This was superseded by more general guidance for interviewing all vulnerable witnesses, published as *Achieving Best Evidence in Criminal Proceedings* (Home Office, 2002).

Central to both the *Memorandum* and *Achieving Best Evidence* was the concept of a phased interview: interviews are expected to have a clear structure that should be evident to an outside viewer. The use of phased interviews is widespread in interviewing children and interviews typically have four phases:

- rapport;
- free narrative;
- questioning;
- closure.

In the *rapport phase*, the interviewer attempts to put the child at ease through discussion of neutral topics prior to the raising of the reason for the interview. This phase is also used for the discussion of *ground rules* designed to challenge any implicit psychological assumptions the vulnerable witness may have about the nature of the interview. For instance, interviewees are reminded that the interviewer was not present at the events and that the interviewee is the only source of information: if they do not understand a question or do not know the answer they should say so. The use of ground rules and rapport are designed to reduce the power differential between interviewer and interviewee and thus reduce suggestible responding (Davies, 2003). In the *free narrative phase*, interviewers encourage the witness to expand in their own words on the central issue of the interview. Interviewers support the witness's narrative by *intelligent listening* ("uh huh . . . yes I see . . . and what happened next?"), a technique that serves to increase the amount reported (Davies, Westcott & Horan, 2000). Free narrative represents the single most accurate source of information available to the investigator (Bull, 1996), however, free narrative will invariably have to be supplemented by a third *questioning phase* to clarify and expand upon the issues raised. Many guidelines encourage interviewers to ask questions of increasing explicitness, though many find such a smooth progression very difficult in practice (Sternberg, Lamb, Davies & Westcott, 2001) and *Achieving Best Evidence* advocates a more general emphasis upon the value of open-ended questions. The final *closure phase* requires interviewers to summarise what the interviewee has said, using his or her own words whenever possible, before reverting to rapport topics to close the interview.

Evaluations conducted on the use of videotaped interviewers in England and Wales found that children giving evidence on tape were perceived as receiving greater social support and more at ease than children giving evidence in open court (Davies, Wilson, Mitchell & Milsom, 1995). Despite some initial scepticism from lawyers, take-up of the facility was extremely rapid and by 1998, 95% of all cases involving allegations of child sexual abuse coming before selected crown courts in England and Wales included applications to show videotapes (CPS Inspectorate, 1998). However, a recent report on vulnerable witnesses paints a less positive picture (Hamlyn et al., 2004): just 42% of all children not involved in abuse cases gave evidence on tape and just 5% of vulnerable adults gave evidence in this way. The same report also highlighted the positive advantages for witnesses of videotaped testimony: 98% of those giving video evidence were satisfied they had been given the opportunity to say all that they wished, compared to only 53% of those in open court.

Concern remains as to whether interviewers are actually following the guidelines proposed by regulatory bodies like the Home Office. A content analysis of over 100 interviews conducted with children by 13 different police forces in England and Wales showed that closed or specific questions made up 75% of all questions, with open-ended questions constituting less than 7% (Sternberg et al., 2001). Given the experimental finding that children appear particularly vulnerable to answering specific questions referring to non-observable events (Waterman, Blades & Spencer, 2000), there is clearly a need for greater training for interviewers in the use of open-ended prompts. One way forward is to be more prescriptive as to the form of questions asked in interviews. *Achieving Best Evidence* offers examples of "off-the-peg" prompts and questions, while the NICHD protocol developed by Lamb, Sternberg and colleagues adopts a semi-scripted approach. The latter technique leads to a demonstrable increase in the number of open-ended questions and in extended narrative elicited from children, but requires a rigorous level of training to first instil and then maintain such skills among interviewers (Sternberg et al., 2001).

Social Support for the Witness

The idea of offering social support to vulnerable witnesses to assist in giving their evidence is sometimes seen as a rival solution to electronic means: this will only be the case in legislatures like those in the United States, which limit access to videotechnology for constitutional reasons (Myers, 1996). In most other common law jurisdictions, the use of social and electronic support will be complimentary. What is meant by social support? It is the provision of information and of trained personnel to support vulnerable witnesses in the period leading up to the court appearance and again when witnesses attend court.

Regarding *pre-trial support*, there is great variation both between and within legislatures in the amount and intensity of provision. A major concern is the *intimidation of witnesses* through threats of violence against them or their loved ones. The UK and the USA are among many countries where the police offer witness protection programmes, which may involve a change of identity and the physical relocation of the witness and, if necessary, their entire family from one place to another (Fyfe, 2001). While such radical measures apply to only a minority of witnesses in the most serious crimes, police have become increasingly proactive against lower level intimidation. A recent survey in England and Wales of vulnerable witnesses reported that police intervened in two-thirds of cases of which they were notified and were successful in stopping intimidation in about half of these (Hamlyn et al., 2004). Police forces in Australia and New Zealand have also been active in mounting successful programmes to deal with such low-level intimidation (Reid Howie Associates, 2002). In the UK, the *No Witness, No Justice* initiative has introduced dedicated witness care units into police forces across England and Wales: pilot projects produced a 19% increase in the number of witnesses attending court (Avail Consulting, 2004).

Fear and ignorance of the courtroom process have been identified as significant stressors for vulnerable witnesses, particularly children (Plotnikoff & Woolfson, 1996). Various initiatives have been introduced to provide *pre-court preparation* for witnesses, which again vary in their scope and ambition. At the lower end, they include the provision of books, CD-ROMS or other educational materials designed to explain how courts operate and the identity and function of the different professionals involved. Information is often provided on legal terminology, as research demonstrates that witness understanding of even common terms used in the courtroom is deficient (Walker, 1993). In many countries age-appropriate materials have been developed for adults and children: in England the National Society for Prevention of Cruelty to Children (NSPCC)-sponsored *Child Witness Pack* includes a pop-up courtroom (Plotnikoff & Woolfson 1995). Many legislatures have provision for a pre-trial visit by the witness to the court, normally accompanied by a supporter, but provision of this basic facility can be patchy, when liaison between the various bodies involved is ineffective (Plotnikoff & Woolfson, 1996).

More ambitious programmes have involved so-called "court schools" run for children and their parents, where witnesses learn about the demands of the legal process, stress reduction techniques, enhancing confidence and meet informally with the judge or prosecutor (Lipovski &

Stern, 1997). Probably the best known of these projects was conducted by the London County Court Clinic (Sas et al., 1991; Sas, Hurley, Hatch, Malla & Dick, 2003). Over a three-year period, child witnesses were assigned to the special eight-week programme or to a control group who visited court and had one brief session on court procedure. Children who completed the full programme enjoyed higher rates of guilty verdicts at trial and showed better subsequent emotional adjustment (see Davies & Westcott, 1995). Similar initiatives for adult witnesses involved in rape and domestic violence cases have also been instituted in Canada, New Zealand and elsewhere (Reid Howie Associates, 2002), but their effectiveness has yet to be rigorously evaluated. Attempts to apply the London model widely have often been frustrated by a combination of high cost, inconsistent attendance by witnesses and concerns among lawyers that witnesses will be coached or otherwise have their evidence contaminated by such interventions (Aldridge & Freshwater, 1993; Mellor & Dent, 1994).

Similar legal anxieties over contamination have frequently interfered with the provision of therapy prior to trial for witnesses who have experienced trauma as a result of offences perpetrated against them. As part of the *Speaking Up for Justice* initiative, the British government launched new guidelines for the provision of therapy for child witnesses (Home Office, 2001) and for adults (Crown Prosecution Service, 2005). The guidance emphasizes that Crown prosecutors have no authority to prevent therapy taking place, but acknowledge the risks involved for the trial process that they believe can be overcome through appropriate questioning by the therapist and proper record keeping. However, there is, as yet, no evaluation as to the effectiveness of this new guidance and experience in other legislatures suggests that witnesses may continue to have difficulty achieving the help they need while legal proceedings are still active (Lipovski & Stern, 1997).

What of *support at trial*? Programmes are available in most common-law countries to provide *supporters* to assist witnesses on the day of the trial, but again provision is often haphazard (Plotnikoff & Woolfson, 2004). In England and Wales, where assistance is provided by the Victim Support Service and the Witness Service, a recent survey found that just 35% of witnesses were escorted to court by a supporter (Hamlyn et al., 2004). The same survey found that 23% of witnesses waited over four hours to give their evidence; here again, the services of a supporter would have been advantageous. Most witnesses (95%) waited in a separate waiting room to the defendant's witnesses, but 44% still encountered the accused prior to giving evidence. The supporter can liaise with court officials and the police so the witness is kept informed of relevant developments and the supporter in turn can appraise the court of any ongoing concerns that may affect the ability of the witness to give their best evidence. Once the witness is called, supporters normally position themselves in the body of the court where they are in sight of the witness. The Scottish courts have shown themselves particularly flexible in their treatment of supporters. The official guidance allows supporters to sit beside witnesses when giving their evidence and even to intervene should a witness break down during examination (Scottish Executive, 2005). Supporters in some legislatures are termed *victim-advocates*: the active presence of such advocates has been shown to be associated with an increased readiness to testify in domestic violence cases in the United States (Dawson & Dinovitzer, 2001) and Australia (Australian Law Reform Commission, 2001).

CONCLUSIONS

This chapter began by setting out the scope of the problem of attrition and listing some of the reasons why vulnerable witnesses in general and victims in particular drop out of the criminal justice system. It then went on to review what can be done to assist witnesses in having their day in court, through the innovative use of videotechnology and social support, highlighting examples of best practice from across the Western world. However, what is required in order to achieve a step-change in the number of vulnerable witnesses is a coordinated programme embracing all aspects of the criminal justice system. As Kelly et al. (2005) note: "From the perspective of complainants, the difference in perceptions between themselves and [the prosecuting authorities] was too often not just a gap but a chasm. If, however, each point in the attrition process is examined in detail, what emerges is a series of smaller gaps, each of which could be bridged by targeted interventions" (p. xii). How might these smaller gaps be bridged?

First, it is critical that vulnerable and intimidated victims/witnesses are identified at an early stage: this may require training for police officers and social workers who in research have been shown to be frequently unaware of vulnerability among witnesses (Gudjonsson, Clare, Rutter & Pearse, 1993). Second, there must be improved levels of support and encouragement for complainants at all stages. This again requires specialist training and the involvement of relevant voluntary agencies (Kebbell & Davies, 2003). There is a need for specially trained, specialist police officers and prosecuting lawyers, to deal with cases involving *all* vulnerable and intimidated witnesses. Sanders et al. (1997) have stressed that the police and the Crown Prosecution Service must be "sensitive to the vulnerable victim's needs, capabilities and sensibilities" (p. 81). Above all, there should be better communication between all authorities and complainants. Psychologists will have a role to play in this process, as court-appointed experts, as researchers and as trainers.

Other areas for improvement concern issues around case handling. There is a need to review the decision making by which cases are judged to meet prosecution criteria, and to review how previous court experiences and outcomes influence such decision making. So often cases revolve around the testimony of the victim and this needs to be supplemented wherever possible by additional evidence "in the form of photographs and reports that can be used at later stages" (Harris & Grace, 1999, p. xiii). At court there is a continuing need for better protection for vulnerable and intimidated victims/witnesses. It is important to ensure equality between defendants and vulnerable victims or witnesses in their treatment by the court, especially with respect to language used and understanding of the court process, and to ensure "advocacy that does justice to the complainant's account" (Kelly et al., 2005, p.xii). As Sanders et al. (1997) note "It is [important] to recognise that normal procedures which create formal equality between defendant and victim often create substantive inequality when the victim is vulnerable" (p. 87). Psychologists, working in tandem with witness support organisations, police and legal personnel, again have an important role to play in realising this demanding agenda.

The logical consequence of coordinated interventions should be more vulnerable witnesses appearing at court. But will this mean more successful prosecutions? In absolute terms this seems likely, but will the proportion of successful prosecutions also increase? This seems much more problematic. While isolated examples of increased success have been noted in the witness preparation literature, there are as many negative instances. For instance, the survey of trial outcomes linked to the introduction of video evidence in England and Wales showed a substantial increase in the number of cases coming forward, but the rate of successful prosecution did not change (Davies et al., 1995).

To tackle this problem requires a re-examination of fundamental common-law principles such as cross-examination, which inevitably discriminate against vulnerable witnesses (Plotnikoff & Woolfson, 2004; Westcott, 1995). Here again, psychologists have an important role to play as researchers, as exemplified by the work of Zajac and Hayne, who in a series of ingenious experiments, have demonstrated that for children, cross-examination leads to the retraction of many truthful as well as false statements to the detriment of their credibility and the truth (Zajac, Gross & Hayne, 2003; Zajac & Hayne, in press). Until the tectonic plates of the legal system begin to shift, many vulnerable individuals will continue to suffer, first as victims and later as witnesses.

NOTE

1 In this and subsequent studies, only selected statistics are reported here –
for example, missing data is not included.

REFERENCES

Aldridge, J., & Freshwater, J. (1993). The preparation of the child witness.
Journal of Child Law, 5, 25–27.

Australian Law Reform Commission (2001). *Access to Justice: Court support
schemes.* ALRC 69, (pp. 1–7). Sydney: Australian Law Reform Commission.

Avail Consulting (2004). *No witness, no justice (NMNJ) Pilot Evaluation. Executive summary.* Retrieved from http://www.cps.gov.uk/publications/docs/
NWNJ_executive_summary_291004.pdf

Bull, R.H.C. (1996). Good practice for video recorded interviews with child
witnesses for use in criminal proceedings. In G. Davies, S. Lloyd-Bostock,
M. McMurran & C. Wilson (Eds), *Psychology, law and criminal justice:
International developments in research and practice.* Berlin: de Gruyter
(pp. 100–117).

Cashmore, J. (2002). Innovative procedures for child witnesses. In H. L.
Westcott, G.M. Davies, & R.H.C. Bull (Eds), *Children's testimony: A hand-
book of psychological research and forensic practice.* Chichester: John Wiley
& Sons, Ltd. (pp. 203–217).

Cashmore, J. & de Haas, N. (1992).*The use of closed circuit television for child
witnesses in the ACT.* Sydney: Australian Law Reform Commission

Crown Prosecution Service Inspectorate. (1998). *Report on cases involving child
witnesses.* London: Crown Prosecution Service Inspectorate.

Crown Prosecution Service. (2005). *Provision of therapy for vulnerable or intimidated adult witnesses prior to a criminal trial: Practice guidance.* Retrieved
from www.cps.gov.uk/publications/prosecution/pretrialadult.html

Davies, G.M. (1994). Editorial. Live links: Understanding the message of the
medium. *Journal of Forensic Psychiatry, 5*, 225–227.

Davies, G.M. (1999). The impact of television on the presentation and reception of children's evidence. *International Journal of Law and Psychiatry, 22*,
241–256.

Davies, G.M. (2003). In the footsteps of Varendonck. In L. Kools, G. Vervaeke,
M. Vanderhallen & J. Goethals (Eds), *The truth and nothing but the truth?
The relation between law and psychology.* Bruges, Belgium: Die Keure
(pp. 1–22).

Davies, G.M. & Noon, E. (1991). *An evaluation of the live link for child witnesses.*
London: Home Office.

Davies, G.M. & Westcott, H. (1995). The child witness in the courtroom: Protection or empowerment? In M.S. Zarogoza, J.R. Graham, G.C.N. Hall, R.
Hirschman & Y.S. Ben Porath (Eds), *Memory and testimony in the child witness.* Newbury Park, CA: Sage (pp. 199–213).

Davies, G., Wilson, C., Mitchell, R. & Milsom, J. (1995). *Videotaping children's
evidence: An evaluation.* London: Home Office

Davies, G.M., Westcott, H. & Horan, N. (2000). The impact of questioning style
on the content of investigative interviews with suspected child sex abuse
victims. *Psychology, Crime and Law, 6*, 81–97.

Davis, G., Hoyano, L., Keenan, C., Maitland, L. & Morgan, R. (1999) *An assessment of the admissibility and sufficiency of evidence in child abuse prosecutions*. London: Home Office.

Dawson, M. & Dinovitzer, R. (2001). Victim cooperation and the prosecution of domestic violence in a specialized court. *Justice Quarterly, 18,* 593–622.

Flin, R., Stevenson, Y. & Davies, G.M. (1989). Children's knowledge of court proceedings. *British Journal of Psychology, 80,* 285–297.

Fyfe, N.R. (2001). *Protecting intimidated witnesses*. Aldershot: Ashgate.

Gallagher, B. & Pease, K. (2000) *Understanding the attrition of child abuse and neglect cases in the criminal justice system*. Unpublished report to the ESRC (R000236891).

Goodman, G.S., Taub, E.P., Jones, D.P.H., England, P., Port, L.K., Rudy, L. & Prado, L. (1992) Testifying in criminal court: Emotional effects on child sexual assault victims. *Monographs of the Society of Research, 57* (5, whole No. 229).

Goodman, G.S., Tobey, A.E., Batterman-France, J.M., Orcutt, H., Thomas, S., Shapiro, C. & Sachsemaier, T. (1998). Face-to-face confrontation: Effects of closed-circuit technology on children's eyewitness testimony and jurors' decisions. *Law and Human Behavior, 22,* 165–203.

Gudjonsson, G.H. Clare, I.C.H., Rutter, S. & Pearse, J. (1993). *Persons at risk during interviews in police custody: The identification of vulnerabilities. Royal Commission on Criminal Justice*. London: HMSO.

Hamlyn, B., Phelps, A., Turtle, J. & Sattar, G. (2004). *Are special measures working? Evidence from surveys of vulnerable and intimidated witnesses*. London: Home Office (HO Research Study 283).

Harris, J. & Grace, S. (1999) *A Question of evidence? Investigating and prosecuting rape in the 1990s*. London: Home Office (HO Research Study 196).

Hill, P.E. & Hill, S.M. (1987). Videotaping children's testimony: An empirical view. *Michigan Law Review, 85,* 809–833.

Home Office. (1992). *The memorandum of good practice on video recorded interviews with child witnesses for criminal proceedings*. London: Home Office

Home Office. (1998). *Speaking up for justice: Report of the interdepartmental working group on the treatment of vulnerable and intimidated witnesses in the criminal justice system*. London: Home Office.

Home Office (2001). *Provision for therapy for child witnesses prior to a criminal trial: Practice Guidance*. London: Home Office.

Home Office. (2002) *Achieving best evidence in criminal proceedings: Guidance for vulnerable or intimidated witnesses, including children*. London: Home Office.

Kebbell, M. & Davies, G. (2003). People with intellectual disabilities in the investigation and prosecution of crime. Special Section, edited by M. Kebbell and G. Davies. *Legal and Criminological Psychology, 8,* 219–266.

Keep, G. (1996). *Going to court: Child witnesses in their own words*. London: ChildLine.

Kelly, L., Lovett, J. & Regan, L. (2005). *A gap or a chasm? Attrition in reported rape cases*. London: Home Office (HO Research Study 293).

Landstrom, S., Granhag, P.A. & Hartwig, M. (2005). Witnesses appearing live versus on video: Effects on observers' perception, veracity assessments and memory. *Applied Cognitive Psychology, 19,* 913–934.

Lipovski, J. & Stern, P. (1997). Preparing children for court: An interdisciplinary view. *Child Maltreatment, 2,* 150–163.

Mellor, A. & Dent, H. (1994). Preparation of child witnesses for court. *Child Abuse Review, 3,* 165–17.

Montoya, J. (1995). Lessons from Akiki and Michaels on shielding child witnesses. *Psychology, Public Policy, and Law, 1,* 340–369.

Murray, K. (1995). *Live television link – An evaluation of its use by child witnesses in Scottish criminal trials.* Edinburgh: The Scottish Office.

Myers, J.E.B. (1996). A decade of international reform to accommodate child witnesses: Steps toward a child witness code. *Pacific Law Journal, 28,* 169–241.

O'Grady, C. (1996). *Child witnesses and jury trials: an evaluation of the use of closed circuit television and removable screens in Western Australia.* Report prepared for the Ministry of Justice, Western Australia.

Orcutt, H.K., Goodman, G.S., Tobey, A.E., Batterman-Faunce, J.M. & Thomas, S. (2001). Detecting deception in children's testimony: Factfinders' abilities to reach the truth in open court and closed-circuit trials. *Law and Human Behavior, 25,* 339–372.

Pigot, T. (1989). *Report of the advisory group on video evidence.* London: Home Office.

Plotnikoff, J. & Woolfson, R. (1995) *Prosecuting child abuse: An evaluation of the government's speedy progress policy.* London: Blackstone Press.

Plotnikoff, J. & Woolfson, R. (1996). Evaluation of witness service support for child witnesses. In *Children in court.* London: Victim Support (pp. 1–92).

Plotnikoff, J. & Woolfson, R. (2004) *In their own words: The experiences of 50 young witnesses in criminal proceedings.* London: NSPCC.

Reid Howie Associates (2002). *Vulnerable and intimidated witnesses: Review of provisions in other jurisdictions.* Edinburgh: Scottish Executive.

Sanders, A. Creaton, J., Bird, S. & Weber, L. (1997). *Victims with learning disabilities: Negotiating the criminal justice system.* Oxford: University of Oxford Centre for Criminological Research.

Sas, L.D., Cunningham, A.H., Hurley, P., Dick, T. & Farnsworth, A. (1995). *Tipping the balance to tell the secret: Public discovery of child sexual abuse.* London, Ontario: London Family Court Clinic, Child Witness Project.

Sas, L., Hurley, P., Austin, G. & Wolfe, D. (1991). *Reducing the system induced trauma for child sexual abuse victims through court preparation, assessment and follow up.* London, Ontario: London Family Court Clinic.

Sas, L.D., Hurley, P., Hatch, A., Malla, S. & Dick, T. (2003). *Three years after the verdict: a longitudinal study of the social and psychological adjustment of child witnesses referred to the child witness project.* London, Ontario: London Family Court Clinic, Child Witness Project.

Saywitz, K.R. & Nathanson, R. (1993). Children's testimony and their perceptions of stress in and out of the courtroom. *Child Abuse and Neglect, 17,* 613–622.

Scottish Executive (2005). The use of a supporter. In *Special measures for vulnerable adult and child witnesses: A guidance pack.* Edinburgh: Scottish Executive.

Sharland, E., Seal, H., Croucher, M., Aldgate, J. & Jones, D. (1996). *Professional intervention in child sexual abuse.* London: HMSO.

Sternberg, K.J., Lamb, M.E., Davies, G.M. & Westcott, H.L. (2001). The memorandum of good practice: Theory versus application. *Child Abuse and Neglect, 25,* 669–681.

Swim, J.K., Borgida, E. & McCoy, K. (1993). Videotaped versus in-court witness testimony: Does protecting the child witness jeopardize due process? *Journal of Applied Social Psychology, 23,* 603–631.

Walker, A.G. (1993). Questioning young children at court: A linguistic case study. *Law and Human Behavior, 7,* 59–81.

Waterman, A., Blades, M. & Spencer, C. (2000). Children's comprehension of questions. In H. Westcott, G. Davies & R. Bull (Eds), *Children's testimony: Psychological research and forensic practice*. Chichester: John Wiley & Sons, Ltd (pp. 146–159).

Westcott, H.L. (1995). Children's experiences of being examined and cross-examined: The opportunity to be heard? *Expert Evidence, 4*, 13.

Westcott, H.L. & Davies, G.M. (1996) Sexually abused children's and young people's perspectives on investigative interviews. *British Journal of Social Work, 26*, 451–474.

Westcott, H., Davies, G.M. & Clifford, B.R. (1991). Adult's perceptions of children's videotaped truthful and deceptive statements. *Children and Society, 5*, 123–135.

Westcott, H., Davies, G.M. & Spencer, J. (1999). Children, hearsay and the courts. *Psychology, Public Policy, and Law, 5*, 1–22.

Zajac, R., Gross, J. & Hayne, H. (2003). Asked and answered: Questioning children in the courtroom. *Psychiatry, Psychology and Law, 10*, 199–209.

Zajac, R. & Hayne, H. (in press). The negative effect of cross-examination style questioning on children's accuracy: Older children are not immune. *Applied Cognitive Psychology*.

CHAPTER 11

Communicating Risk
to the Court

DON GRUBIN

INTRODUCTION

It is not unusual for evaluators to reach different conclusions about risk
even though their assessments were carried out in a similar manner
and the same information was available to both. Although such disagreement may be fundamental to adversarial systems of law, it suggests uncertainty about the nature of risk assessment and highlights
the misconceptions that can occur in the determination of risk in offenders. Confusion can arise from a number of sources. The questions
asked by those requesting an assessment are not always what is being
answered by those carrying it out, but this discordance is frequently
obscured by the fact that both make use of the same terms. Lack of
clarity in terminology may be compounded by the absence of a coherent
framework with which to understand risk, leading to an idiosyncratic
application of "evidence" that varies between assessors, and varies over
time in the work of an individual examiner. These factors can also result in potentially unedifying arguments about the merits of actuarial
as opposed to clinical approaches to risk assessment, and vice versa.

The confusion in the nature of risk assessment, and a model to assist
in unravelling it, are explored in this chapter. (See also the chapter by
Howells and Stacey in this book for a discussion of the characteristics
of individual offenders.)

Practical Psychology for Forensic Investigations and Prosecutions.
Edited by Mark R. Kebbell and Graham M. Davies. © 2006 John Wiley & Sons, Ltd.

THE MEANING OF RISK

When applied to offenders, risk is a much more complex concept than it appears on the surface. It comprises an unstable mix of the likelihood of an individual carrying out a specific action, the degree of harm that action might cause, its imminence and its potential frequency over the longer term – although applied to an offender, it in fact relates to the offender's behaviour. This is masked by the condensation of risk into categories such as "low", "medium" and "high". As the two examples below illustrate, these classifications conflate different aspects of risk in ways that may not be immediately clear when cases are considered on their own:

> GS is a 36-year-old man due to be released from prison following a conviction for the sexual murder of a 20-year-old woman that took place 15 years ago. The victim's body was found on wasteland near to her home. Her clothes were ripped but only partially removed, there were bite marks on both breasts, and there were other indicators of a sexually sadistic attack. GS met his victim while drinking in a pub with work colleagues, and he admitted to being with her before her death, but he claimed amnesia for the offence, attributing his lack of recall to alcohol consumption. When his residence was searched a large collection of sexually sadistic pornography was found, and in prison he disclosed a rich sadistic fantasy life. He was living alone at the time of the offence, and he had never been in a long-term relationship. He had little in the way of offence-specific treatment in prison, but he denied any sexually deviant fantasies for a number of years.
>
> KD is a 24-year-old man with seven convictions for indecent exposure, although he is known to have exposed himself on hundreds of occasions. His offending always follows a common pattern: he approaches young women in public parks and similar places, attracts their attention and then exposes himself while masturbating. He never approaches his victims or says anything to them, and on the few occasions when he has been confronted he runs off. He reports that he offends at times of stress. Apart from indecent exposure he has a number of convictions for burglary, but none for violence. He has received treatment in the past from a psychiatrist, and he has been dealt with by the courts with fines, probation orders and short prison sentences.

Few would argue that when compared with GS, KD has a greater likelihood of reoffending, and any reoffending by him will probably be sooner and of a higher frequency. Many would be uncomfortable, however, in concluding that KD is a "higher" risk than GS given the different consequences associated with their offending. This may be lost when KD is considered in isolation, with his risk qualified only when contrasted with GS, and varying aspects of risk move into the foreground.

When assessing an offender, at least five different types of risk need to be considered:

- likelihood of reoffending;
- imminence of reoffending;
- frequency of reoffending;
- consequences of reoffending;
- escalation of offending.

As the cases above illustrate it is easy to slip between these distinct aspects of risk unawares, with the risk of further offending (likelihood) in particular becoming blurred with the risk of harm (consequences). When sentencing decisions are being made, considerations of likelihood and consequences tend to dominate, but when management plans are being determined imminence and frequency become more pertinent (an offender who is at high risk of reoffending soon is of more concern than one who is at high risk of reoffending sometime). Assessing these diverse types of risk requires different approaches and involves differing considerations.

PREDICTION VERSUS ASSESSMENT

Courts, and others involved in the management of offenders, typically want to know whether or not an individual will reoffend, or sometimes more bluntly, whether he or she is "dangerous". Evaluators, however, are not capable of answering such questions in a dichotomous, yes or no manner. Human behaviour is dependent on the myriad ways in which circumstances may come together but which no one, except perhaps biblical prophets, can claim to foresee – in other words, events are conditional on certain things happening. Evaluators, therefore, resort to probabilistic determinations of the likelihood of future harm (Steadman, 2000), using words such as low, medium, high, possible, probable, likely and a range of similar terms. By doing so they are making assessments, or judgements, of risk, not predictions of events.

While it is relatively straightforward to prove whether or not a prediction is right – the event predicted either happens or not – this is not the case with assessments. A weather forecast that states there is a 60% chance of rain tomorrow is not incorrect if it does not rain tomorrow, and can only be shown to be wrong if it doesn't rain on 60% of the tomorrows for which the forecast is made. Another way to illustrate this point is to consider the risk of an accident in an 18-year-old driver who has just bought a high-powered sports car and who is fond of driving at high speeds with a fair bit of alcohol inside him. Most would say that this driver's risk of having an accident is high, but if he does not have an accident over the next year it does not mean that the original risk assessment was wrong, and that his risk was really low all along.

This difference between assessment and prediction is not always understood, even by those carrying out assessments. Variables in the research literature that have been shown to "predict" reoffending can be applied clinically, but when they are, this is as an evidence base to support the assessment, not as a predictor. Unlike a research study, the evaluator is not "wrong" if a high risk offender does not reoffend, or when a low risk offender does, and it makes no sense to talk in the research vernacular of "false positives" and "false negatives" in clinical settings.

THE MEANING OF LEVEL OF RISK

Even when different aspects of risk are clearly teased out, there remains the issue of clarifying just what terms such as low, medium, high etc., mean. Often they are little more than markers of subjective belief: an offender who is a "medium" risk of reoffending (focusing on *likelihood* of reoffending for present purposes) is a greater risk than someone who is rated as "low", but not as much of a risk as someone judged as "high"; similar functions are performed by terms such as "possible", "probable", "more likely than not". The lack of precision inherent in these concepts makes them ripe for challenge, and difficult to defend (Edwards, Elwyn & Mulley, 2002). This has led to attempts to quantify risk – if an evaluator can state that the risk of reoffending is 60%, for example, than it can be left to decision makers to determine whether this should be considered as medium, high, very high, probable or whatever.

But quantification brings with it its own sources of confusion. While accepting that risk assessments are probabilistic statements, the "meaning" of this probability still needs to be clarified. A 60% likelihood of reoffending, for example, does not entail that a specified individual will reoffend 60% of the time; it is not the same "type" of probability as that involved in saying that over time the number 3 will occur on one in six rolls of a dice. Nor does it mean that if we only had enough information our probability estimate would approach 100%, as it would if we knew the precise physical characteristics of the dice and the forces applied to it when it is rolled – it is unlikely that we will ever have such knowledge of the laws of human behaviour, or all the relevant "variables" to enter into our equations. More information in these circumstances does not improve accuracy, only certainty.

The probability involved in risk assessment determinations are not statements about the individual being evaluated, but about people "like" him. The conclusion that an offender has a 60% likelihood of reoffending means that over time, 6 out of 10 individuals with characteristics similar to him will reoffend. In other words, the offender is being assigned to a group; the more individuals in the group who reoffend, the higher risk the group represents overall.

The importance of distinguishing between individual and group probabilities becomes clear when one considers the misunderstanding that is sometimes associated with a determination that an offender has a "50% chance of reoffending". As a probability statement about an individual such a finding would suggest a 50–50 risk of reoffending, no better than flipping a coin. The apparent randomness disappears, however, when one recognizes that the statement really means that one in two people like this individual will reoffend. If there is a 50% chance of rain you might consider bringing a raincoat to the picnic, whereas you would probably leave your raincoat at home if the chance of rain was 10% (although even then the decision would also depend on how adverse you were to getting wet).

THE FORMATION OF RISK GROUPS: ACTUARIAL VERSUS CLINICAL ASSESSMENT

Approaches to the determination of risk in offenders often polarize into debates about the merits or otherwise of actuarial versus structured clinical types of assessment (Dolan & Doyle, 2000), even though this restricts the issue to the likelihood of reoffending.

Actuarial assessments are based on risk tables developed from studies involving large numbers of offenders, using variables that are defined and scored in specified ways and then combined according to predetermined rules, in a manner similar to the way in which risk is established in insurance settings (Grove & Meehl, 1996). In theory, there is no room for subjective bias, either in terms of the variables chosen for analysis or the weight given to them – insurance premiums are not decided by the mood of the person taking your details on the end of the phone, or whether that person likes you or not.

Structured clinical assessment involves consideration of a much wider information base obtained from both interview and documentation that focuses on clinical areas known to be associated with reoffending, usually leaving it up to the evaluator to decide which variables are most important in individual cases. Supporters of structured clinical judgement maintain that in highlighting characteristics of concern it provides more meaningful statements of risk than those associated with actuarial instruments (Hart, 1999; Webster, Douglas, Eaves & Hart, 1997).

It has been demonstrated consistently that actuarial type assessments are more accurate than assessments derived from more amorphous clinical experience, whether structured or otherwise. This is the case for both violent (Grove & Meehl, 1996; Mossman, 1994) and sex offending (Hanson & Morton-Bourgon, in press). But while proponents of clinical assessment accept that actuarial techniques are superior in creating risk groups, they argue that mechanical procedures and actuarial tables cannot take into account information pertinent to specific individuals within the groups, limiting the applicability of actuarial assessment. They also note that actuarial scales achieve at best only moderate levels of accuracy associated with ROC-AUC figures of between 65% and 80% – in other words, correctly classifying offenders two-thirds to just over three-quarters of the time – reasonably accurate but insufficiently so to be clinically useful (Mossman, 2000).

These arguments, however, tend to be at cross purposes. They imply that actuarial and clinical assessments are mutually exclusive, ignoring their potential to work together. For example, some researchers argue that any attempt to adjust actuarial findings with clinical information only makes the former less accurate and thus should never be done (Harris & Rice, 1997, 2003), although this leaves a big gap in reaching decisions about "medium risk" groups with offending rates between 15% and 40%. Similarly, clinical purists cannot ignore what insurance companies base their survival on – actuarial assessment works.

Before looking more specifically at actuarial and structured clinical tools, therefore, it is worth considering in more detail how actuarial and clinical assessments can complement each other.

THE PROCESS OF RISK ASSESSMENT

Consider how a doctor might go about assessing the risk of myocardial infarction in one of his patients. A man aged 20 with a marked family history of heart disease – having a number of close relatives who died in their 40s from myocardial infarctions – would be said to have a high *long-term* risk of having a myocardial infarction himself. This long-term risk is on the whole static and unchanging (although it may reduce when he has reached his 50s). Once aware of the risk, however, attention can be paid to factors that will influence it, such as raised blood pressure or high blood cholesterol levels (which may in the end turn out to be the underlying mediators of his risk). These are relatively stable characteristics, but can be modified by treatment, although they tend to return to baseline when treatment stops. There

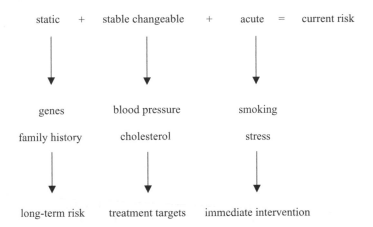

Figure 11.1 Risk assessment in myocardial infarction (see text)

is also another set of factors that will have a more immediate impact on the risk of myocardial infarction, such as smoking and stress. These are risk factors that fluctuate over short periods of time, and can be modified straightaway through intervention. The individual's *current* risk, therefore, will depend on the interplay between these three types of risk factor (Figure 11.1), but regardless, his long-term risk of myocardial infarction will remain high.

Risk assessment in offenders can be thought of in a similar manner (Figure 11.2).

Static risk factors, based on historical characteristics such as past convictions, offence type and age, provide an estimate of *long-term* risk. Long-term risk is relatively inert and changes only passively.

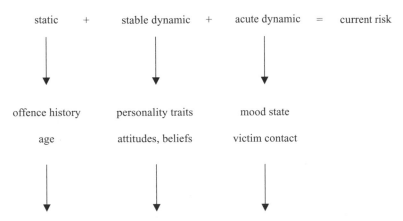

Figure 11.2 Risk assessment in offenders with examples of risk factors

Individuals get older, and they may commit more and different types of offences, but static factors change in only one direction – an offender cannot reduce the number of offences he has committed, or lower his age.

Whether or not this long-term risk manifests itself in reoffending is dependent on other, dynamic factors that are more proximal to offending. Hanson and Harris (2000) refer to these as stable dynamic and stable acute risk factors:

> *Stable dynamic* risk factors relate to, for example, personality traits, attitudes, beliefs, response styles and similar features that determine what an individual is like and how he functions. These have been described as the psychological underpinning of offending, and recourse to them can help explain what it is about an individual that makes him a risk. They also represent appropriate targets for treatment.
>
> *Acute dynamic* risk factors change more rapidly than static ones, and relate to circumstances, states and behaviours rather than to underlying psychological characteristics. They include such things as mood state, intoxication and activities that bring an offender into contact with potential victims.

A determination of the consequences of offending must also be incorporated into the overall assessment, which in the case of myocardial infarction was explicit from the outset. This type of model is probably best developed in respect of sex offenders (Hanson & Harris, 2000; Thornton, 2002).

Different approaches, instruments and techniques are more appropriate for each of these three stages:

- Actuarial assessments are best suited for the first stage in the process, the determination of long-term risk. They address a single issue only: the likelihood of reoffending over a set period of time. They provide a baseline on which an overall assessment can be anchored, but say nothing about the consequences, imminence or frequency of offending, or the possibility of escalation in offence severity.
- Having assigned an offender to a risk group, actuarial assessments are silent regarding the specific individuals who comprise the groups. To determine the nature and extent of any stable dynamic risk factors, more clinically focused evaluations are required, of the sort provided by structured clinical judgement and psychometric examinations.
- Because of the motivation many offenders have to conceal information of concern about them, assessment interviews and testing are of only limited use in identifying acute dynamic risk factors. Instead, monitoring and techniques like tagging and polygraph examination

(Grubin, Madsen, Parsons, Sosnowski & Warberg, 2004) provide a means to assist in detecting relevant changes in circumstances or behaviours.

Combining an assessment of long-term risk with the identification of dynamic risk factors enables the development of a coherent risk management strategy, regardless of whether the concern is about a patient having a heart attack or an offender committing another offence.

ACTUARIAL INSTRUMENTS

Most use is made of actuarial instruments in North America, where they are fundamental to identifying high risk offenders as defined by civil commitment laws (Janus & Meehl, 1997). In England they also play a role in assessing individuals labelled as having a Dangerous and Severe Personality Disorder (Home Office/Department of Health: http://www.dspdprogramme.gov.uk/). While their objective nature and quantifiable outcome makes them in theory well suited for this task, in practice evidence with which to validate specific instruments is sparse, and published peer-reviewed research is limited to a very small number of validation studies.

What actuarial instruments appear to do well is to identify a small group of offenders with a potentially high rate of reoffending. Their reasonably good specificity means that attention can be focused on a group of individuals who are genuinely high risk of committing another offence. However, the sensitivity of these instruments is less good – significant numbers of offenders in lower risk groups also reoffend. Although this does not mean such individuals have been wrongly classified (lower risk drivers still get in accidents), one must clearly avoid equating lower risk with no risk (Sjostedt & Langstrom, 2001).

Actuarial instruments can only apply to populations similar to those on which they were developed – an actuarial assessment of the risk of a car accident cannot be derived from a database of house burglaries. Because of the relatively large numbers needed to create an actuarial scale, actuarial instruments for reoffending are available only for adult male offenders, and these cannot be generalized to women or adolescents. It is also worth noting that because actuarial instruments are dependent on follow-up data from large cohorts of offenders, they are dated even before they are used. One cannot simply assume that the offenders on whom the scales are based, convicted 10 or 20 years ago, are similar to the offenders of today. This has become particularly pertinent, for example, with the emergence of sex offenders whose crimes relate to the internet, for whom very different factors may be associated with their offending than more typical sex offenders.

In this respect it is worth noting that the assessment of risk of reoffending is not equivalent to the assessment of offending in the first instance, and existing actuarial tools relate to the risk of reoffending only. Variables associated with reconviction are not necessarily the same as those that relate to offending in the first instance. For example, while there is a higher prevalence of sexual abuse in the histories of sex offenders than in the population as a whole (Hanson & Slater, 1988), such a history does not distinguish sex offenders who reoffend from those who do not (Hanson & Bussiere, 1998). Likewise, the importance of characteristics found in sex offenders may have limited relevance in non-offenders; rape fantasies, for example, are not uncommon among young males (Crepault & Couture, 1980), but their contribution to risk will differ between rapists and men who have not offended. The lessons of the criminal courts, therefore, cannot simply be transported to the civil arena.

There are a large number of risk assessment protocols for use with offenders, in particular for sex offenders; Doren (2002), for example lists over 20 for this latter group. A few of the better known tools are referred to below.

Violent Offending

The Violence Risk Appraisal Guide (VRAG) is a 12-item scale that was developed based on a Canadian maximum security hospital population. As such, all those in its developmental sample had convictions for serious offences as well as mental disorder, and it is not clear whether the instrument can be generalized across the offending spectrum. It is reported that virtually all those rated in the highest risk group will reoffend (Harris, Rice & Cormier, 2002), but the numbers in this group are so small, and the characteristics of the offenders in it so extreme, that this claim must be viewed cautiously.

More recently, the Classification of Violent Risk (COVR) actuarial instrument was developed from data collected in the MacArthur Violence Risk Assessment study (Monahan et al., 2005). This tool is more sophisticated than typical actuarial instruments, using a classification tree methodology that allows for a range of combinations of risk factors to be considered but requiring computer software to run. Although a less severe group than the one on which VRAG is based, it is still composed only of mentally disordered subjects.

Risk Matrix 2000 – Violence (RM 2000-V) is a 3-item scale used in Britain, with a development sample that was prison based. Unpublished data suggests that about 60% of offenders in its highest risk group will be reconvicted for a violent offence and it is of moderate accuracy overall, but there is no published data for this scale.

Comparisons between these scales is difficult because of the paucity of independent assessments relating to them that have been carried out. Their AUCs (see endnote 1 above) all seem to fall in the moderate range, but small numbers mean that confidence intervals are wide.

Sex Offending

Actuarial and quasi-actuarial instruments related to sex offenders all tend to tap into two domains, one related to general criminality (that is, factors that predict reoffending generally such as young age and past number of convictions), the other to sexual deviance (Hanson & Thornton, 2000). As such, they make use of similar variables, although they differ in the numbers of variables involved and the weightings each variable is given.

The Rapid Risk Assessment for Sexual Offence Recidivism (RRASOR) and Static-99 (Hanson & Thornton, 2000) are probably the most widely used sex offender actuarial assessments. RRASOR is composed of just 4 items (age, past sex offences, having unrelated victims and having male victims), while Static-99 is a 10-item inventory (which includes the four RRASOR variables). The 2 highest risk groups in the former are reported to have 10-year reconviction rates of about 50% and 75% respectively, while the highest risk group in the latter has a reconviction rate of approximately 50% over 15 years.

The Sex Offender Risk Appraisal Guide (SORAG) – a sister to VRAG – is another popular inventory, made up of 15 items (Quinsey, Harris, Rice & Cormier, 1998). As with VRAG, its developmental sample came from a high secure psychiatric hospital, and it requires substantially more, and less easy to obtain, information than do RRASOR and Static-99, such as the presence of personality disorder, substance use and childhood behavioural problems. Its developers report over 90% reconviction rates in the highest risk group, but again this includes very few individuals indeed. The Minnesota Sex Offender Screening Tool – Revised (MnSOST-R), a 16-item scale, is similarly dependent on clinically derived but more difficult to ascertain material (Epperson, Kaul, Huot, Goldman & Alexander, 2003).

In Britain, Risk Matrix 2000-Sex (RM 2000-S) is the standard actuarial assessment employed by the prison, probation and police services (Thornton et al., 2003). It is a 7-item scale that allocates offenders to low, medium, high and very high risk groups with reconviction rates of 60% in those rated very high risk.

Although independent validation of these scales is limited (Barbaree et al., 2001, being 1 of the few in the literature), and there is variation in accuracy reported in different samples, on the whole they all fall within a similar range of accuracy, with AUCs in the 0.70s. Apart from simplicity in use, there does not seem much to recommend 1 over the other.

There are as yet no actuarial scales appropriate for use in sex offenders under the age of 18, but 2 are in development: the Juvenile Sex Offender Assessment Protocol (J-SOAP; Prentky, Harris, Frizzell & Righthand, 2000), and the Estimate of Risk of Adolescent Sex Offender Recidivism (ERASOR; Worling, 2004); published information about either is limited.

Non-actuarial Scales

The most widely used protocols for structured clinical judgement have been developed on the west coast of Canada: the HCR-20 (Webster et al., 1997) for the assessment of violent risk; Sexual Violence Risk – 20 (SVR-20) (Boer, Hart, Kropp & Webster, 1997) and the Risk for Sexual Violence Protocol (RSVP) (Hart, Kropp & Laws, 2003) in relation to sexual risk; and the Spousal Assault Risk Assessment Guide (SARA) (Kropp, Hart, Webster & Eaves, 1995) have all spread internationally. They aim to provide a systematic review of a range of risk factors (historical, clinical and lifestyle related) that have been demonstrated to be associated with violent behaviour rather than produce a risk score, although broad risk "categories" of low, medium and high are created. Given the absence of quantification it can be difficult to test these types of scale, although there is evidence to indicate that reoffending is greater among those considered to be higher risk (for example, Douglas, Ogloff, Nicholls & Grant, 1999 in respect to the HCR-20).

A structured type of clinical assessment that nonetheless makes use of scoring algorithms is under development in North America in relation to sex offenders (Hanson & Harris, 2000). Referred to as the Dynamic Supervision Project, it comprises behavioural rating scales made up of stable and acute dynamic risk factors (for example, general and sexual self-regulation, important social influences, cooperation with supervision) that supervisors can score repeatedly over time, but which are anchored by an initial assessment on Static 99. It is being evaluated in a prospective design, which is rare in research of this kind; preliminary unpublished findings suggest that both the actuarial and dynamic components of the assessment contribute independently to outcome.

Although a different sort of assessment, the Psychopathy Checklist – Revised (Hare, 1991), a 20-item personality assessment for the presence of psychopathy, is widely used in risk assessment as those with high scores have been consistently shown to have higher rates of violent offending (Barbaree, Seto, Langton & Peacock, 2001); psychopathic traits include being manipulative, parasitic, grandiose and impulsive, among other characteristics. The Psychopathy Checklist is included as part of the structured risk assessments referred to above, as well as in some actuarial instruments. However, one must be cautious in its application as while the presence of psychopathy is a good indicator of a risk of violence, its absence does not equate with low risk.

Psychometric instruments have been advocated as a means of identifying stable dynamic risk factors, and a number have been employed, ranging from personality assessments to those that focus on specific psychological areas of functioning. While they can contribute to an overall evaluation, assisting in the identification of psychological factors that may underpin offending such as cognitive distortions, emotional dysregulation and poor life management skills (Thornton, 2002), the temptation to apply them in isolation is something that needs to be resisted as none have been demonstrated to be strongly predictive of reoffending.

Obtaining Information

An important difference between patients being evaluated for cardiac risk and offenders assessed for risk of reoffending is that the latter are generally less likely to disclose fully (or sometimes at all) the types of information required by the evaluator. Although this is not usually an issue in respect of static risk factors such as previous convictions used in the simpler actuarial measures, offenders may not report reliably, or even recognize, relevant aspects of their histories or current behaviour. In contrast, the doctor does not have to rely on a patient's self-report of diet in order to determine blood cholesterol levels, and there is little for a patient being treated for angina to gain by not telling the doctor that he smokes. In any case, the patient who hides important information from his doctor in the end harms only himself, but offenders who do so put others at risk from his reoffending.

Since the 1990s, the polygraph has become increasingly used in the management of offenders, particularly sex offenders, in the community. The information disclosed in polygraph examinations has been found to add to what is known about an offender's criminal background and the behaviours, not necessarily criminal in themselves, that are associated with it. Thus, offenders report more victims, different offence types and an earlier start to offending than was known based simply on official records and self-report (Grubin et al., 2004). Most of this work, however, is done in post-conviction settings, and it remains to be seen whether and how it can be integrated into assessments carried out for the courts.

CONCLUSION

Even the most careful of assessments can be skewed by irrelevant considerations. Personal feelings about an offender can lead to either an over- or underestimation of risk, and pre-existing assumptions, such as "everyone knows" that an individual is dangerous even though he scores lowly on assessment tools, can exert an invisible influence on outcome. The structure imposed by systematic assessment, however, increases the likelihood that external factors will become more transparent.

In communicating all this to the courts, it is important that clear statements are made about long-term risk and how this is determined, the consequences of any likely offending, the stable dynamic factors that "explain" the risk (for example, a strong sexual interest in children and a lack of emotionally intimate adult relationships), and the sort of acute factors (for instance, an ability to gain access to potential victims) that would suggest how imminent any reoffending might be. Although experts may continue to disagree in individual cases, decision makers will then be in a position to understand the basis of the disagreement, and to make their own determinations accordingly.

NOTE

1 Receiver Operator Characteristics (ROC) are a good measure of predictive accuracy where the base rate for the relevant outcome measure is low. It is reported in terms of the Area Under the Curve (AUC). An AUC of 0.5 indicates performance no better than chance, while an AUC of 1 would be perfect prediction. In practice, an AUC of 0.60–0.80 is usually considered to represent a moderate effect, while one of 0.80 or greater a large effect. In terms of outcome, the greater the AUC, the more likely it is that a randomly selected reoffender will come from a higher risk group than a randomly selected individual who has not reoffended.

REFERENCES

Barbaree, H.E., Seto, M.C., Langton, C. & Peacock, E. (2001). Evaluating the predictive accuracy of six risk assessment instruments for adult sex offenders. *Criminal Justice and Behavior, 28*, 490–521.

Boer, D.P., Hart, S.D., Kropp, P.R. & Webster, C.D. (1997). *Manual for the Sexual Violence Risk – 20: Professional guidelines for assessing risk of sexual violence.* The British Columbia Institute Against Family Violence; The Mental Health, Law and Policy Institute, Simon Fraser University.

Crepault, E. & Couture, M. (1980). Men's erotic fantasies. *Archives of Sexual Behaviour, 9*, 565–581.

Dolan, M. & Doyle, C. (2000). Violence risk prediction: Clinical and actuarial measures and the role of the Psychopathy Checklist. *British Journal of Psychiatry, 177*, 303–311.

Doran, D.M. (2002). *Evaluating sex offenders: A manual for civil commitments and beyond.* London: Sage.

Douglas, K.S., Ogloff, J.R.P., Nicholls, T.L. & Grant, I. (1999). Assessing risk for violence among psychiatric patients: The HCR-20 violence risk assessment scheme and the Psychopathy Checklist: Screening version. *Journal of Consulting and Clinical Psychology, 67*, 917–930.

Edwards, A., Elwyn, G. & Mulley, A. (2002). Explaining risks: Turning numerical data into meaningful pictures. *British Medical Journal, 324*, 827–830.

Epperson, D.L., Kaul, J.D., Huot, S., Goldman, R. & Alexander, W. (2003). Minnesota Sex Offender Screening Tool – Revised (MnSOST-R) technical paper: Development, validation, and recommended risk level cut scores. HTTP://129.186.143.73/Faculty/Epperson/Mnsost_Download.htm.

Grove, W. & Meehl, P. (1996). Comparative efficiency of informal (subjective, impressionistic) and formal (mechanical, algorithmic) prediction procedures: The clinical–statistical controversy. *Psychology, Public Policy and Law, 2*, 293–323.

Grubin, D., Madsen, L., Parsons, S., Sosnowski, D. & Warberg, B. (2004). A prospective study of the impact of polygraphy on high risk behaviours in adult sex offenders. *Sexual Abuse: A Journal of Research and Treatment, 16*, 209–222.

Hanson, R.K. & Bussiere, M.T. (1998). Predicting relapse: A meta-analysis of sexual offender recidivism studies. *Journal of Consulting and Clinical Psychology, 66*, 348–362.

Hanson, R.K. & Harris, A.J.R. (2000). Where should we intervene? Dynamic predictors of sex offense recidivism. *Criminal Justice and Behavior, 27*, 6–35.

Hanson, R.K. & Morton-Bourgon, K.E. (in press). The characteristics of persistent sex offenders: A meta-analysis of recidivism studies. *Journal of Consulting and Clinical Psychology.*

Hanson, R.K. & Slater, S. (1988). Sexual victimization in the history of sexual abusers: A review. *Annals of Sex Research, 1*, 485–499.

Hanson, R.K. & Thornton, D. (2000). Improving risk assessments for sex offenders: A comparison of three actuarial scales. *Law and Human Behavior, 24*, 119–136.

Hare, R. (1991). *Manual for the Fevised Psychopathy Checklist.* Toronto: Multihealth Systems, Inc.

Harris, G.T. & Rice, M.E. (1997). Risk appraisal and management of violent behaviour. *Psychiatric Services, 48*, 1168–1176.

Harris, G.T. & Rice, M.E. (2003). Actuarial assessment of risk among sex offenders. *Annals of the New York Academy of Sciences, 989*, 198–210.

Harris, G.T., Rice, M.E. & Cormier, C.A. (2002). Prospective replication of the *Violence Risk Appraisal Guide* in predicting violent recidivism among forensic patients. *Law and Human Behavior, 26*, 377–394.

Hart, S.D. (1999). Assessing violence risk: Thoughts and second thoughts. *Contemporary Psychology, 44*, 6–8.

Hart, S.D., Kropp, P.R. & Laws, D.R. (2003). *Risk for Sexual Violence Protocol (RSVP): Structured professional guidelines for assessing risk of sexual violence.* Burnaby, BC: Mental Health Law and Policy Institute, Simon Fraser University.

Janus, E.S. & Meehl, P.E. (1997). Assessing the legal standard for predictions of dangerousness in sex offender commitment proceedings. *Psychology, Public Policy, and Law, 3*, 33–64.

Kropp, P.R., Hart, S.D., Webster, C.D. & Eaves, D. (1995). *Manual for the Spousal Assault Risk Assessment Guide* (2nd edn). Vancouver: British Columbia Institute on Family Violence.

Monahan, J., Robbins, P., Appelbaum, P., et al. (2005). An actuarial model of violence risk assessment for persons with mental disorders. *Psychiatric Services, 56*, 810–815.

Mossman, D. (1994). Assessing predictions of violence: Being accurate about accuracy. *Journal of Consulting and Clinical Psychology, 62*, 783–792.

Mossman, D. (2000). Commentary: Assessing the risk of violence – Are "accurate" predictions useful? *Journal of the American Academy of Psychiatry and the Law, 28*, 272–281.

Prentky, R.A., Harris, B., Frizzell, K. & Righthand, S. (2000). An actuarial procedure for assessing risk with juvenile sex offenders. *Sexual Abuse: A Journal of Research and Treatment, 12*, 71–93.

Quinsey, V.L., Harris, G.T., Rice, M.E. & Cormier, C.A. (1998). *Violent offenders: Appraising and managing risk.* Washington DC: American Psychological Association.

Sjostedt, G. & Langstrom, N. (2001). Actuarial assessment of sex offender recidivism risk: A cross-validation of the RRASOR and the Static-99 in Sweden. *Law and Human Behavior, 25*, 629–645.

Steadman, H.J. (2000). From dangerousness to risk assessment of community violence: Taking stock at the turn of the century. *Journal of the American Academy of Psychiatry and the Law, 28*, 265–271.

Thornton, D. (2002). Constructing and testing a framework for dynamic risk assessment. *Sexual Abuse: A Journal of Research and Treatment, 14*, 139–153.

Thornton, D., Mann, R., Webster, S., Blud, L., Travers, R., Friendship, C. & Erikson, M. (2003). Distinguishing and combining risks for sexual and violent recidivism. In R. Prentky, E. Janus, M. Seto & A.W. Burgess (Eds), Understanding and managing sexually coercive behavior. *Annals of the New York Academy of Sciences, 989*, 225–235.

Webster, C.D., Douglas, K., Eaves, D. & Hart, S.D. (1997). *HCR-20 Assessing risk for violence* (2nd edn). Vancouver: Simon Fraser University.

Worling, J.R. (2004). The estimate of risk of adolescent sexual offence recidivism (ERASOR): Preliminary psychometric data. *Sexual Abuse: A Journal of Research and Treatment*, 16, 235–254.

CHAPTER 12

Future Directions for Applying Psychology to Forensic Investigations and Prosecutions

MARK R. KEBBELL AND GRAHAM M. DAVIES

The traditional way to conclude a book of this nature is to say that we have achieved a lot, the future looks bright for forensic psychology and we have to do more research. To some extent this is what we will do now, and to a large extent this is true. Contemporary knowledge concerning forensic psychology, which is relevant to forensic investigations and prosecutions, has been summarized broadly in the preceding chapters. As we have seen, forensic psychology can be usefully applied to initial investigations. This can involve identifying offenders and offences with appropriate eyewitness interviews and identification processes, assessing the credibility of witness evidence, offender profiling, effective interviewing of suspected offenders, ensuring the innocent do not falsely confess and detecting deception. Similarly, forensic psychology is of relevance to decisions to prosecute, supporting witnesses providing evidence, understanding offenders and their motives and informing courts of the risk that offenders pose.

Clearly then, psychology has a lot to offer the justice agencies in the investigation and prosecution of crime, and in the last 20 years, tremendous strides have been made both in the theoretical and practical uses of psychology. During that time, investigators and prosecutors have become more aware of what psychology has to offer, and in turn psychologists have become more aware of what investigators and

Practical Psychology for Forensic Investigations and Prosecutions.
Edited by Mark R. Kebbell and Graham M. Davies. © 2006 John Wiley & Sons, Ltd.

prosecutors need from them. Nevertheless, much remains to be done. Improvements have to be made to the research methodologies we use, and the way our knowledge is communicated to users. We would like to take this opportunity to elaborate on these critical issues.

METHODOLOGIES

Most research in psychology has been conducted using the experimental method. Independent variables (for example a witness interview technique) can be manipulated to determine the effect on dependent variables (for example volume and accuracy of witness recall). The experimental method has been described as the "royal road to causality" (Robson, 1993), because every detail is held constant apart from the independent variable, and so causality can be attributed. However, while this methodology is powerful, much of its use has been with undergraduate students, a point which raises obvious questions concerning how well we can extrapolate from this population to a forensic population. For example, if one were to look at the most heavily researched areas of forensic psychology, eyewitness testimony and jury studies (Ogloff, 1999), where literally thousands of studies have been published, only a handful were conducted with forensic populations. This has three important implications.

First, the results from "real" studies are often very different from those found in laboratory studies. For example, Yuille and Cutshall (1986) found that real eyewitnesses who had witnessed a shooting first-hand, showed much higher levels of accuracy and much lower levels of suggestibility than is conventionally found in the laboratory. Clearly, this is a concern if we are attempting to extrapolate from laboratory findings to the real world (see Bermant, McGuire, McKinley & Salo, 1974 for a discussion of the external validity of legal decision research).

Second, by removing themselves from real-world situations, researchers remove themselves from the situations in which they are likely to be able to determine what needs to be researched and what has real-world implications. For example, the first author had conducted laboratory research on eyewitness evidence for a number of years but only became aware of the large numbers of false allegations that were being made by people with intellectual disabilities when he started conducting field research with these populations. Relatedly, the second author, when working with forensic eyewitnesses, finds that many were under the influence of alcohol at the time of witnessing the offence but there is little research concerning the influence of alcohol, especially large amounts of alcohol, on witness memory.

Similarly, if one simply looks at laboratory studies, one would expect the cognitive interview to be incredibly successful for interviewing witnesses, however, in practice it frequently is not (see Sternberg et al., 2001). The reason appears to be that many interviewers find it incredibly difficult, or are unwilling to follow even simple instructions such as not constantly interrupting witnesses. Clearly, this body of research would have benefited from a greater focus on field studies (for a discussion see Milne & Bull, 1999), rather than endless laboratory studies that were essentially replications of earlier work with similar results.

Third, conducting field research, and particularly conducting research that shows *effectiveness* in the field, means that results are more convincing to users because the methodology is less abstract. Of course, a major drawback of field research is that it is time consuming and involved. Further, it requires much closer relationships between the researcher and users. The fact that the research is so difficult and time consuming means that there is tremendous pressure on researchers to take the easy route and simply not bother. After all, you can probably get 10 laboratory studies published in the time it takes to do 1 field study, plus you are likely to encounter difficulty getting that field study published because of potential confounds. In short, unfortunately, most researchers get the message and go for the easy route of laboratory studies with undergraduate students, in place of field studies with "real" participants.

In addition, while the experimental method is the most effective way of determining causality, and experimental field studies are particularly important, qualitative methodologies are also relevant. We will not argue that qualitative methods should replace experimental studies, but we do argue that they should be used more frequently to supplement experimental work. Qualitative research has the potential to shed light on many issues that are not suitable for the experimental method. For example, how sex offenders felt about their victims or how they were thinking when they were interviewed by the police, is not something that can be readily accessed with experimental methods.

A related point is the importance of acknowledging and pointing out what we do not know either because of methodological limitations or because an area has not been researched. For example, an offender profiler who gives a profile which acknowledges uncertainty, adds caveats and genuinely reflects our current knowledge of the area, is likely to be perceived as less impressive than someone who, either through ignorance or machiavellian instincts, misrepresents his or her profile as being both highly specific and highly accurate. In these cases it is important for psychologists to inform users not only of what they know, but also of what is not known at the current time, to prevent others making false claims and untoward comparisons.

TRANSFERRING KNOWLEDGE

When the first author had his first academic journal article published he went excitedly to the University of Liverpool library to look at the completed article in all its glory. Once there, an important point struck him. There were no police officers, lawyers or other members of the justice system there. In fact there were few students there either (and this is before the internet made journal articles available online!). The implication of this is clear. If we are to communicate psychological information to investigators and prosecutors, we cannot rely on investigators and prosecutors to trawl through dull and often incomprehensible journals to find the information they require. We must communicate the information in other ways. This is an important task that should be considered (incidentally this was the reason for selecting the authors who submitted chapters for this book – their ability to combine academic excellence with clear communication to users).

One way for researchers to communicate their knowledge, is to directly inform stakeholders of their research. This can be achieved by writing in a clear concise manner in publications that users are likely to read. But, perhaps most importantly, it can be communicated by direct face-to-face communication, a task that many academics do not excel at. Research, particularly academic research, tends to favour particular characteristics. People succeed at research if they enjoy reading and writing, and are particularly fond of focusing on a relatively narrow area of research that they may concentrate on for years (if not decades). Idle conversation and socializing often impair academic performance, and hence, can be neglected. This focus means that "people" skills are often poorly developed. This is unfortunate, because to work with investigators and prosecutors, good interpersonal skills are required. A clear implication of this is that interpersonal skills must be developed. Too often investigators and prosecutors are influenced by people who have excellent interpersonal skills but little knowledge, and conversely are not influenced by knowledgeable individuals who lack excellent interpersonal skills.

Of course, knowledge transfer is a two-way process and another way of encouraging the dissemination of information to users is to encourage users themselves to attend courses, or to complete research degrees with academics. This is happening increasingly, particularly with police officers. However, even for these students it is also necessary to help them "sell" psychology to users, particularly when psychological techniques may conflict with what experienced users "know" to be the case.

FINAL CONCLUSION

To conclude, psychology has come a long way with regards its application to forensic investigations and prosecutions. The information this book contains, summarizes what we currently know and can be used to facilitate improving the investigation and prosecution of crimes. Nevertheless, there is much more we can do. We must focus on improving our methodology, particularly regarding field studies and qualitative research, and we must improve our ability to sell psychology to those who are interested in buying it.

REFERENCES

Bermant, G., McGuire, M., McKinley, W. & Salo, C. (1974). *Criminal Justice and Behavior, 224*, 229–232.

Milne, R. & Bull, R. (1999). *Investigative interviewing: Psychology and practice.* Chichester: John Wiley & Sons, Ltd.

Ogloff, J.R.P. (1999). Law and human behavior: Looking back and reflecting forward. *Law and Human Behavior, 23*, 1–7.

Robson, C. (1993). *Real world research: A resource for social scientists and practitioner-researchers.* Oxford: Blackwell.

Sternberg, K.J., Lamb, M.E., Davies, G.M. & Westcott, H. (2001). The memorandum of good practice: Theory versus application. *Child Abuse and Neglect, 25*, 669–681.

Yuille, J.C. & Cutshall, J.L. (1986). A case study of eyewitness memory of a crime. *Journal of Applied Psychology, 71*, 291–301.

Index